One-volume edition first published in 1981
Copyright © 1973 by George L. Flynn
Library of Congress Catalog Card Number 81-50401
ISBN 0-442-22540-7

Van Nostrand Reinhold Company
135 West 50th Street, New York, NY 10020

Van Nostrand Reinhold Ltd.
1410 Birchmount Road, Scarborough, Ontario M1P 2E7

Van Nostrand Reinhold Australia Pty. Ltd.
17 Queen Street, Mitcham, Victoria 3132

Van Nostrand Reinhold Company Ltd.
Molly Millars Lane, Wokingham, Berkshire, England RG11 2PY

First published 1973 in two volumes by New York Graphic Society

16 15 14 13 12 11 10 9 8 7 6 5 4 3 2 1

VINCE
LOMBARDI
on FOOTBALL

Edited by George L. Flynn

Introduction by Red Smith

VAN NOSTRAND REINHOLD COMPANY
NEW YORK CINCINNATI TORONTO LONDON MELBOURNE

Contents

Red Smith

In a tower suite in Milwaukee's Hotel Pfister, Vince Lombardi sat chatting with half a dozen sportswriters on the afternoon of Dec. 22, 1967. In something like 20 hours the Green Bay Packers would go after their third straight championship of the National Football League's Western Conference, playing the Los Angeles Rams, who had upset them two Sundays earlier. As relaxed as he ever could be on the eve of a game, the coach held forth on the theme that was the core of his existence—the commitment to excellence and to victory.

"As St. Paul wrote in one of the Epistles," he said, " 'Know ye not that they which run in a race run all, but one receiveth the prize? So run, that ye may obtain.' "

In the fading twilight, his visitors exchanged sidewise glances. Some had been taking an occasional note but nobody broke in to say: "Just a minute, coach. Would you take that over a little slower?" In a little while the gathering broke up.

"How about that?" a man said in the corridor outside. "St. Vincent de Paul!"

"The Gospel according to Lombardi," another said.

They scattered to their own rooms to check chapter and verse in the Gideon Bibles. The man had it right.

"Vince has a knack," the Packers' all-pro guard, Jerry Kramer, said later, "for making all the saints sound like they would have been great football coaches."

I don't know why this incident keeps coming back to mind unless it is because it illustrates the paradox that was the essence of Vince Lombardi—a deeply religious man who worshipped the God of peace and taught a game of cruel violence, with total dedication to both.

In a comparatively brief career as a head coach, Vince was incomparably the best in his profession. The sorriest team in pro football, only once a winner in twelve starts, won seven of twelve the first season he was in charge. In the eight years he remained after that, the Packers won the conference championship six times and finished second twice. They won five of six playoffs for the league championship, winding up with an unprecedented three in a row. When Vince resigned, two Super Bowl games had been played. The Packers had won both. He was the best coach in the world, meaning he was 12 inches better than Tom Landry of Dallas. That's how far Bart Starr carried the ball to beat the Cowboys for the championship 13 seconds before the end of Vince's last season as the Green Bay coach.

If the private man was a paradox, his public image was a mass of contradictions. Alive, he was pictured as a despot combining the finer qualities of Captain Bligh and Tomas de Torquemada. "Winning is not everything," went the line most frequently attributed to him. "It's the only thing." Then cancer took him away with terrible swiftness, and many who had painted him as a tyrant nominated him for instant canonization.

The truth, of course, is that he was neither sadist nor saint. He was emotional, mercurial, sentimental, quick-tempered, profoundly loyal, fiercely honest. A perfectionist, he made harsh demands on his players to prepare them for the harsher demands of combat. By his own authority, what he really said was: "Winning is not everything—but making the effort to win is." In short, he was a good man who was supremely good at what he did.

I suppose *Vince Lombardi on Football* could be described as Vince's text on how to do the job as well as he did it. No doubt it is important to an aspiring young coach to know that the Packers played their defensive tackles 18 inches off the ball on second and long yardage, but it isn't important to me. The parts of these books that are important to me are those that bring my old friend back to life.

Red Smith
New Canaan, Conn.

Editor's Foreword

The genesis of these volumes began in the fall of 1961 when Red Smith agreed to help me publish a unique series of sports books. Our intention was to get the best professional in his sport together with an outstanding writer, and let them tell about his profession in the most literate manner possible. Our choice for the first book was Vince Lombardi, the writer was W. C. Heinz, and the book was called *Run To Daylight!* Like Lombardi's teams, the book became the standard of excellence for sports publishing.

Vince Lombardi and I, as his editor and publisher, became close friends, and over the years we worked together on other projects. One of them was a film series, *Vince Lombardi's The Science and Art of Football*, intended for coaches and players. The scripts and narration for that series have provided the basic blueprint on which these volumes were constructed. The additional material has come from the many conversations I had with the coach as well as some material that was used in *Run To Daylight!*

Vince Lombardi's success, I am convinced, lay not only in his inspirational personality but also in his ability to *teach*. He was a teacher. He could communicate an idea to his players, explain it so that they understood it—not only how to execute it but why! Throughout these books you'll notice a conciseness of text. This is how he taught, right to the heart of the matter, without frills or gimmicks. And throughout, there comes across the demands he made on the intelligence of his team. You had to be smart to play for Lombardi. In a split second a lineman had to read and react to the move of his opponent, and react correctly—so for all players, both offense and defense. Of course the physical talent was there, but all teams in professional football have that. The ability of his teams to do the right thing—cut the right way, block the right man, read the key correctly—these are the reasons for the championships.

This book comprises what Vince Lombardi thought was necessary to know about the game of football and what he felt could be understood by anyone, fan or coach or player or even publisher. We have tried to make everything as clear as possible by supplementing the basic text with accurate and entertaining illustrations and line drawings to explain the intricate maneuvers on the field.

This volume brings you the fundamentals of the game of football as Vince Lombardi gave it to his Green Bay Packers. We hope it will give some insight to and understanding of what a great man Vince Lombardi was.

George L. Flynn
Editor

Bart Starr

Because of the Green Bay Packers' success under Vince Lombardi, thousands read of his beliefs, desires and principles but few really knew him. I was one of the privileged pro football players to play for him. I knew this complex man, this man of many moods, better than most because, as his quarterback, I spent more time with him.

Lombardi felt that every fiber in your body should be used in an effort to seek excellence, and he sought this goal every day of his life with complete dedication. He stated this thought eloquently to us one day in a meeting: "The quality of a man's life is in direct proportion to his commitment to excellence, regardless of his chosen field or endeavor."

I considered this to be the finest statement he ever made to the Packer squad. It is typical of the man: direct, sharp, inspirational, encompassing. Notice the word 'football' is not mentioned. He never treated football as an end result, but rather a means to an end. He was concerned with the full, total life. It emphasizes his commitment and flaming desire to excel. He was tough on his players because he was tough on himself. He never expected more from us than he was willing to give of himself. He would not tolerate excuses or compromises, but was interested only in results. Tough, demanding, abrasive, he was also compassionate and understanding. For though he recognized that absolute perfection is never attainable, he believed the quest for it can be one of the most challenging races an individual can run.

I know that, as you read this book, his dedication, his desire, his pride of performance, his confidence and his teaching ability will be vividly displayed in the diagrams and words which so fully illustrate and describe the genius of this great man.

Bart Starr
Green Bay, Wis.

Glossary of Terms

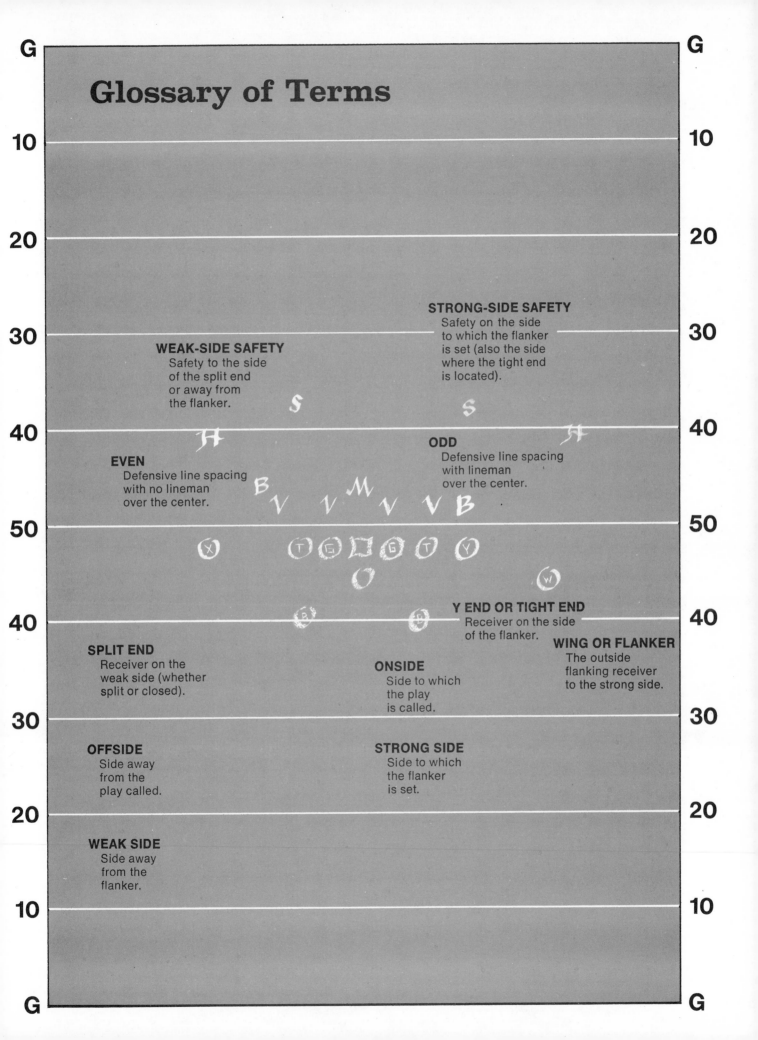

WEAK-SIDE SAFETY
Safety to the side
of the split end
or away from
the flanker.

STRONG-SIDE SAFETY
Safety on the side
to which the flanker
is set (also the side
where the tight end
is located).

EVEN
Defensive line spacing
with no lineman
over the center.

ODD
Defensive line spacing
with lineman
over the center.

SPLIT END
Receiver on the
weak side (whether
split or closed).

ONSIDE
Side to which
the play
is called.

Y END OR TIGHT END
Receiver on the side
of the flanker.

WING OR FLANKER
The outside
flanking receiver
to the strong side.

OFFSIDE
Side away
from the
play called.

STRONG SIDE
Side to which
the flanker
is set.

WEAK SIDE
Side away
from the
flanker.

1

My Life
and Football

I owe almost everything to football, in which I have spent the greater part of my life. And I have never lost my respect, my admiration or my love for what I consider a great game.

For over thirty years I have been coaching football—in high school, in the college area and at the professional level. Yet I've never had the time, in all those years, to put together my thoughts on the game and what I consider to be the fundamentals. That is what I propose to do here: talk about the fundamentals of football, from the basic techniques of the individual player to the most sophisticated offensive and defensive formations.

To me football is more than diagrams and techniques. It is a lot like life in demanding a man's personal commitment to excellence and to victory. But to achieve success, whatever the job we have, we must pay a price for success. It's like anything worthwhile. It has a price. You have to pay the price to win and you have to pay the price to get to the point where success is possible. Most important, you must pay the price to stay there. Success is not a "sometimes" thing. In other words, you don't do what is right once in a while, but all the time. Success is a habit. Winning is a habit.

Unfortunately, so is losing.

We have all watched people and teams achieve success—a promotion or a championship—and then be unable to repeat the next year. Winning the first time is a lot easier than repeating as champions. To succeed again requires dedication, perseverance and, above all, discipline and mental toughness. Truly, I have never known a really successful man who deep in his heart did not understand the grind, the discipline that it takes to win.

Through the years, for better or worse, I've picked up a reputation for being tough. I must admit I have mixed emotions about that. I guess what it comes down to is that success demands singleness of purpose and I demanded "mental toughness" from all my players. There has been a lot written about the mental toughness I have supposedly instilled in my teams. I guess the best way to explain it is that once you have established the goals you want and the price you're willing to pay for success, you can ignore the minor hurts, the opponents' pressure and the temporary failures.

I remember the opening day of practice in Green Bay when I was a head coach for the first time in pro football. Afterward, when I walked back into a locker room, I wanted to cry. The lackadaisical, almost passive attitude was like an insidious disease that had infected the whole squad.

The next day there were almost twenty players in the trainer's room waiting for diathermy or the whirlpool or a rubdown. I blew my stack.

"What is this?" I yelled, "an emergency casualty ward? Get this straight! When you're hurt, you have every right to be here. But this is disgraceful. I have no patience with the small hurts that are bothering most of you. You're going to have to live with small hurts, play with small hurts, if you're going to play for me."

The next day when I walked into that room there were only two players there. So maybe that's how you start building mental toughness. And later on, as our success continued, our mental toughness kept us going in games that looked impossible to win. And the many hurts now seem a small price to have paid for winning.

Football is a game of many lessons in courage, stamina and teamwork. It's a spartan game and requires spartan qualities. Sacrifice, self-discipline, dedication—these are spartan qualities.

There are other lessons in football that apply to life. For example, in the early stages it requires exhausting hard work, to the point of drudgery.

It's a game in which hundreds of thousands of Americans take part, and yet it is completely uninhibited by racial or social barriers.

It is a game of strategy and quick decisions.

Winning requires the right psychological and emotional attitudes.

The only true satisfaction a player receives is the satisfaction that comes from being part of a successful team, regardless of what his own personal ends are. More important, each man contributes to the spirit of the whole, and this spirit

I've known many fine people in and out of football, and George Halas is one of my most treasured friends. He has done so much for football and I've admired and respected him for many years.

The rivalry that exists between his Chicago Bears and the Packers is the most intense in all of pro football. Unless you have played or coached in a Bear-Packer game, it is impossible to understand fully what happens on the field. Whether the Packers and Bears are playing for first place or last, the intensity of this rivalry is such that each team feels it has had a winning season if it has beaten the other.

is the cohesive force which binds forty talented men into an indomitable team.

I have been quoted as saying, "Winning is the only thing." That's a little out of context. What I said is that "Winning is not everything—but making the effort to win is."

Lately, in our society, it seems that we have sympathy only for the losers and misfits. Let us also cheer for the doers and the winners. The zeal to be first in everything has always been American, to win and to win and to win. Not everyone can be a winner all the time but everyone can make that effort, that commitment to excellence.

And if we fall a little short of our goals, at least we have the satisfaction of knowing we tried. As President Theodore Roosevelt said: "It is not the critic that counts. . . . The credit belongs to the man who is actually in the arena . . . who strives valiantly, who errs and often comes up short again and again . . . who, at the best, knows in the end the triumph of high achievement, and who at worst, if he fails, at least fails while daring greatly, so that his place shall never be with those cold and timid souls who know neither victory nor defeat."

Each Sunday, after the battle, one group savors victory; another lives in the bitterness of defeat. The practice and the hard work of the season seem a small price for having won. But there are no reasons that are adequate for having lost. For the loser there must be one hundred percent determination and dedication to win next time.

And each day, each week, each year, there is a new encounter, a new challenge. But all of the cheers and all of the color and all of the display linger only in the memory. The spirit, the will to win and the will to excel—these are the things that endure and these are the qualities that are so much more important than any of the events that occasion them.

And I say that the quality of any man's life has got to be a full measure of that man's personal commitment to excellence and to victory, regardless of what field he may be in.

2
The Lombardi Sweep

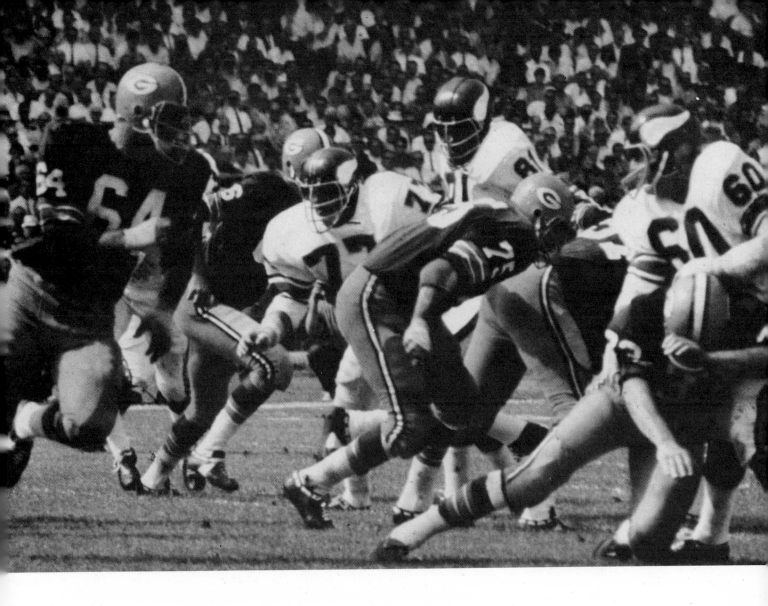

Every football team eventually arrives at a lead play. It becomes the team's bread-and-butter play, the top-priority play. It is the play that the team knows it must make go, and the one the opponents know they must stop. Continued success with the play, of course, makes for a No. 1 play, because from that success stems your confidence, and behind that is the basic truth that it expresses the coach as a coach and the players as a team and they feel complete satisfaction when they execute it and it's completely right.

My No. 1 play has been the power sweep, sometimes called the Lombardi sweep. It began to be a part of me during my days at Fordham. I was impressed playing against the single-wing sweep the way those Pittsburgh teams of Jock Sutherland ran it. And I was impressed afterward when I attended coaching clinics and the single wing was discussed.

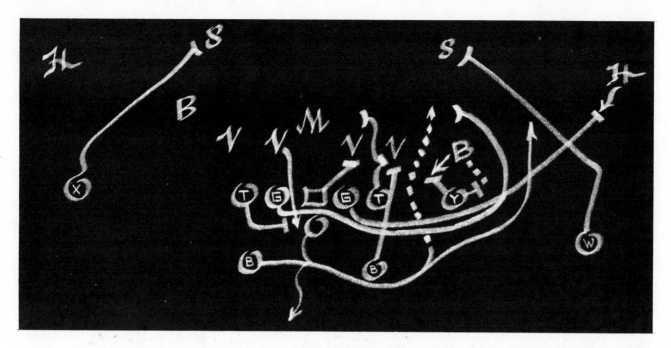

Today, our sweep has a lot of those Sutherland qualities, the same guard-pulling technique, the same ball carriers' cutback feature. And there is nothing spectacular about it, it's just a yard gainer. But on that sideline, when the sweep starts to develop, you can hear those linebackers and defensive backs yelling, "Sweep!" "Sweep!" and almost see their eyes pop as those guards turn upfield after them. But maybe it's my No. 1 play because it requires all eleven men to play as one to make it succeed, and that's what "team" means.

We have it illustrated here against a 4–3 defense. One of the advantages of this play is that we feel we can run it against any defense, even or odd. We will also show it against an over defense, wherein the defensive line is overshifted to the strength of the formation and the linebackers are shifted weak, given an Oklahoma setup on the weak side. In the under defense the linemen are shifted weak with the linebacker shifted strong, given an Oklahoma look on the strong side. Here is a 4–4 defense, one that has even spacing of the defensive linemen, with the middle linebacker shifted strong, sometimes referred to as a 6–2 defense.

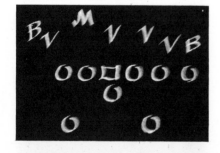

This play can be blocked either odd or even and it is the center's decision how it is to be blocked. Of course, in these two defenses, the over and the under defenses, there is no decision—it's odd to start with. There's a man playing directly on top of the center; therefore he will make the odd call. The tackle will make the cutoff block on the middle linebacker. The call of odd also determines the block of the offensive

Sweep left: hand-off perfect, guards pulling hard, back reading blocks, following guards into hole.

back. On an odd call by the center, that back must drive the man between himself and the ball—in this case, the defensive tackle.

OFFENSIVE LINEMEN BLOCKING RESPONSIBILITIES

The Y end's rule is to open up to a position somewhere between 6 and 9 feet from his tackle. We ask the Y end to do this so we can isolate the defensive man or linebacker over the Y end and the Y end himself so that the ball carrier can either cut inside the block of the Y end or outside of that block.

COACHING POINT: We tell the Y end that under no circumstances should he allow penetration to the inside. We do not care how much penetration the defensive man gets to the outside. There is a particular technique which we ask the Y end to use here. We tell him to set as on a pass. In other words, he uses exactly the same technique here as we ask the offensive lineman to use in protecting the passer. We ask him to put his weight on his inside foot, keeping his eyes right on the numbers of the defensive man so that if the defensive man does come to the inside quickly, the Y end, with his weight on the inside foot, can drive that defensive man down the line.

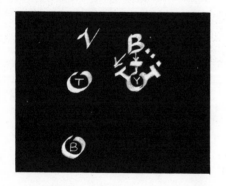

This is the ideal way to run the sweep, getting that defensive man to come to the inside. The worst thing that can happen to the defense is to have the sweep get to the outside. Usually what happens is that the defensive man playing over the Y end will penetrate to the outside. In this case, we have a different technique. Here, we ask the Y end to open up with his outside foot, keeping his eyes again on the numbers, and when the numbers of the defensive man are outside his eyes he wheels him out—just a plain wheel block—to keep him on the outside so that the back can cut inside.

COACHING POINT: I would like to repeat that the Y end's, or the tight end's, rule is to set as on the pass and drive the man over him in the direction of that man's angle. Never, and I repeat never, allow penetration to the inside. We don't care too much about penetration to the outside, where it usually happens. Because of the pull of the guard, the linebacker will usually do one of two things: he'll try to penetrate inside or he'll try to penetrate outside. Very seldom will he try to come directly over the Y end.

The halfback keys the block of the Y end, who drives that linebacker in the direction he wants to go.

Onside tackle

On an even call by the center the rule of the tackle is to drive the defensive man if that man is over him. If no man is over him, he slams the defensive end and seals inside for the middle linebacker.

The fullback

The fullback, working in coordination with the offensive tackle, drives the first man outside the offensive tackle—usually the defensive end. If the defensive end should go inside, then the fullback would go by that end and seal inside for the middle linebacker.

COACHING POINT FOR THE FULLBACK: The fullback must make a direct attack almost over the outside leg of the offensive tackle. The fullback drives right at the first man that shows; I mean, the first defensive man the fullback sees. If no one shows, in other words, the defensive end has moved inside the offensive tackle, the fullback seals inside for the middle linebacker.

SECOND COACHING POINT FOR THE FULLBACK: The fullback is to take a direct approach, a straight-line approach at that defensive end. A very common error that we find even in the professional ranks is that most of the fullbacks try to take a roundabout approach or a circle approach. As a result, the defensive end can make a quick penetration coming way inside the fullback and knocking off the guards. Penetration here by the defensive end is as bad as it is by the outside linebacker. So we ask the fullback to go as fast as he possibly can in a straight approach, a straight line to make this block. In fact we even tell him, if it's necessary, to cheat up on the line a little bit, to move up toward that end before the ball is snapped. We don't care who knows it or who sees it. The reason, of course, is so that he can make that block as quickly as possible. Penetration is the one thing we do not want on this play.

Excellent illustration of the even defense: the linebacker is over the center, about 1½–2 yards deep. Stance of center and quarterback is perfect.

Here is the view of the sweep as it looks from behind. The fullback is blocking on the end, the guards are in full power, the back has the ball from the quarterback and is reading the blocks.

Odd call

On an odd call by the center both the tackle and fullback are affected. An odd call, even on an even defense, means that the center feels he cannot make the onside block on the defensive tackle. In this case, he will now call odd, making the cutoff block on the middle linebacker. This now tells the offside tackle that he must drive the man between himself and the ball, the defensive tackle. It also tells the fullback that right now he's got the defensive end.

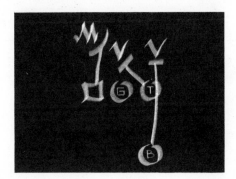

Onside guard

A rule for the onside guard or right guard, in this case, is to pull onside and drive the first man outside the block of the Y end. The guard's technique is to pull on a 45° angle. His first leg or his lead foot will be at a 45° angle as he leaves the line of scrimmage. He must be aware, of course, of the

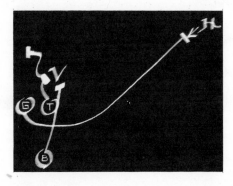

fullback passing in front of him. He allows the fullback to pass in front of him and he quickly pulls behind him.

One of the common errors, of course, is that the guard is so quick to get out there that he cuts off the fullback's block.

So, he must come behind the fullback. The fullback comes up to take the tackle, and the guard comes behind him. Preferably we would like the guard to continue on the outside of the Y end's block. And the reason for this is that it forces the defensive man, that linebacker who is playing over the Y end, to continue on the outside. Later on, as the guards become more experienced, we will sometimes allow them the freedom to come inside the block by the Y end and to go outside to block on the cornerback.

Offside guard

The offside guard's technique is to pull flat. And the reason he has to pull flat is so that he will not interfere with the quarterback. So his first move is flat. By flat I mean that he pulls on a direct line down the line of scrimmage. After the guard gets by the position of the quarterback he will then

Here is the sweep being run against an odd-man line. The tackle (No. 71) was lined up over the center and is just getting by the center's block as the guards get away to lead the ball carrier.

belly out or roll out. He keeps looking inside and will take the first daylight or the first hole he sees. He will then turn up into that hole and he, too, will seal inside, looking for the defensive pursuit.

The offside tackle has what we feel is a very difficult assignment on this play. What he has to do is prevent any kind of plugging by the first man, the defensive tackle, to his inside, and his technique is to pull deep. One of the most common errors is to pull too flat. In essence, his pull is a direct opposite of that of the offside guard. If he should pull too flat, this gives the defensive man a great area in which to pursue the ball carrier because of the hole opened by the pulling offside guard. So what we ask the offside tackle to do is to pull as deep as he possibly can, almost the same technique the

Offside tackle

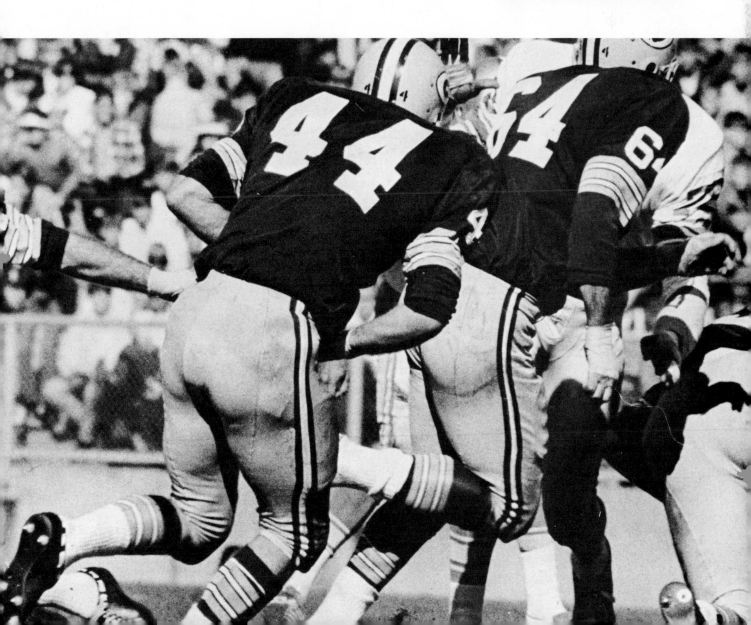

onside guard uses in pulling for that cornerback. The deeper the offside tackle moves, we feel, the better the position for the block.

If the defensive tackle were to go in pursuit in back of the line of scrimmage, the offside tackle would continue and take the first hole and seal it just like the offside guard. Usually, however, what happens is that the defensive tackle comes into the hole to chase the ball carrier from behind; and now we're in a position to make the cutoff block on him or to run up his back, which is perfectly legal since all this action takes place on the line of scrimmage.

Weak-side end

The weak-side end, or split end, releases for the weak-side safety, just a straight release, and sometimes he may split away from the line of scrimmage, about 3 yards.

Wingback

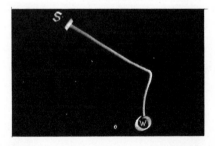

The wingback's technique is to come off the line of scrimmage to try to drive the defensive halfback back. We feel that the longer he can delay that halfback from coming up to meet this play, the better the play will run. So, his technique is to come off the line and to simulate a pass so as to drive the halfback back.

However, he must be very aware of the safety man. If

Led by Fuzzy Thurston (No. 63), Hornung is into the secondary and racing downfield for a long gain.

the safety man comes up and forces quickly, the wingback has got to come off that line and drive down on the safety. His assignment in this case is the safety man.

If it's zone coverage or a coverage where they're rotating to the strength of the formation, where the defensive halfback is doing the forcing and the safety man is covering the corner, the wingback will run right by the halfback for the safety man. The quick force by the safety, of course, determines that the wingback has got to come off his fake and drive down for the block on the safety.

The halfback

The ball carrier on the power sweep right is usually the halfback, and I've been fortunate to coach a couple of great all-around backs who made the sweep their personal play, Paul Hornung and Frank Gifford. Though neither had that blinding speed, they both were quick, intelligent runners who could "control" their running so that they used their blockers and got every possible yard out of each play.

The fullback (No. 31) has launched his block on the linebacker as the guard (No. 64) and offside tackle (No. 78) turn upfield. The ball carrier (No. 25) is already looking downfield. This is a perfect execution of the sweep.

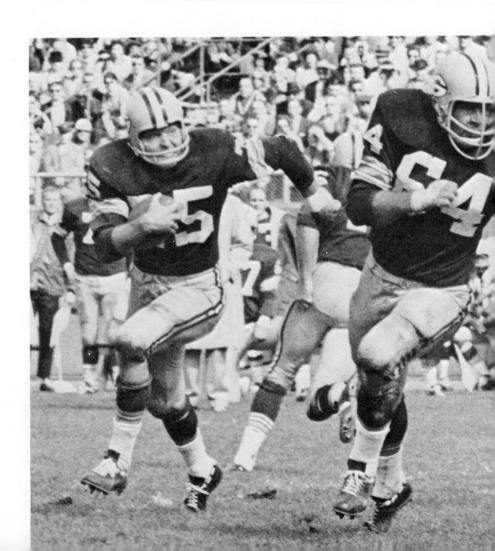

The halfback's technique is to lead-step to his right and to come across parallel to the line of scrimmage just as hard and as fast as he can, in a straight line. Now, as soon as the halfback gets the ball from the quarterback who opens up in an open pivot, he seats the ball and then comes under control with a slight belly or dip. We ask him to come under control and to belly slightly so he can key the block of the Y end on the linebacker or the man who's playing over the Y end. This is most important because the halfback has to make a decision on whether to go inside or outside of that block by the Y end. Also, if the back comes across too fast, not only will he be unable to make the cut back inside—he will cut off the guards or beat the guards out into their blocking area.

So we ask him to come under control to key that block by the Y end. If the defensive man or the defensive linebacker is driven to the outside the back will cut inside. If the linebacker makes a move to the inside the back will continue and go to the outside of the Y end block.

That's one of the great advantages to this play. It really

has two holes. We are looking for an isolation between the Y end and the linebacker, and we also want to create an alley between the linebacker and the defensive end. That's what we're looking for—the block out by the Y end on the linebacker, the block by the guard on the halfback and the block by the wingback on the safety man. The seal by the tackle and fullback cutting off pursuit and the isolation of the Y end and linebacker give the ball carrier two alleys in which to run.

Actually, I've seen this play run inside the defensive end, who, reading sweep, sometimes makes a violent move to the outside, but because of the belly of the halfback, because of the controlled running of the halfback, the halfback sees this and he comes off that outside foot and "bing!" he brings it right back inside that defensive end. That's what makes it one of the great plays, I believe; because it opens up so many holes for us to hit.

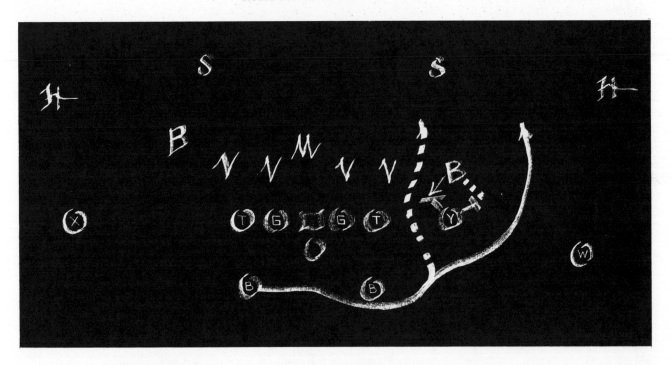

ATTACKING ADJUSTMENTS TO THE SWEEP

Once a team establishes a lead play, the play they like to run and the one the opponents know they must stop, the defenses around the league begin to make adjustments to it. In our case, teams began making defensive plays that were unusual but effective in stopping the sweep. I never meant

that teams could not stop the sweep, but to do so they had to make unusual adjustments. In making these adjustments it left them vulnerable to plays that looked like the sweep but took advantage of the defense and its changes. Of course, this required that we have personnel of intelligence and ability to recognize the adjustments and in a split second counter the defensive plan. While there are many adjustments the defense can make, when they do they leave themselves open to other areas of attack.

Here is the perfect illustration of the back taking the hand-off from the quarterback, seating the ball and coming under control. Note how he has begun to belly slightly and his eyes are on the blockers. The hand is gripping the ball in such a manner that he can quickly bring it up to pass.

Sucker play or influence play

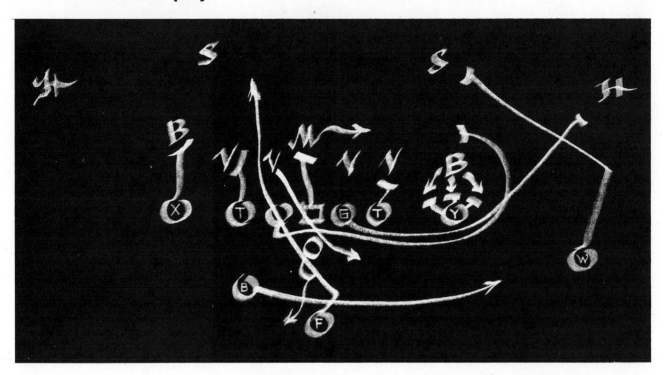

We have just explained the block of the offside tackle. That offside tackle has the difficult assignment of blocking the defensive tackle that pursues quickly into the vacated areas of the pulling offside guard. Also, with the center blocking onside for the other defensive tackle or even going after the middle linebacker, a large area is left for a quick tackle to pursue the ball carrier and possibly tackle him from behind the line of scrimmage. Many of these defensive tackles in our league are as quick as running backs and when they see the pull of the guard they read sweep and come through the hole like a shot. Tackles who do this, however, leave themselves vulnerable to what we call an influence play or a sucker trap. It is not a play that is used unless you have made that defensive team conscious of the sweep and have a quarterback who knows when to call it and an offensive team that can execute and adjust.

We line up exactly as we do when we are going to run the sweep. The Y end splits 6 to 9 yards outside his tackle. The backs are split just as they are on the sweep. Now, with the snap of the ball, the guards pull just as they do on the sweep, the quarterback pivots just as he does on the sweep and the halfback comes across just exactly as on the sweep.

The fullback makes his start toward his block just as he does on the sweep. With the pull of the guards and the flow of the backfield and the line to the right, it opens the hole for that defensive tackle to pursue the halfback. The fullback, however, takes only a jab step toward his blocking assignment, then comes back against this flow and takes the ball from the quarterback in an underneath handoff and goes into the hole vacated by the pulling guard on the offside.

The defensive tackle pursues the pulling guard and the halfback, and by the time he reads "trap" the fullback is by him and into the hole without a block on that tackle. That's why we call it a sucker play. We fake sweep, suck him into following the halfback and then run the fullback right into his area. After this has happened to that tackle, he will be a little leery about chasing the sweep so quickly.

The sucker play: the fullback (No. 36) is already through the hole and into the secondary as the defensive tackles (Nos. 71 and 74), following the back (No. 22 in the background), turn to see the result of the sucker play.

In our championship game with Dallas in 1967, we put in the sucker play, or influence play, because of the exceptional talent of their great defensive tackle, Bob Lilly. And it again shows what a team can do when it is prepared to take advantage of an opponent's strength. Bob Lilly is the heart of the Dallas defense, and his speed, strength and quickness gave us trouble on the sweep because he was so quick to get into that hole vacated by the pull of the offside guard.

One of the reasons Bart Starr is such a great quarterback is that he has the intelligence and patience to be ready for the right call. All through the game we had run the sweep to the right, and Dallas and Lilly had done pretty well in stopping it. Now it was our ball on their 11-yard line, first down, less than a minute, with them leading 17–14. Starr called the play, and it was one of the great calls in championship football history. He had waited all game until the situation was right, and many times earlier he had been tempted to make the call. But he waited till the last minute, actually less than a minute. We lined up in the sweep formation, the ball was snapped. Gale Gillingham, the offside guard, pulled hard, the halfback came across hard and Lilly charged hard. Starr opened up just like the sweep handoff but instead gave the ball to the fullback, Chuck Mercine, who blew into that hole vacated by the defensive tackle, and he got to the 3-yard line of Dallas before being tackled. It was superb football.

This is what the sweep looks like from behind: the pulling guards, the ball carrier getting the handoff, the fullback and tackle taking their men, and the ball carrier in full control, following his lead blocker, the guard (No. 64).

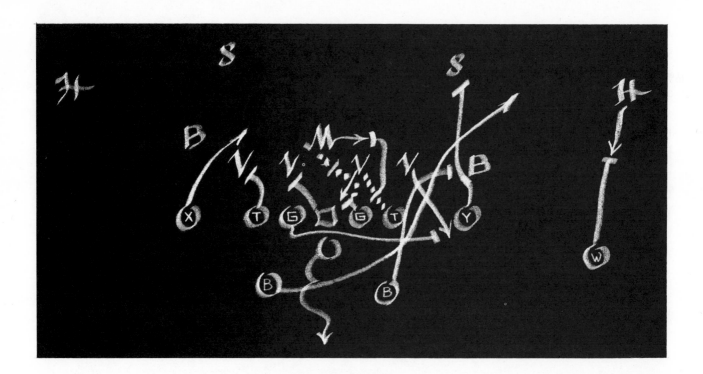

The quarterback lets the fullback go in front as the guard pulls flat and hard down the line of scrimmage. The ball carrier (No. 23) comes across to take the ball from the quarterback. The middle linebacker (No. 55) is held by the fake of the fullback, allowing the fullback to get to him and block him.

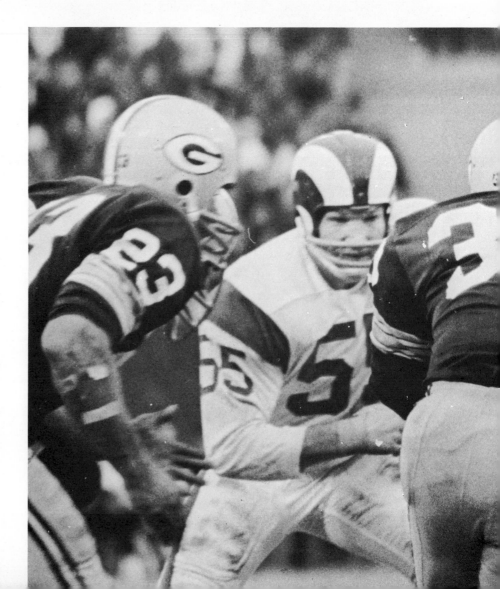

Another adjustment to stop the sweep is to have the defensive end make a hard, quick, deep outside move to cut off the guards and to force the sweep deep. This is a very common adjustment to the sweep.

Now, when we feel that the defensive end is doing just this, we run the play inside of him. A lot of defensive ends became so sweep-conscious that they would do this every time we lined up in our sweep formation. So to counter their hard outside charge we would run what we call the long trap. We have broken more long runs against this particular defense than any other type of adjustment that has been made to stop our sweep.

Everything is set up to look exactly like the sweep and everyone's position is the same. The position of the fullback, the position of the Y end is exactly the same. The fullback influences the defensive end even a little more. He will drive right at the outside leg of that man exactly as he does on the

THE LONG TRAP

sweep to pull him up the field even that much more, and then will go through the hole trying to seal off the linebacker over the Y end so that the linebacker cannot fall off and come back and make the tackle inside. This is very, very important.

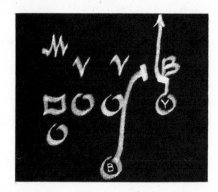

The onside guard and the onside tackle will use a do-dad type of operation. The offensive right guard drives with his outside shoulder right at the inside of the defensive tackle, all the time looking at the middle linebacker. If the linebacker were to come in hard following the back the onside guard would leave this block and take the middle linebacker. The onside tackle leads with his inside foot for the outside hip of the defensive tackle. If the defensive tackle goes to the inside the offensive tackle will seal for the middle linebacker. If the defensive tackle comes to him, he will block and the onside guard will lead and seal on the inside.

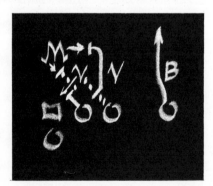

The Y end releases immediately from the linebacker over him on the inside to block on the safety man. The center blocks back, down-blocks to his outside or down-blocks to his back side on the defensive tackle. The offensive left guard pulls on the trap close to the line of scrimmage. He gains

The back is keying the block of the offensive guard on the linebacker and will cut inside that block.

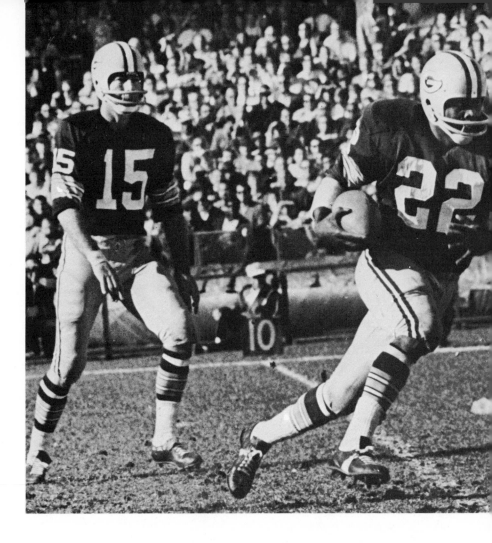

ground down the line and kicks out into the defensive end and blocks him out. The halfback comes across straight, the quarterback pulls out hard exactly as he does in the sweep except now it's an underneath hand-off to the halfback to give him a better approach to the trap and to the hole.

In our Western Conference playoff game against the Los Angeles Rams in Milwaukee in 1967, the long-trap play got us our first touchdown. We had been beaten by the Rams in L.A. two weeks earlier when they blocked a punt and then scored with a little less than a minute remaining.

Now we were facing them again and they were coming into the game as the favorite. No team of mine had been an underdog since my first year at Green Bay. Even a lot of the Packer fans were saying that we had had it, that no team would ever win three NFL titles in a row. We had won in '65 and '66 and now had to beat the Rams to qualify for the chance to win the third consecutive title.

Their front four presented a serious problem because of

The halfback is cutting behind the trap block by the guard (No. 68). The guard has the force man in his sights and is driving on him. The form is excellent.

their size and quickness and experience. But I knew that we would win because now we were in the playoffs and this is where my teams were at their best. There was no way the Rams were going to beat us, and I told the team that. Before that game we were sky-high in the locker room and even though the Rams scored first, it was just a matter of time before we caught them. The weather was mild for December in Milwaukee, so the footing was good for the running game.

I remember giving the team a slogan for that week and it was, "Run to win." I took it from St. Paul in the Bible. To beat the Rams we had to run on them and we had to beat their strength, which was Deacon Jones and Merlin Olsen, and that offensive line of ours did the job.

The first touchdown we scored came off the long trap on Jones and we broke it for about 45 yards. We worked it just like the diagrams say, and as soon as that back was into the secondary you could see our linemen raising their arms to signal touchdown.

Here's the form of the guards pulling flat and hard on the weak-side sweep. The quarterback is handing the ball to the running back, who is keying the block of the halfback on the defensive end or linebacker. Note the uniformity of the motion of the guards.

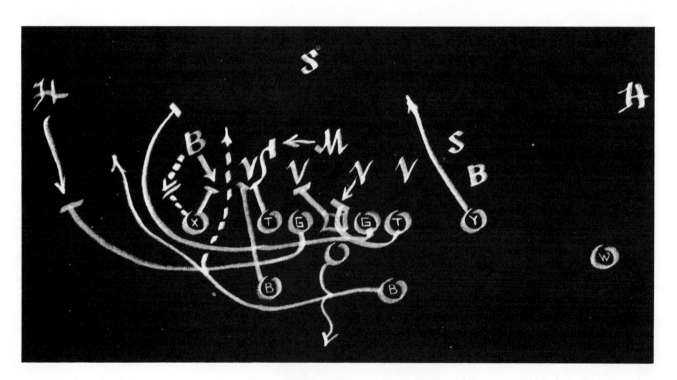

Weak-side sweep

Not all the sweeps are run to the right wtih the halfback carrying the ball. The alternate is the weak-side sweep with the fullback as the ball carrier. As with all our running plays, we require our backs to be able to block, and in the power-sweep right the fullback must block on the end or linebacker. Now the halfback, in the weak-side sweep, must be the lead blocker.

At Green Bay, we had excellent blocking backs in Paul Hornung and Jim Taylor. Paul may have been the best all-around back ever to play football, and his blocking was one of the reasons for that. Jim Taylor would have been the best if they had let him carry the ball while blocking, but he still was excellent.

The key to the quarterback in calling the weak-side sweep is the position of the defensive backs, especially the safeties. Often, to stop the sweep, the strong-side safety will move close to the Y end in order to be able to hit quickly into the flow of the play before the blockers can form and turn downfield. When the strong-side safety moves closer to the

Y end, the weak-side safety will compensate, or pull to the strong-side safety's side of the field, or more closely to the middle of the field.

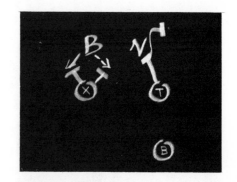

Now, if we run to the weak side we'll be missing the block of the flanker. There is no flanker on the weak side so the split or X end now takes the same distance from tackle as the Y end and he takes the man over him—either the defensive halfback or the weak-side linebacker. And instead of the Y end we now run it toward the X end. The X end takes the same spacing, the 9-foot split—he opens up 9 feet against the man over him. He takes the man in any direction he wants to go. It's exactly the same thing we tell the Y end.

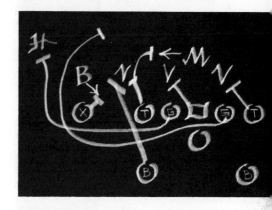

The onside tackle, or left tackle in this case, influences the defensive end and then seals for the middle linebacker. By influence we mean he drives out at the defensive end, hits him, then comes off that block to seal for the middle linebacker.

The center blocks the onside tackle. The backside tackle or offside tackle cuts off from the back or blocks the defensive offside tackle.

The onside guard pulls and kicks out on the first man he sees and the second guard, the offside guard, pulls and turns up anyplace he can turn up with the same instructions we gave the backside guard on the sweep going the other way, and then he seals.

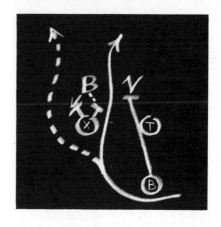

The halfback now, of course, blocks on the defensive end. The fullback is now the ball carrier. He comes across, loses a little bit of ground—exactly the same instructions we gave the halfback—keying the block of the halfback and the tackle. If the linebacker goes out he breaks inside the halfback's block, if the linebacker comes inside he goes outside and runs it as a regular sweep. It's a very good play against a rotating defense.

In Super Bowl I we ran this play against Kansas City to score our second touchdown. Max McGee had a great game that day as a receiver, but on this play his block actually knocked down three men. From his split position McGee cracked back on the linebacker, pushing that man into the defensive end who was trying to get into the pursuit, and that end fell into the path of the middle linebacker, holding him up. It was quite a parlay. Jim Taylor followed the guards and, as they drove the defensive halfback out, he cut back and ran 14 yards for the touchdown.

Here you see the pull of the guard leading the fullback on the weak-side sweep. The weak-side tackle has tried to make penetration but has been cut off, and the blocker is in full flight.

THE HALFBACK OPTION

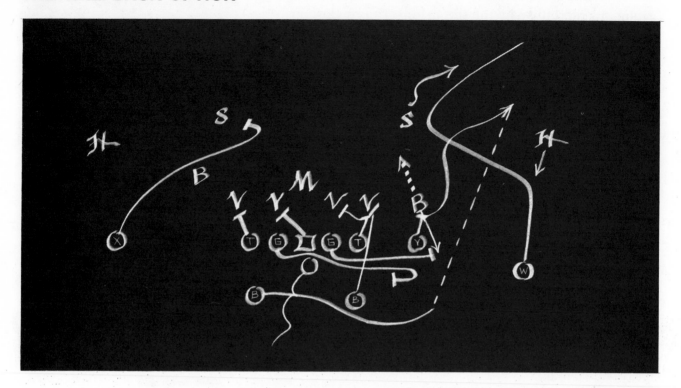

Another effective play to counter defenses that have the defensive halfback and safety forcing quickly to stop the sweep is the halfback option. In fact, if you want to make the sweep go you must be able to execute the halfback option where the back can either run or throw. This play puts a great deal of pressure on the defensive linebacker, the defensive halfback and the safety, and properly executed can often bring a long gain.

The halfback option began for me when I left West Point and joined the New York Giants as offensive coach under Jim Lee Howell back in 1954. Frank Gifford was with the Giants then and I remembered him from the Southern Cal.–Army game because we played them in the mud at Yankee Stadium and he put on a great show.

But I had not seen much pro football while at West Point so that winter I studied game films of all the Giants' games and all the other teams in the league to familiarize myself with every defense and offense.

Watching Gifford, I remembered that great day he had against us not only as a runner but as a fine passer. Since the Giants ran from the T-formation and the halfback option is basically a single-wing play I had to figure out how we could utilize Gifford's tailback talents.

The first thing I had to do was to flank the right halfback (in this case Alex Webster). This gave me the necessary two receivers on the onside going downfield. But now I needed blocking since I was losing my right halfback as a blocker. So I pulled the two guards and either faked the fullback into the line or sent him out ahead as a blocker. Later that right halfback became a flanker and the backfield had only two backs—the halfback and the fullback, which is today's standard pro set.

Paul Hornung had been a quarterback at Notre Dame and when I got to Green Bay the same process took place. I studied films of the Packers and Hornung in action as a halfback and fullback, and knew he had as much ability as any back in football. So the halfback option came to Green Bay.

Halfback option

Everything is made to look exactly like the sweep but there are a number of changes in the assignments of the flanker, the Y end, the offside guard and, of course, the halfback.

The flanker, who in the sweep is responsible for blocking the safety, comes downfield exactly the same way, trying to drive back the halfback but always watching the safety. He comes downfield and drives in on the safety. He does not block the safety but continues on past him and runs a deep corner pattern. If the safety does not force but stays with the flanker, the flanker continues on a deep fly pattern to keep the safety deep.

The Y end sets up on the sweep and takes the man over him in the direction he wants to go. In order to make the man over him move he'll set, pump his feet a little and, after contact, he'll count to about three: one thousand one, one thousand two, one thousand three. Then he releases his block and runs a flat route about 12 to 15 yards downfield.

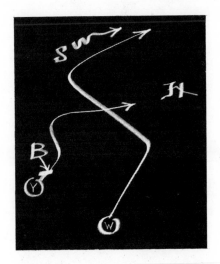

Tackle & fullback   Solid blocking by the tackle and fullback takes the defensive end inside.

Onside guard   The onside guard pulls just as in the sweep, and now he looks for the man released by the Y end. He's got to block that linebacker if the linebacker tries to force the play. If the defensive halfback forces, the guard would take him, since the linebacker would be responsible for the Y end. This very seldom happens.

As the safety forces, the halfback brings the ball up and passes downfield to the open receiver.

The center blocks back on the offside defensive tackle. Offside guard pulls and then turns back when he gets to the area behind the strong-side defensive end, and he turns back to pick up anyone chasing from behind, the middle linebacker or anybody who might have broken through and is chasing the play. The offside tackle will drive-block on the defensive end. The X end runs a crossing pattern trying to get in front of the weak-side safety.

The quarterback opens up exactly as he does in the sweep and hands the ball to the halfback coming hard and flat to the right. The halfback seats the ball and comes under control. He keys the block of the onside guard on the force man, either the linebacker or the defensive halfback. Now he makes his decision—if the Y end is open he throws to him, if the flanker is open he throws to him. That's ideal, of course, because if the safety has come up hard the flanker will be all alone downfield and it's six points.

But many times the defense smells the option. They read pass so there is no force and the linebacker drops back, the defensive halfback covers the Y end and the safety has the flanker. So now all the halfback does as he reads these keys is yell "run" to the guard and he follows the guard upfield for a good gain.

Remember, all these plays are successful only after the defense has been forced to respect the sweep, our No. 1 play. Only then can these adjustments be made to work for us against the defense.

Center, offside guard, offside tackle, X end

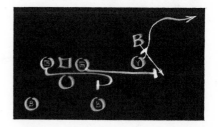

Quarterback, halfback

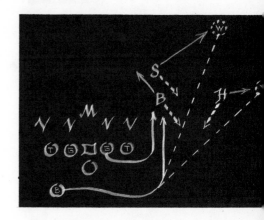

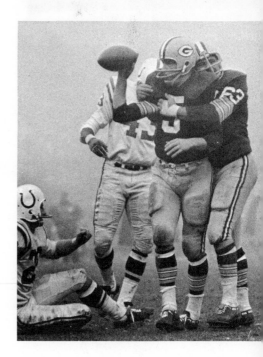

3

Offensive Line Play

One play can win a football game. One game can make a season and one player, any player, can make the difference between winning and losing. No one knows when the big play is coming up; therefore, every player must go all out on every play. In other words, every player has a responsibility on every play, and that responsibility begins with the proper use of his given talents.

It takes a special kind of man to play on the offensive line. He must have the determination and the mental discipline to practice the various blocks constantly. He must be dedicated to perfection and recognize that perfection can be achieved only through the drudgery of practice. There are no shortcuts to success in football. The individual who tries to find them will lose his way.

At the level at which we teach up here, we are dealing with players who have behind them six, eight, ten, twelve or more years in the game, and yet we find, when we analyze why the performance of an individual or a team declines, that it declines because of a breakdown in fundamentals.

Each day, each player, all-pro or rookie, must discipline

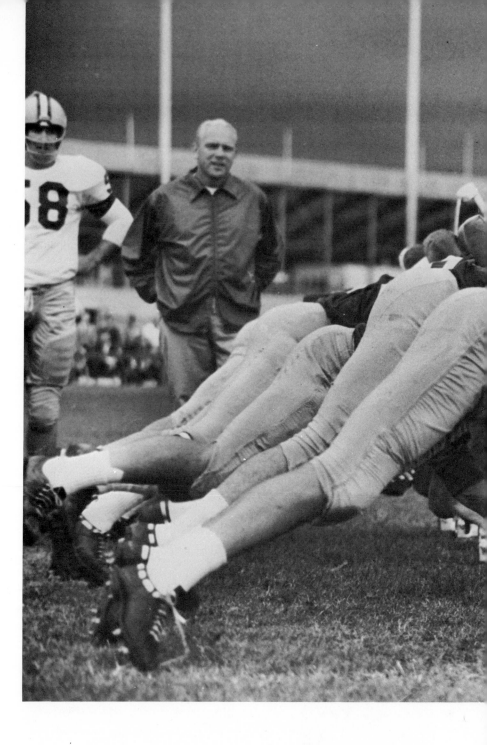

himself mentally and devote himself physically to fundamentals. Only then will his actions become automatic and his excellence instinctive, as it must be for the offensive linemen called upon in the split point of a second to initiate those blocks that make the offense go.

A lineman seldom finds his name in headlines. I know, for I was one myself. The band seldom plays for him, but when he does his job he knows it.

The drudgery of practice and the concentration on the fundamentals are prime ingredients for successful football. The offensive linemen, hitting that blocking sled, show that perfect form that comes from constant practice.

Blocking is the key to winning offensive football. Offensive linemen seldom get the credit due them, but their personal satisfaction lies in knowing that they are part of the successful whole.

Good offensive line play is based on good stance, explosive start, body control, correct hitting position on contact, a forceful delivery of the blow and the follow-through. When the offensive line comes off the ball, it must come off not like the keys of a typewriter but as one man. Uniformity in line play is an absolute necessity. No man can adopt a substitute technique even though he may sometimes be successful with it. There is only one right way to execute each block—the correct way.

The development of all talent is founded on the fundamentals, and in football the first of the fundamentals is the

basic football position: feet spread, knees flexed, a slightly sitting position with the weight evenly distributed. It is from this position that all football movements must stem. All players, whether on the offense or defense, assume this position or move to it, for it is the basic position from which everything, as I have said, will stem, including the basic offensive stance.

All the offensive linemen are doing their thing the correct way. The ball carrier has but to follow his blockers for a good gain.

The offensive football stance is with the feet spread just slightly outside the width of the shoulders with the right foot staggered in the right-handed stance, the toe of the right foot even with the heel of the left foot; the right hand is down with the weight now evenly distributed on the fingers and the two feet. The right arm is just inside the knee of the right leg. The buttocks are slightly higher than the shoulders and the shoulders are square. Sometimes it is difficult to get the shoulders square.

This is the basic offensive linemen's stance: feet spread and slightly staggered, weight evenly distributed on the fingers and the two feet, shoulders square, head up, aiming at the chin of the opponent.

COACHING POINT: To make sure the shoulders are square, drop the left arm to the same position as the right arm, and then lift the left arm and keep it just about even with the knee—this will keep the shoulders square.

Both heels are off the ground slightly, with the right heel somewhat higher than the left heel. It is from this position that the football player uncoils. This is the offensive stance: feet and shoulders properly positioned, head up, neck firm but not straining, and tail slightly higher than the shoulders.

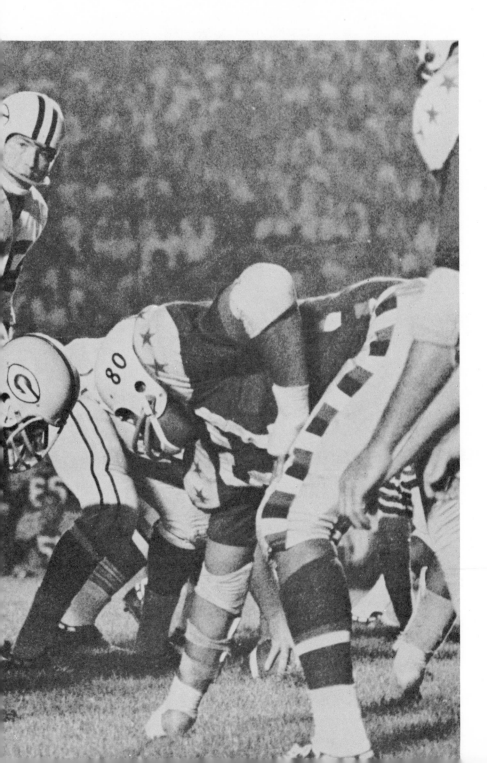

The drive blocker, the guard (No. 64), feet pumping, drives his man as the back cuts behind the block.

The basic block in offensive football is the drive block. The essentials of the drive block are the approach, the delivery of the blow and the follow-through. In the approach the player drives off the rear foot over his front foot and aims his head right at the chin of his opponent, striking him a blow with his head. As the defensive player moves, the blocker takes that man in the direction of his angle. If the defensive man moves to his left, the blocker pinches him on his left shoulder with his head and his left shoulder.

If the defensive man wants to go to his right the same basic approach is used by the blocker, driving off the rear foot over the front foot, aiming his head at the chin of the defensive man, striking him a blow with the forehead.

The purpose of the drive blocker centering his head upon his opponent and driving with the head is that if the defensive man makes a quick move in either direction the blocker can get a piece of him with either shoulder.

As the offensive man drives out he aims his head for his opponent's chin. By the time he has passed the line of scrimmage, however, that chin will not be there because the defensive player will naturally rise. What the blocker will see is the numbers and he drives his head into those. In other words, this is what the drive blocker will see as his target: the chin and the numbers.

Another phase of the offensive block is the speed of the offensive blocker getting to the defensive man. The faster he can get there, the easier it will be to control the defensive man. Once he makes contact he must follow through. One of the reasons we have so many blocking failures is the lack of follow-through, the lack of the continuation of the block. So he must not only make contact but, more important, he must follow through with quick, driving steps, his feet still kept in the same width that they were originally in that stance.

Remember, however, that if the blocker's explosive charge exceeds his ability to control his body, he becomes too extended, making it easy for his opponent to discard or control·him; therefore, the blocker's charge must be a continuous drive—powered and sustained by the piston action of his legs. You cannot drive a man if he is lower than you are; therefore, the blocker must be lower and achieve that balance between body control and explosive charge.

Drive block

This is daylight. An excellent seal by No. 64 and a good drive block by the tackle (No. 75) open a gaping hole in the defense.

As he drives his head into his opponent, the blocker's back is straight and he brings up his forearms and shoulders to broaden his base of contact.

As he starts to drive that man, the blocker will be able to tell from the defensive man's pressure the direction in which that man wants to go. The blocker takes him in that direction, always keeping in mind his own blocking assign-

ment and the hole to which the ball carrier is running. He sustains that drive until the whistle blows.

To summarize: the blocker explodes with the snap, making contact with his head, bringing the forearms and shoulders up and into his man, keeping his legs under him and moving, driving his man out and opening the hole for the runner.

This is the result, and this is what the Packers are all about. Our third consecutive NFL title won against a great defense and the elements—something no team has ever done before: Bart called the wedge, Kramer, with Bowman, drove out their tackle, and Bart took it in. A courageous decision. It climaxed one of the great touchdown drives in football history, and showed the poise, determination and guts not to let any obstacle stand in their way.

Now here is a drive block that was not only perfectly executed but was also the key to a touchdown that won the National Football League championship. There were 16 seconds left in the game and we were trailing 17–14. We were going after our third consecutive NFL title, something no other team in modern professional football had ever accomplished. After a magnificent drive downfield, we had been stopped twice by Dallas on the goal line. Bart Starr called our last time out, came over to me and I said to call the drive play. No question about a rollout or a pass or a field goal. Run it! And he did. Bart took it himself rather than risk the backs slipping away as they had on the two prior plays. He made that decision. I called the play and the line did the blocking!

In this instance, because of the importance and the drama of the game, the right guard (Jerry Kramer) who threw the block was singled out and rightly celebrated. But what of the center (Ken Bowman) to his left and the offensive tackle (Forrest Gregg) to his right and the rest of the line? They all came off that ball together—each did his own job, whatever it was, unseen and uncelebrated.

The second of the essential line blocks is the cutoff block used to prevent pursuit. The blocker makes his first step in the direction of the man he is assigned to block. He pushes off the rear foot and drives over the front foot. He throws his arms, shoulders and head beyond the far leg of the opponent. He goes to all fours and keeps moving in a crablike motion.

Notice that his arms, shoulders and head are in front of the defensive man.

Cutoff block

Down block

Now let us discuss a block where the defensive man is to the inside of the blocker. We call this the down block.

In the down block, again as in the drive block, the blocker takes his first step with his near foot, that is, the foot closer to the man he is going to block. It is a short step and the blocker aims his head at the crotch of his opponent. He must aim at the crotch if he is to keep his head in front of the defensive man and prevent penetration. He makes his contact with the far shoulder. If the defender tries to roll out, the blocker continues to scramble and sometimes this will work into a reverse body block.

The blocker has driven down on the man to the inside and cut him off as the runner goes to the hole outside that block.

A good down block by the center quickly springs the runner into the hole.

Pinch block

Still another type of block is the pinch block, sometimes referred to as the post-drive block or the double-team block, usually used to drive the defensive man back off the line of scrimmage and usually in power or short-yardage plays.

In the pinch block, it is the post man's responsibility to nullify the defensive man's charge and prevent his penetration. The post man moves out with a short step of the foot closer to his drive man; the head is aimed at the midsection of the defensive man, and the post man's objective is to break the charge of that man. He must prevent the defensive man from penetrating between the pinch man and himself.

The pinch man's first step is with the foot closer to the post man because he is also concerned with preventing the defender from coming between the post man and himself. His second objective is not to allow the defensive man to roll out of the block. To sum up: post man—short steps, head aimed at the midsection of the defensive man breaking his charge; pinch man—down block into the side of the defensive man.

This is an excellent example of the pinch block. The post man, the guard (No. 68), has raised his opponent as the pinch man (No. 71) down-blocks into the side of the defensive man.

Pulling linemen

One of the most important techniques that all interior linemen must master is the technique of pulling on traps and sweeps. Guards and tackles must be able to pull with power, speed and precision. The beginning movement in the pull is the basic and most important move. It consists of two parts:

1) the snap of the lead arm on the side to which the pulling lineman is going; the lead arm is pulled back with the elbow close to the body.

2) the direction of the lead step. The direction or the positioning of the lead foot is determined by whether the pull is long or short. For the short pull, as used on trap plays, the blocker's first step is a quick jab step with the eyelets or eyes of the lead foot looking down the line of scrimmage where the blocker wants to go. It is important for the pulling blocker to shift his weight immediately onto that lead foot or he will rise too high as he takes off.

As he approaches his objective, the trap blocker must remember not to launch his block too soon; in fact, he should be close enough to his opponent so that he is almost stepping on the opponent's toes. Just before reaching his man, the blocker must make a small dip. Then he drives through that man. If he does not move the opponent, the play will be piled up. The technique is the same for all interior linemen, whether they play to the right or to the left of center.

For the long, deep or belly pull used in the sweep, the first step is almost an about-face away from the line of scrimmage. As with the trap block, when pulling, both of these actions—the snap of the lead arm and the lead step—must be made as one motion. The second step is normal in length and the blocker takes off running low and hard and pumping his arms. He bellies his pull to a depth of 4 or 5 yards and, wheeling into the hole, he moves upfield toward his assignment.

The pulling lineman, the guard (No. 68), shows power and speed as he charges through the defensive man to lead the runner upfield.

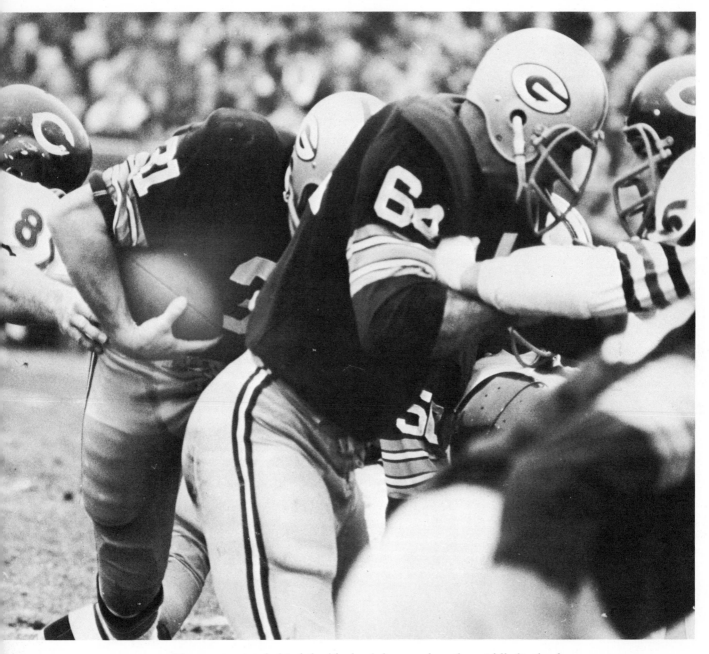

The runner cuts behind the block of the guard on the middle linebacker.

Fold block A very effective block used by the guards and the center is referred to as the fold block, in which the center blocks back in either direction and the guard folds, or falls, behind that block and goes for the middle linebacker. It is usually used in the power plays up through the middle. The fold blocker will take a delaying step, allowing the center to pass in front, and then his technique is the same as that of a drive blocker.

Here the guard (No. 64) folds behind the center (No. 57) as he drive-blocks on that middle linebacker.

Do-dad blocking

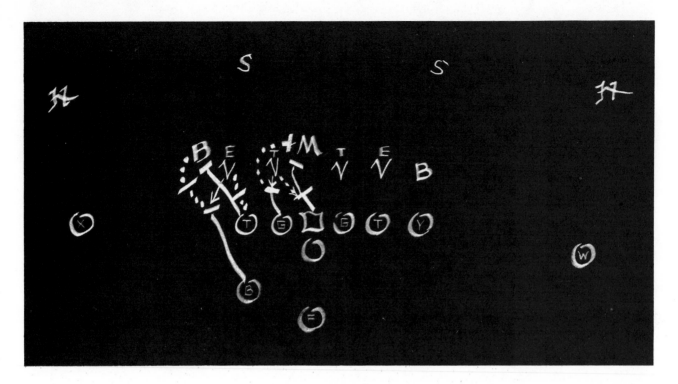

On illustrating the do-dad, or the area block as it is sometimes called, we will talk about just the offensive center, the offensive left guard in this case, the offensive left tackle and the halfback. The guard and the center do-dad or area block the defensive tackle and the middle linebacker. Do-dad blocking is used against stunting lines or lines that stack one defensive man behind the other. In the case where the defensive tackle has an inside charge and the middle linebacker is keying the fullback and has the outside responsibility, the middle linebacker will, with the snap of the ball, move immediately to the hole, making it impossible for the offensive center to cut him down because of the middle linebacker's key on the fullback. In this case we will use do-dad blocking.

The center is the lead blocker—the apex. He will lead-step, the same technique as the down block, for the crotch of the defensive tackle. The offensive guard, using the same technique as he does in the drive block, will aim for a point which is outside the hip of the defensive tackle. If the

In this do-dad block the center has taken the defensive tackle as the guard (No. 63) comes off his block to seal for the middle linebacker.

defensive tackle has an inside charge, the guard immediately releases the tackle, picking up the middle linebacker who would be moving with the key of the fullback toward the hole. The center, since the tackle is moving into him, would pick him off.

If the defensive tackle has an outside charge, that means that the middle linebacker would first have responsibility to the inside. Remember, however, that the middle linebacker still has the key of the fullback. But the fact that he has inside responsibility would hold him long enough so that the center, coming off the down block on the defensive tackle, could recover and pick off the middle linebacker.

The worst that could happen is that, with an outside charge by the tackle and inside responsibility by the middle linebacker, the center could not recover—and he cannot always recover from his start at that defensive tackle. So we would have a double team block on that defensive tackle, driving him back and often cutting off the pursuit of the middle linebacker.

Another illustration of do-dad blocking is the do-dad between the offensive tackle and the offensive halfback against the defensive end and the linebacker. The same principle applies: outside charge by the defensive end, inside responsibility by the linebacker—inside responsibility by the defensive end means outside responsibility by the linebacker. The two offensive men—the offensive tackle and the halfback—will do-dad with these two defensive men—the defensive end and the linebacker. The inside man or offensive tackle again is the apex in the blocking. He lead-steps for the crotch of the defensive end. If the defensive end goes to the outside—or if he disappears, in other words—the offensive tackle off his lead step would immediately look for the outside linebacker who usually would have the inside responsibility on that particular deal between these two men.

If the defensive tackle came to the inside, the tackle would pick him, releasing the offensive halfback who would now pick the outside linebacker. The halfback leads for the outside hip of the defensive end. If the defensive end disappears to the inside, he takes the outside linebacker. If the defensive end comes out into him, the halfback would take the end, leaving the outside linebacker for the offensive tackle to block.

Do-dad blocking can be used anyplace on the offensive line with any two offensive linemen—offensive tackle and end, offensive tackle and guard—against any combination of defenses that are stacked or that deal.

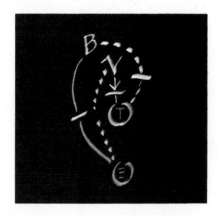

Here's a do-dad between the guard (No. 68) taking the tackle as the tackle (No. 72) comes off to seal on the linebacker.

Tight end or Y end as a blocker

In rule blocking, the blocker takes the man over him in the direction that man wants to go. Here No. 64, the guard, is driving on the defensive tackle and the back, keying his block, will go in the opposite direction.

The tight end is first a blocker, second a receiver, and third a runner. In other words, he must be able to execute all the blocks of the interior linemen as well as catch the ball and run with it. And one of his most important blocks is the one required in the power sweep.

We ask the Y end blocking for the sweep to split 6 to 9 feet from the offensive tackle in order to isolate the defender or linebacker who usually is playing over him. He takes his

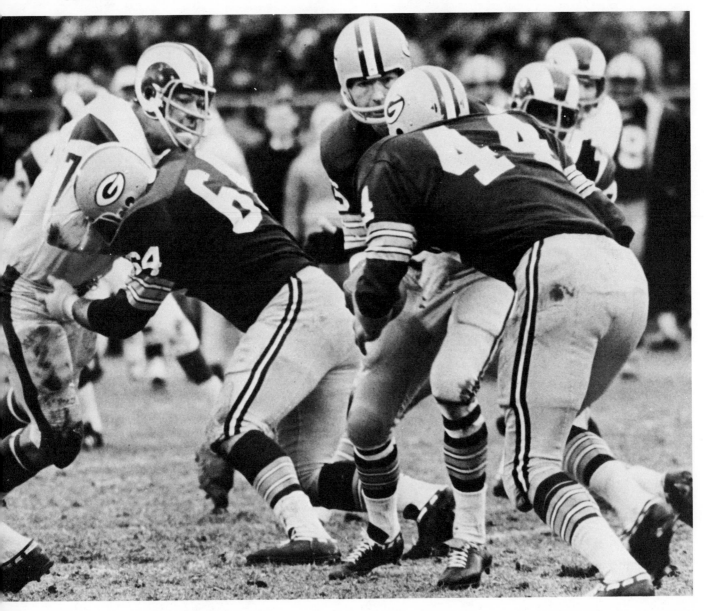

regular three-point stance and his rule is: on the snap he sets as on the pass. It is the same technique an interior offensive lineman would use to pass-block. His weight is on the inside leg, and his eyes are on the numbers of the defensive man playing over him. If that defensive man tries to penetrate to the inside, the Y or tight end will drive him down the line of scrimmage. The Y end is prepared to take that defensive man, to drive the man over him in the direction that he wants to go.

COACHING POINT: Never allow penetration to the inside! Because we cannot have penetration, the Y end's weight must be on the inside of his foot, his eyes on the numbers of that defensive man, and he must be ready at all times to drive the man down the line if he tries to penetrate.

On an outside move by the defensive man the same technique is used: the weight is still on the inside and now we tell the Y end to drop back his outside foot, keeping his eyes on the numbers, and not to make his move until the man is even with him. In other words, the numbers on the defensive man are beyond his eyes. When the numbers are beyond the eyes, he wheels and takes him out.

And on the practice field, of course, is where good blocking begins. It begins with the proper stance, the proper angle of the approach, the proper follow-through, the linemen driving off the ball as one man and hitting as one man. It is stance, approach, hit and follow through. And they must come off as one man. One man coming off late will permit penetration. So they must all come off the ball together, as we have practiced over and over again until they are all one— one single driving unit.

Rule blocking

Today our whole running offense depends upon the speed and power with which we drive off that line. And one of the reasons we can operate with such speed is that we no longer allow the defense to dictate the blocking of the offensive line. In other words, each lineman knows his assignment and, no matter what the defense does, he has "a rule" to adjust to it.

When I played this game we were all position blockers. We took the first step to get into position and we launched off the second step. When I joined the Giants, they were blocking according to the defense they were facing on any play. The defense dictated the man the offensive lineman was to block, so this was in effect a defensive approach to offensive football.

I'll never forget that first team meeting at Salem, Oregon, when I went to the board knowing that the players on the Giants were skeptical of any "college stuff" I might want to introduce. I know I was very positive but they weren't, and even on the practice field they were still not sure. When I gave it to them, this rule blocking, they thought I was crazy and thought they would have to break me in to the game of professional football. But I had complete authority of the offense and could put in what I wanted, so eventually they came around to my way.

Rule blocking simplified the blocking for those offensive linemen because they no longer had to learn a different assignment for each defense and they bought it big! Now the defense was no longer calling the shots.

For instance, if there is a man over the center he'll drive-block him or cut him off. If no man is over the center then he becomes a seal man and cuts off pursuit. Same thing for the guard: no man over you—seal for the first inside linebacker; man over you—take him in the direction he wants to go.

Center's blocks

The center makes two blocks more often than any other offensive player. These blocks are the cutoff block and the down block.

The cutoff block is used to prevent pursuit. One example of the cutoff block is that the center must get the middle linebacker who is starting in the direction of the play. The center, pushing off the rear foot and driving over the front foot, makes his first step in the direction of the man that he is assigned to block. On contact with that man he throws his arms, shoulders and head beyond the far leg of his opponent. He then will drop to all fours and keep moving in a crablike motion. If he is going to release his man he must release him to the rear.

The down block or the block back is used by the center when he must block a defender who is set to either side of him or when that defender is attempting to penetrate, as in a gap or a goal-line defense. The center's first step is with his near foot. It is a short step and he aims his head at the crotch of his opponent, anticipating that the defensive man will move on the snap of the ball. If the center does not get his head in front and aims at the hips he will lose his man because that man will beat him across the line of scrimmage. He must aim at the crotch. He makes his contact with the far shoulder and keeps his head in front of the man. If the defensive man does not penetrate, the center moves into a reverse body block to prevent the defensive man from spinning out.

Here the center has already made a good down block on the defensive player as the guard (No. 63) fold-blocks behind him, and the offside guard (No. 64) has pulled and is leading the ball carrier.

Receivers

Receivers, of course, are also called upon to block. The tight end or Y end, for example, is first a blocker, then a receiver. He must be able to execute the drive block and the down block, and also fulfill his role in the two-on-one block, or the pinch block. The split end or flanker, however, is first a receiver and then a blocker; and he must also be able to

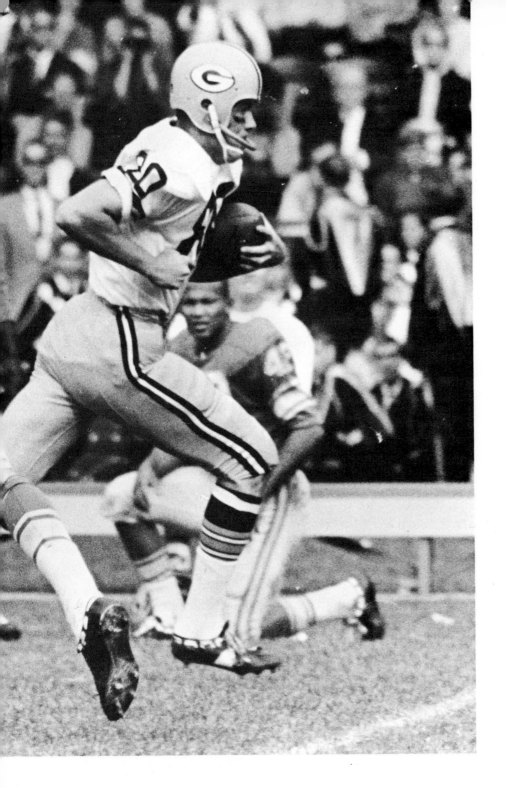

When the flanker (No. 84) cracked back on the safety, his block sprung his teammate, the split end, for a long gain.

execute the crack-back block against linebackers and defensive backs.

On the crack-back block the blocker must get down the line quickly before the linebacker can penetrate. On contact he puts his head in front of the linebacker at his waist and he pinches him with the outside shoulder and keeps driving.

SUMMARY

As I said, it takes a special kind of person to play on the offensive line. He must have the strength to block those huge defensive linemen, the quickness and agility to pull and get in front of the speedy runners, the mental ability to adjust to sudden changes in the fraction of a second and the speed to get downfield into the secondary to block for the runner. When you find all of that in one player you really have a man. And you must have tackles who are big and strong enough to play guard and guards who are quick enough to play tackle. Versatility in an offensive lineman is a plus and, with my teams, a must, because you never know when an injury will strip you of one of your linemen.

Injuries are part of the game of football, and the speed and abandon at which the game is played dictates that you are going to have some each season. You can only hope that the physical conditioning program you have put them through in the summer keeps injuries to a minimum and, with luck, that the big injury will escape you. But injuries occur, each game and each season. When an injury happens to an offensive lineman, it can be very damaging because of the loss of timing and rhythm to that line. Timing and rhythm are a subtle thing: when you have it, the whole team moves like a finely tuned drill team; take out one of the parts and that offensive line can look like a bunch of rookies, destroying the best plays devised.

The anonymity that the offensive lineman lives in can be relieved somewhat if you stress, and he believes, that without him there is no glory for the backs and receivers. But the drudgery of practice, the boredom of running the same play over and over, makes it imperative that the coach, at least, gives those linemen all the credit they deserve. The newspapers and television broadcasters never will. I know.

What it comes down to is that the offensive lineman, to be successful, must be willing to pay the price, even if in that success someone else gets the headlines. Great teams are built on successful line play, offensively and defensively. The individuals on that offensive line—Thurston, Ringo, Skoronski, Kramer, Bowman, Gillingham and Gregg—were all talented, but their greatness was as a team, one single driving force that over the years proved itself in so many winning games.

Forrest Gregg is, quite simply, the finest football player I ever coached.

4
The Running Game

The running game—this is football. The running with the ball is what makes football. The running game is the heart of football.

This is what I believe and believe strongly. It is the running game that puts a team in position to command. It is the running game that makes the passing game go. A pass play may succeed through the coordination of two, three or four men. But it takes the coordination of everybody, the cohesion of all eleven men to make the running game go. Thus, the satisfaction derived from the successful running play is supreme, but so are the demands.

Football is two things: it is blocking and tackling. You block and tackle better than the team you're playing, and you win. Some people try to find things in this game or put things into this game which do not exist. I do not believe the game is as complex as many people think it is and as some try to make it. At the same time, I do not think it's as simple as it was thirty years ago. We try to make it as uncomplicated as we can, because I believe that if you block and tackle better than the other team, and the breaks are even, you're going to win.

When I first came into this league and after I had spent all those months studying the movies, it seemed to me that while the passing game was great, the running game was like a half try. In those days everybody was saying you just couldn't sustain a running game against the pros, that their defenses were too large and too mobile. Well, they're still large and mobile today. What they forgot was that everything in football, as in physics, is relative, and that the people you could put on that offense could be every bit as big and just as mobile as the people on the defense.

What I think they really liked about the throwing game was that only two or three key men had to be coordinated on the pass play, but on a running play it required split-second timing of at least seven or eight people. It is difficult not only to develop the running game but to keep this coordination required for its success because, if you want to scrimmage once the season starts, you have to run your first team offense against your first team defense and you are risking injury. What it comes down to is that to have a good running game you have to run as a coach. You have to derive more creative satisfaction from the planning and the polishing of the coordination of all eleven men rather than just three or four.

When I first got to Green Bay I tried to make the offensive linemen's job both easier and harder at the same time by introducing them to option-blocking or rule-blocking. Instead of squaring off as they had in the past with the opposite man and locking horns like two giant dinosaurs, the option-blocker was expected to contact his opponent to determine

Here is a good illustration of a back reading the blocks of his offensive linemen. The guard has the middle linebacker with a firm drive block, and he has raised his opponent and is controlling him. The center has taken the defensive tackle, and the tackle has the good position on the defensive end. The back is cutting away from the center and between the block of the guard and the tackle. If that linebacker had moved farther to the left, the guard would have taken him that way and the back would have cut between the guard and the center—again it is run to daylight.

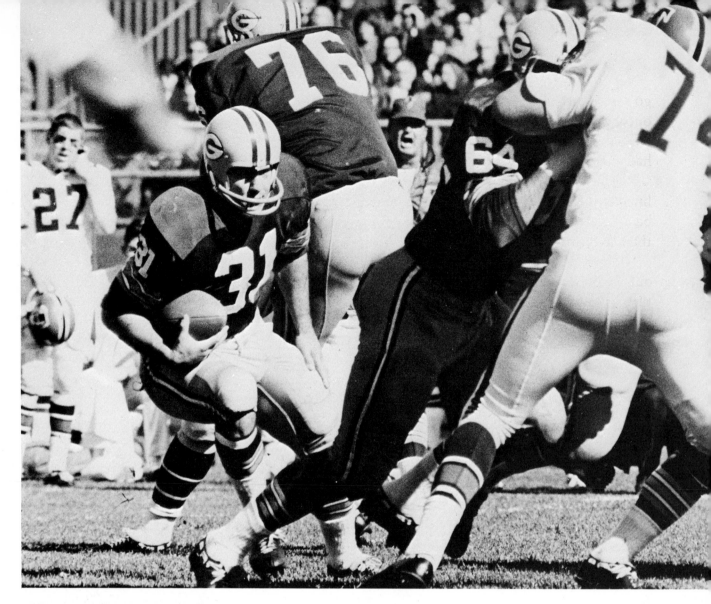

The guard (No. 64) is driving out the defensive tackle in the direction that tackle wants to go. The back (No. 31), keying that block, cuts to the outside of that defensive tackle. This is a perfect example of the running back reading the block of his offensive lineman.

the thrust of the opponent's drive and assist him in that direction; in other words, "take him in the direction he wants to go." Well, the back, reading the block of his offensive linemen, had that split-second choice to make his decision of which way to run or "to run for daylight."

The first time I realized that in pro football it was to your advantage to run to daylight and not to run to a specific hole was when I started coaching with the New York Giants. We put in a belly play for Frank Gifford and it was designed to go inside the left end and our right guard would pull and take the left end out. But, with all of the emphasis on an inside run, the defensive end started to read the play and pinched so hard that you couldn't get him out of there. So Gifford, as the defensive end, would close inside, would fake inside and go outside. If the end, instead of closing down, went to the outside, then Gifford just followed the block of the guard and went inside. In other words, the offensive linemen no longer had to go head to head with those monsters.

The thing that was more difficult for those offensive linemen was that they had to be aware of all the options, be able to read their defensive linemen and be able to take them in the direction they wanted to go.

Running to daylight is a very glamorous description of our running game, but it requires the split-second coordination of the offensive linemen and the intelligence of those linemen in making their blocks, and the backs, who have poise and confidence, to make the quick decision necessary if the running-to-daylight option is to work.

In our 1961 championship game in Green Bay against the Giants, they undershifted their line to try and stop Jimmy Taylor on the off-tackle slant whenever we got into that formation. So we countered by running the ball right at the middle linebacker who is normally in the middle. But because the Giants' defensive line was overshifted to the weak side to stop Taylor, the middle linebacker was playing over the guard. With straight-ahead zone-blocking or option-blocking all we did was have the center drive-block the tackle over him. The guard would take the middle linebacker in the direction he wanted to go and the offensive tackle took the defensive end to the outside. This gave Taylor three holes to hit. If the middle linebacker came to the right, he went to the left; if the middle linebacker went to the left, he went to the right; and if the defensive end closed down hard to the inside, then Taylor just went outside of that defensive end's force and the offensive tackle let the defensive end come to the inside. With the tight end cutting off the linebacker over him, Taylor got a great deal of daylight to run to. And on one particular play Jimmy broke it for about a 45-yard run.

The success of the running game, while it is based on the dedication, coordination and efficiency of all eleven men on the offensive team, is also based, of course, on the ability of the quarterback and his offensive team to take advantage of the weaknesses and the habits of the defensive team they are facing. The success or failure of one play will always set up another play that can be worked.

THE RUNNING BACK

Every back has his own natural way of running. Some shuffle their feet, some pick up their knees. For obvious reasons, the back who has natural high knee action and great leg drive has the advantage. But if a runner tries to overemphasize picking up his knees, he'll end up just running in one place. All good running backs should have quick feet no matter what the stride, and neither foot should be on the ground any longer than it takes to push off it. And when that back is about to be tackled, he must make himself as compact as possible to save himself punishment and also to inflict it. It is much better to give than to receive.

We no longer teach our backs to run to a specific hole. They know, of course, where that hole is supposed to be, but we school them to run to daylight, wherever it is. The habits formed on the practice field are the habits that the player will carry into the game and throughout a career; therefore, every time that running back runs the ball in practice he must run it as close to perfection as possible.

Running-back stance

In the running-back stance, the feet are straight ahead and parallel to the line of scrimmage. The toe of the rear foot is opposite the arch of the forward foot. The weight is balanced on the balls of the feet. The fingers of the down hand are extended and touch the ground lightly to form a tripod with the two feet. The shoulders are squared with the back parallel to the ground. The running back's head is up, the eyes looking straight ahead and not at the area to which the back is going to run.

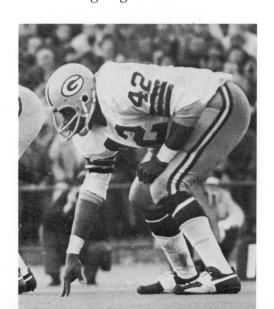

Here is the result of that high, driving knee action by the back. Sometimes Jimmy Taylor (No. 31), when he broke into the secondary, would look for those defensive halfbacks just so he could "sting 'em a little."

Out on the practice field is where we perfect the techniques of all phases of the game of football. Here we see the form of the back with his inside arm back and out of the way, and the forearm is forward and parallel to the line of scrimmage, fingers extended. The quarterback, coming down the line of scrimmage, has the responsibility for placing the ball in the belly of the back, and all the back does is keep his eyes on his blockers. Notice the uniformity of the leg action of the offensive line as they drive off the ball.

At the hand-off the inside arm is back and out of the way. The outside forearm is forward and parallel to the ground with the outside stop hand open, fingers extended, and now the eyes are on the hole.

We use a little different technique, I think, than most teams in the position of the back receiving the ball from the quarterback. We like to have the stomach completely open. Our back takes a natural running action, arms pumping. It is the quarterback's responsibility to place the ball in the belly of the back. So all the back does is keep his eyes on the hole to which he is running.

It is very important that he keep his inside arm back behind his hips so that the whole stomach is exposed. There is nothing there to stop the ball, there is nothing there to hit the ball, there is nothing there to cause a fumble.

The back, in assuming a natural running position as he is going to get the ball, has his hand back, forearm of the outside hand parallel to the ground, stop hand next to the outside part of his stomach with the palm open. This prevents the ball from coming all the way across the body. At the same time he is watching the blocking take place in front of him. As the ball comes in, he stops it with his outside hand, and as the ball is seated his inside hand comes underneath the ball and he cradles it. The quarterback has stepped down the line of scrimmage. His eyes are focused on the belly of the back. The back has his near arm removed, his other forearm parallel to the ground, his hand open to stop the ball. His eyes are on the hole. The quarterback plants the ball so the back can feel it.

In our 1965 championship game against Cleveland we found the draw to be a very effective play with Jimmy Taylor running it. Here is an excellent close-up of the handoff by the quarterback to the fullback on a draw play. Note the tackle on the left-hand side setting as if to pass and the hard charge of the defensive end coming after the quarterback. The ball is handed off as the fullback waits for the quarterback. It means that the fullback had set as a pass blocker and the quarterback came back to him and made the hand-off.

There's another important variation of the hand-off and that is the one that is employed in the draw play. Draws are effective in combating excessive pressure by the defense in its rush to the passer and as a change of pace for the offense. For the draw to be effective, however, everyone must simulate pass, including the running back who is going to receive the ball. That means that the back will not be moving toward the hole. He will be set as he does as a pass blocker and the

quarterback will come to him to make the hand-off. The back will sit there and wait for the ball to be seated in his stomach. Once it is seated, the runner will key the block of his offensive right guard. If the offensive right guard takes his man to his right, he will run the draw play to the inside. If the offensive right guard takes his man to the left, he will run that draw play to the right side. This is a classic example of running a play to daylight.

Hand-off on slant plays

On slant plays the quarterback uses a reverse pivot. The quarterback has complete responsibility for placing the ball. The back's eyes are on the hole. The slant has long been a favorite play of mine because it gets the back to the hole almost as quickly as the dive play yet it gives the back the opportunity to run to daylight.

Pitchouts

Note the concentration of the quarterback on the area where he is going to place the ball, and the eyes of the running back are looking toward the area to which he is going to run.

Of course, not all running plays are designed for the quarterback to actually hand the ball to the running back. Sometimes, if we want to get outside the defensive perimeter quickly, we use pitchouts. There are two types of pitchouts, of course, which are the one-handed or the underhanded spiral pitchout, and the two-handed toss to either side. The

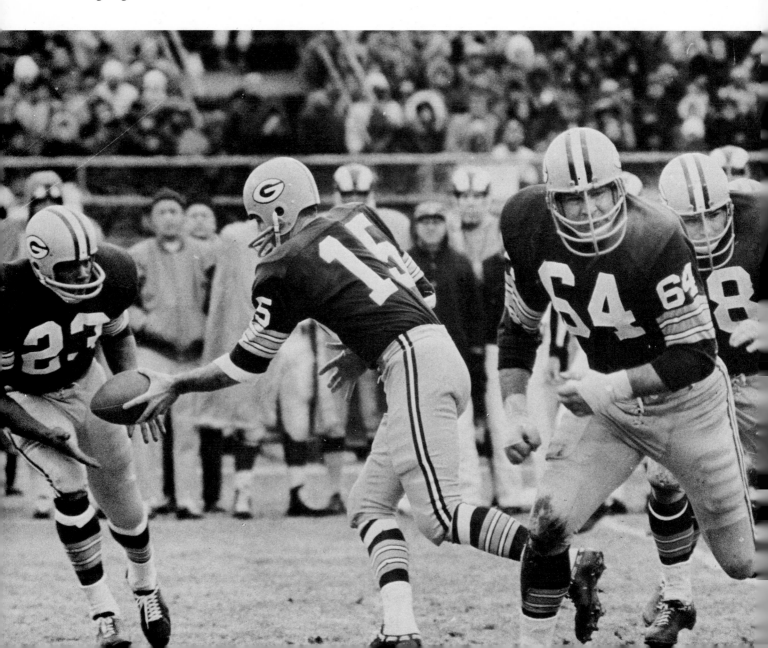

two-handed lateral, which is a soft lateral, is usually made with a reverse pivot to the right, and to the fullback, who is going wide on a sweep action.

Another type of lateral that is used, usually to the halfback on a quick pitchout going to the right, is done with a reverse pivot and with a spiral action of the ball; and again the ball is thrown from the stomach by the quarterback. Also, again, the quarterback has complete responsibility for putting the ball in the hands of the halfback going out. The successful pitchout, or any running play, however, is not just the result of a partnership of two or three men. It is the result of the coordination and concentration of all eleven men, each of whom has made himself a master of the fundamentals on which winning football is founded.

Below is an illustration of the two-handed lateral to the fullback going wide on a sweep action. Note the concentration again of the quarterback getting the ball to the fullback, and the position of the arms of the fullback is just as on any running play—open, and making it easy for the ball to come into him.

THE PLAYS

Now let me discuss some plays that have been the nucleus, the bread and butter, of my running game. Let us first recognize the formations from which we run them. In the Brown formation the fullback lines up directly behind the quarterback and the center, about 3 to 3½ yards deep. In the Red formation, the fullback takes his position not in line with the quarterback and center as he does in the Brown formation but behind the offensive tackle.

Veer play

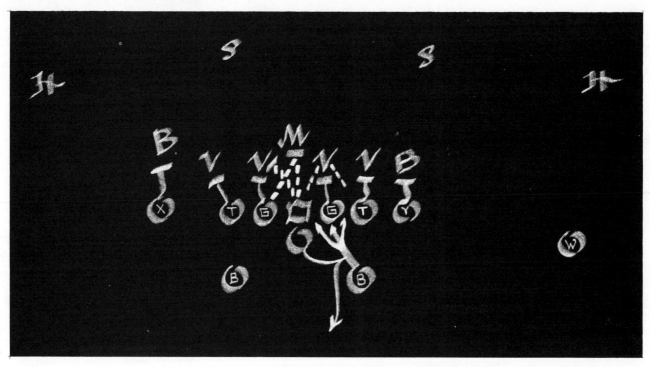

The veer play, which is really a take-off on the dive play, is a favorite of mine because it gives the back the opportunity to read the block of his guard and center and to be able to run to daylight.

In the veer play the outside end or Y end blocks the man over him. The onside tackle and guard do the same. The center has a choice here—he can block on the middle linebacker or he can block down on the defensive tackle to his outside. Offside tackle and offside end drive-block the men over them.

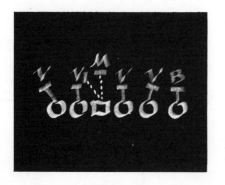

The fullback, the ball carrier, starts with his inside foot off his stance straight at the rear of his onside guard. The quarterback on an open pivot gains ground approximately

three steps and hands off to the fullback. The quarterback continues around the ball carrier after the hand-off.

The ball carrier then veers into the hole. The key to the runner in this play is the straight drive blocking by the offensive linemen, taking the men over them in the direction they want to go.

In the veer play the fullback will read the blocks of the offensive guard and center and of the offensive left guard, and will run to the hole according to the direction in which the defensive man is taken. For instance, if the middle linebacker closes to the hole toward the right guard, the center will take him that way and the back will veer around the

In our Western Conf. championship against the Rams, the veer play got us our final touchdown.

The fullback, Chuck Mercine, has just cut behind the block of his guard on the defensive tackle. . . .

center's block and into the hole vacated by the middle linebacker. If the right guard takes his man, the defensive tackle, toward the center, the fullback will go straight through that hole.

And, sometimes, with the middle linebacker and the defensive tackle closing the hole to the right of the center and a hard inside charge by the defensive tackle on the left on the offside guard, that offside offensive guard will take that defensive tackle the way he wants to go and that back will

The safety tries to stop him, but he's driving and headed for that goal line. . . .

break it off and veer outside of that defensive tackle into that hole.

We do many things with the left halfback in this veer play depending upon what we think the keys of the linebackers are. If the middle linebacker is keying the left halfback, we will move the left halfback to the right, making that linebacker move with him, opening up the hole even more for the fullback. If the outside linebackers are keying the left halfback, we will move the left halfback to the left, keeping

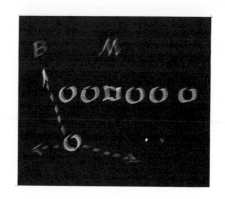

He drives through the tackle of the safety and into the end zone for the touchdown. . . .

the linebackers out so that they cannot fall off into the play. In some defenses we would drive the halfback right at that outside linebacker.

The veer play is very effective against the odd formation; in fact, I believe that's what makes it one of the great plays. The blocking is the same in the odd formation as in the even formation, whether it's 4–3 over or 4–3 under. The offensive linemen take the men over them in the direction they want to go. The center is the key blocker against the odd defensive line. He takes the man over him in the direction he wants to

The joy of winning can be clearly seen in the expressions of the running back and his teammates.

go. The ball carrier must also recognize the odd defense since it sets up the blocking for his hole. He knows, for example, by the alignment with which the center has a man over him, that he must key the block of the center. If the center takes his man to the left, the back goes up to the right. If the center takes the man over him to the right, the back will veer behind his block and go up to the left.

That's why we like this play; we don't care what kind of defenses they're going to throw at us, we're going to run this veer play on them!

Off-tackle play

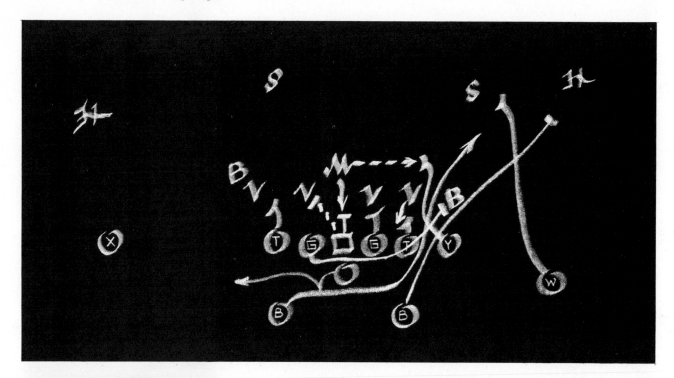

The off-tackle play is one of the oldest plays in football, reminiscent of the days of the single wing, but it remains a fundamental play that teams must be able to execute and execute well. The flanker is in a near position, that is, 5 to 8 yards split from his Y end. The flanker releases for the strong-side safety.

The Y end downblocks on the first man to his inside. If the defensive end goes to the inside, he pulls off the double-team block or pinch block with his right tackle on that defensive end and seals for the middle linebacker.

The right tackle aims his head at the crotch of the defensive end and drives him. If that end has an inside charge he makes that block with his left shoulder, allowing the Y end who is double-teaming with him to slide off and seal for the middle linebacker. If the end comes upfield we use

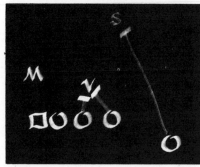

Here's the off-tackle play to the weak side with the running back following the pull of his guards. The onside guard kicks out for the safety man and the offside guard turns upfield into the hole and the running back follows the offside guard into the hole.

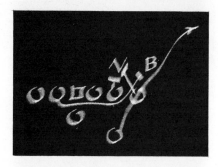

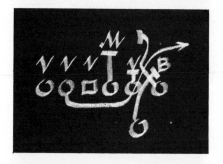

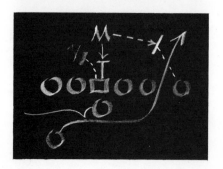

a double-team block between the Y end and the offensive tackle.

The right guard drives and cuts off the man over him. The center cuts off the man over him. If there is no one over him, he drives offside to help on the defensive tackle.

The fullback moves up to get an outside position on the linebacker and drives the first man outside of the Y end's block. The offside guard pulls onside behind the center, also driving the first man outside the Y end's block. If the guard sees the fullback has the block on that linebacker, the guard turns up through the hole looking to the strong-side defensive halfback.

Offside tackle against an odd-man line pulls with the offside guard and cuts off the first man between himself and the center. As is true with every play, all offensive players must recognize whether the defense is odd or even. Against an even-man line he cuts off the defensive end or linebacker, whoever has the inside responsibility. The offside end releases inside the offside linebacker looking for the safety.

The quarterback opens up to the left halfback and makes the hand-off almost directly behind the center, being very careful not to force the left halfback too far from the line of scrimmage. The left halfback comes across parallel to the line of scrimmage and drives through the hole.

COACHING POINT: On this play there is a special technique for the center. It is sometimes called a look-and-see block. If the center were to block down on the offside defensive tackle, the middle linebacker could go through that hole and make the tackle behind the line of scrimmage. On the other hand, if the center releases for the middle linebacker immediately, it is possible for the defensive offside tackle to follow the play and make the tackle behind the line of scrimmage. So what we ask the center to do is "look and see." He hesitates slightly for a fraction of a second on the line of scrimmage. Actually what the center does is key the middle linebacker. If the middle linebacker goes in pursuit of the back, the center blocks back on the defensive tackle. If the middle linebacker blitzes over him, the center takes him because now he knows that the offside tackle has outside responsibility on the weak side.

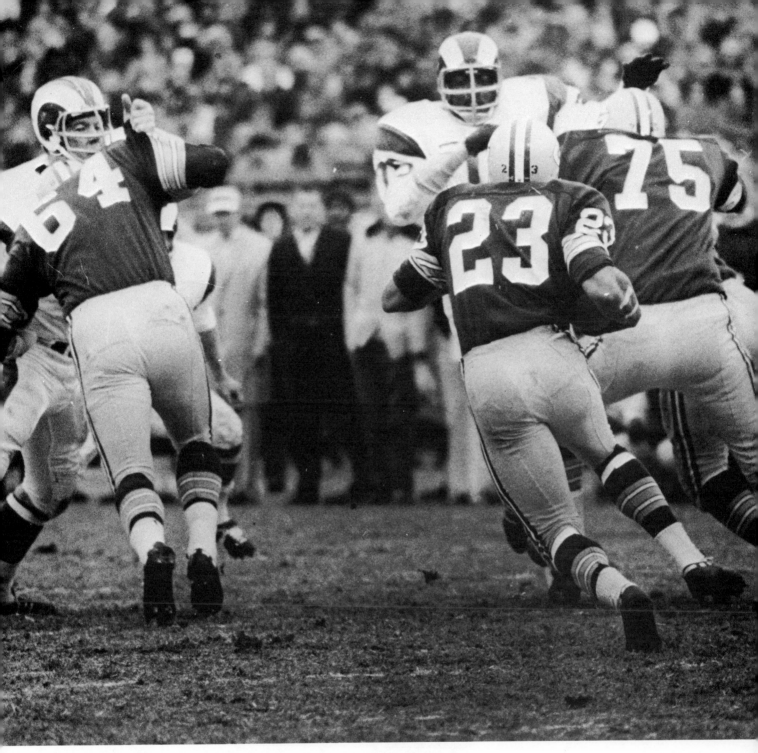

A good example of a running back keying the blocks of his offensive linemen. The back plants that inside foot and cuts back inside the block of No. 64 on the defensive tackle.

Strong-side pitchout

The strong-side pitchout is used when the strong-side defensive end is slow or when the strong-side linebacker is holding up the Y end on his outside release. It is a play that will break in a number of places and its element of surprise is based on getting the ball to a fast back led by a fast tackle.

The flanker splits 10 to 12 yards from the Y end, comes down the line of scrimmage and cracks back on the strong-side linebacker just about when the strong-side linebacker has pushed off the Y end's outside release. If the Y end has taken the linebacker, the flanker will turn upfield for the safety man. In other words, they switch assignments. The Y end drives hard through the outside hip of the strong-side linebacker and releases outside for the strong safety.

COACHING POINT: When the Y end feels that the linebacker is going to blitz, the Y end will take the linebacker trying to hook him, in which case the flanker will turn upfield and block the safety.

This is how that strong-side pitchout looks to the safety man (No. 48). That tackle (No. 75) is bearing down on him and, cutting behind his blocker, the fullback (No. 33) takes it upfield.

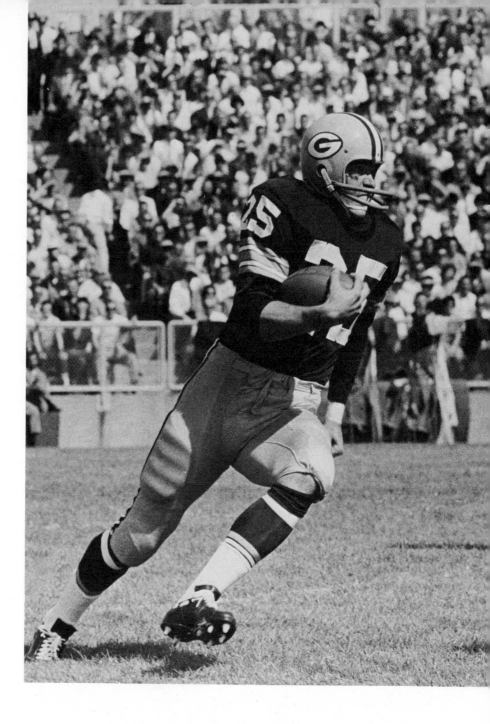

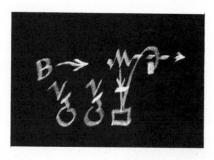

The onside tackle pulls to the onside and as soon as he passes the flanker he turns upfield to maintain an inside-outside position on the strong-side defensive halfback or the corner man to block him out. The onside guard pulls onside to cut off the defensive end. The center releases onside to cut off the middle linebacker. If that middle linebacker is gone the center will fan-back block close to the line of scrimmage. The offside guard, the offside tackle and the offside end release inside the men over them to cross the field and try and get in

The back, on a strong-side pitch-out, is now into the secondary, and still has his lead blocker in front of him.

front of the ball carrier. The halfback or the offback runs a quick trap action trying to cut off the offside defensive tackle. The quarterback releases and gives a quick pitch or toss to the fullback.

The fullback comes under control and loses a little ground until he gets the ball. The idea is to get that ball to the fullback as quickly as possible so he can look and run to daylight, keying the block of the strong-side tackle and the Y end.

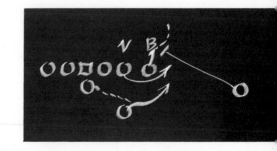

Fullback toss weak

The fullback toss weak is a special type of play designed to get the fullback to the outside on the weak side as quickly as possible. It should be run against a defensive end who is playing rather tight and also against a safety who is favoring the strong side of the formation or is lining up to the strength of the formation or the side to which the flanker is.

The reason I say this about the safety is, as you'll notice from the diagram, we have only one blocker to the outside who must be used to crack back on that first inside linebacker or the first linebacker to his inside. There is no one else to block the safety, and as the guard pulls and turns upfield, he kicks out on the corner man, so there is really no one else who can get to that safety man if he were too far over. We do expect, however, the offside tackle to release and get in front of that safety man as best he can. The offside Y end also releases and tries to get out in the secondary.

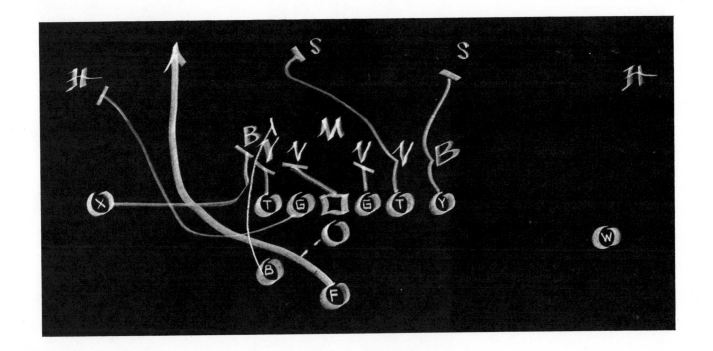

This is a good example of the fullback toss weak, with the quarterback pitching the ball softly to the running back. The eyes of the quarterback are on the area to which the ball is headed, and the running back, with that natural motion, has his stomach exposed and hands ready to make it easier for the quarterback to complete the pitchout.

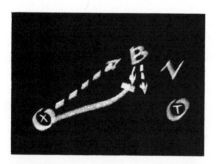

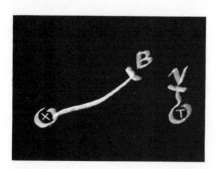

The fullback toss weak is a play in which the fullback gets the ball very fast from the quarterback and he turns upfield just as quickly as he can. The technique here for the X end is to crack back on the linebacker.

COACHING POINT: In any crack-back block, whether it be from the flanker or the X end, the first step is not at the man he's going to crack down on but rather flat down the line of scrimmage. And the reason is that if the defensive man were to come across quickly to meet the play, the crack-back blocker is in position to take him. However, if the crack-back blocker moved at the man in his position at the snap of the ball and that man were to blitz or to come across hard, there is no way the crack-back blocker could get back to make the block on that man. If he comes down flat and the defensive linebacker stays where he is, the blocker can always turn and go upfield to get him.

This is the tough area to score: down by the goal line. There is an excellent cutoff block by the guard (No. 63), and the fullback (No. 31) is reading the blocks of the linemen and his blocking back (No. 5).

Halfback & tackle

These two men work as a team exactly the same way as they did on the weak-side sweep. In other words, the tackle's rule is to drive the man over him; if no defensive player is over him, he slams the first man to his outside, releases inside and seals for the middle linebacker. The halfback's rule is to take the first man outside, the offensive left tackle in this case. None, in other words, if the tackle has taken in the defensive end, the halfback would go through and he would do the sealing for the linebacker. The onside guard pulls exactly as he does on the sweep. He kicks out on the corner man. The center does the same thing as he does on the sweep; he makes the onside cutoff block on the defensive tackle. The off guard cuts off the offside defensive tackle and releases; the off tackle releases inside and goes for that safety, and the Y end releases inside, also for a defensive back.

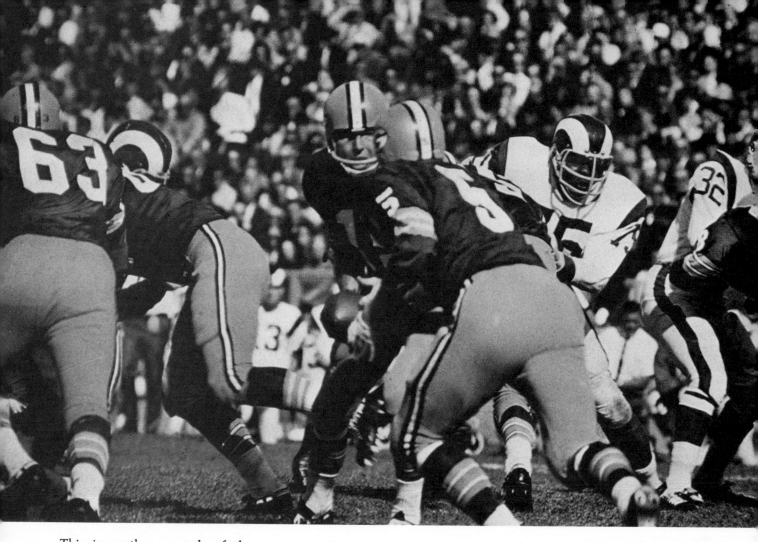

This is another example of the trap block. The guard (No. 63) is folding behind the center for the middle linebacker; the back (No. 5) is reading the guards and getting ready to accept the ball from the quarterback. This play is a quick trap, and the quarterback has opened up quickly to give the ball carrier all the room he'll need to read the guard's block. Note the good drive block by the right guard, the right tackle and the tight or Y end.

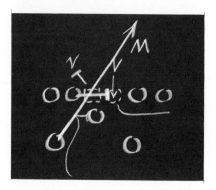

Quick trap

The quick trap is usually used when we are getting undue pressure on the quarterback in a passing situation from one of the inside defensive people or when the middle linebacker is playing quite deep, or when the middle linebacker leaves his position entirely.

For example, if the middle linebacker lines up here in front of the fullback, in a Red formation, we will automatically go to a quick trap in between the two defensive tackles. It can be run by either one of the backs. It can be run from the Red formation or it can be run from the Brown formation. It can be run from the Brown formation with the fullback hitting right up into the center. That's a quick trap. It can be run by the halfback with the halfback hitting in behind the guard.

The quick trap is a play in which the center down-blocks or drives back the defensive tackle; the guard, the left guard in this case, pulls across him, makes a quick trap on the man over the right guard. The right guard, whose man is going to be trapped, can do one of two things. He can pull in order to influence the man over him, or, if it's a passing situation, he may set as on a pass, drawing that man into a quick move and then, of course, moving out to help keep that man from falling back into the play.

The onside offensive tackle on this play pulls across and blocks on the middle linebacker. The off-tackle seals on the defensive end. The off-end seals on the outside weak-side linebacker. The onside end releases outside the linebacker as he does in the pass and goes for the safety man, the flanker releases for the defensive halfback.

The fullback, as we explained in the veer play, can do many things, again depending upon what we think the keys are for those linebackers. He could come across in back of the runner to bring the linebacker with him; or he could lead toward the right side of his offensive tackle; or he could come straight across to the outside; or he could dive straight ahead. Any one of those particular moves can be used.

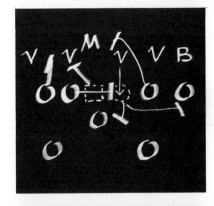

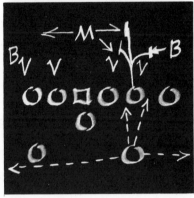

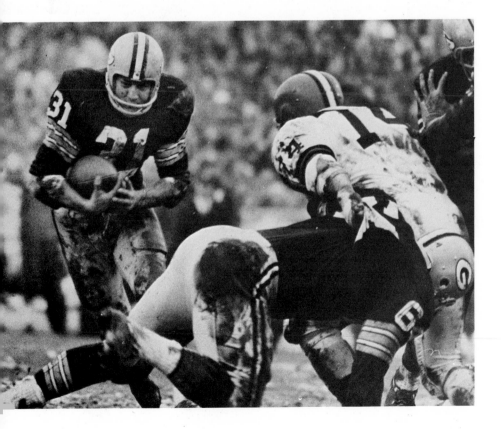

A good down block by the guard (No. 64) and the cutback off the block by the fullback (No. 31) is another excellent example of run to daylight.

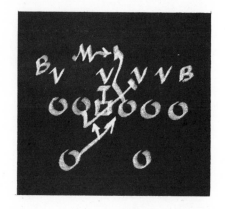

The quarterback uses a slice pivot; he opens up quickly to the halfback who is going to be the ball carrier. The halfback hits right off the center's block. Actually, the center's got to get a stand-off block on the defensive tackle, and the guard who is doing the trapping must really get the drive block on that outside defensive tackle.

We like this play, too, because it's as effective against the odd defenses as it is against the even defenses. In fact, we automatic to it against the odd. It becomes the same play against the odd as is the veer play. Everybody uses zone blocking, straight-ahead blocking, and again the back cuts to either side of the center's block.

Inside belly play

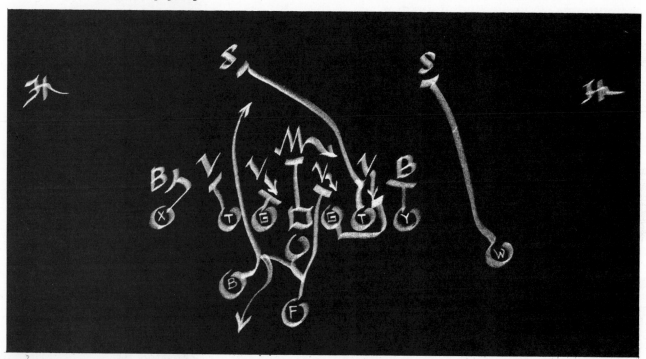

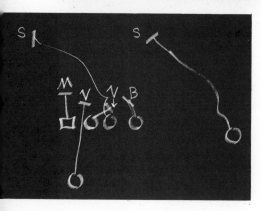

The inside belly play is designed to take advantage of defensive tackles who are reading and reacting to the pull of the guards. The inside belly play is a hard, quick-hitting play with the running back hitting behind the block of the left guard.

The flanker splits 5 to 7 yards and releases for the strong-side safety. The Y end drives and cuts off the strong-side linebacker over him. The onside tackle releases inside the man over him for the offside safety. The onside guard pulls onside and blocks the man over him or beyond the offensive tackle. The near back or fullback drives up the area the right guard vacated to block the defensive tackle there. The back can be in either the Brown or Red formation. The center blocks the man over him either on the line or off the line. The offside guard drives the man over him in the direction that man wants to go. This is the key block. The offside tackle drives and cuts off the man over him or the first man to his outside. He must be very careful to make sure that the defensive end does not release inside of him. The offside end drives and cuts off the linebacker over him. The quarterback opens toward the fullback and gives a reverse hand-off to the left halfback. The left halfback, the ball carrier, takes a lateral step to his right and drives back into the hole.

The principle here is to begin the flow one way and then run back against the flow. The runner keys the offside guard's block going inside or outside as that guard takes the defensive tackle in the direction he wants to go.

This is the result of good faking by the quarterback and what happens to a middle linebacker when he reacts instead of analyzing first. The back (No. 44) is into the hole and the linebacker (No. 51) is going after the fake by the fullback. The fullback, by the way, has made an excellent block on the defensive tackle.

Fullback slant

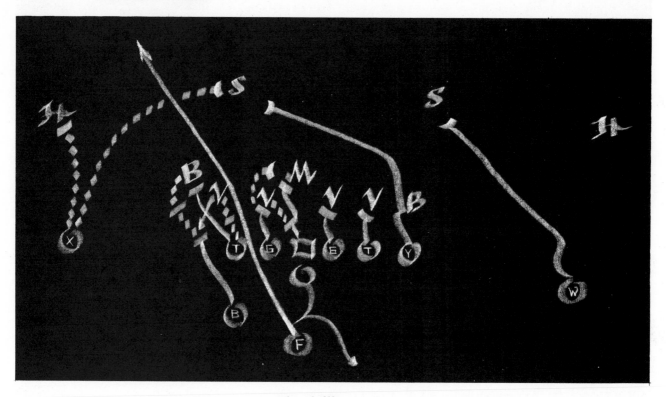

The fullback slant is a weak-side smash over the left tackle. The split end comes downfield and makes his decision to take either the weak-side corner man or the weak-side safety, depending on which one forces the play. The onside left tackle works with the left halfback as a team even as the defensive end and outside linebacker work as a team. The onside tackle aims his head at the crotch of the defensive end. If that end moves to the outside the tackle drives his head past the inside hip of the defensive end and continues upfield to block the linebacker.

The left halfback runs a course at the outside hip of the defensive end. If that end moves to the outside, the halfback will block him. The halfback's approach and the block must have the speed and quickness to stop the penetration by either the end or the linebacker, whoever has the outside responsibility.

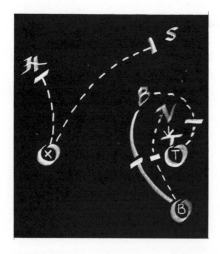

The onside left tackle: If the defensive end comes inside, the tackle aiming his head at the crotch will be able to pick up that end.

The left halfback: If the defensive end comes inside, the left halfback aims his head at the outside hip of that end but

In this weak-side slant the fullback keys the block on the outside linebacker (No. 82). Now he's into the secondary and being chased by the middle linebacker. It was in our 1962 NFL title game against the Giants, one of the most bitterly fought games I've ever seen.

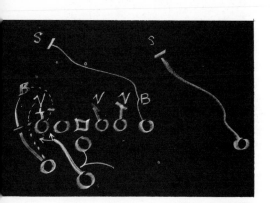

continues on and takes the linebacker who now has outside responsibility. It is a do-dad situation.

The onside left guard and the center also work as a team. The left guard drives his head past the outside hip of the defensive tackle, continues on past him and looks and turns to the inside for the middle linebacker who is going with the flow of the play. The center makes an onside cut-off block on the tackle over the left guard. On a call by the center, the left guard will drive out and cut off the man over him. The center's assignment then is to cut off the middle line-backer. By call I mean that the center feels that he cannot make the cutoff block on the defensive tackle because the tackle is split too wide or is too quick; he then tells the guard to take the tackle and the center releases for the middle line-backer.

The offside right guard drives and cuts off the man over him or outside of him. The offside right tackle drives and cuts off the man over him or outside of him. The Y end releases inside the man over him for the onside safety or halfback. The flanker releases to block the offside safety. The quarter-back reverse-pivots to the fullback making the handoff as deep as possible to give the fullback more time to read the halfback's and left tackle's block. His basic key is the do-dad block of the tackle and the halfback.

COACHING POINT: Often this play will be run back to the in-side. It is run back to the inside because of the play of the de-fensive tackle and the defensive end and, therefore, it is important that the cutoff blocks by the right guard and right tackle be sustained. The play, however, may break to the out-side of the halfback and the onside tackle. It's another run-to-daylight play.

As we know, one play will establish another. For ex-ample, we have just talked about the fullback slant. Now let's discuss another fullback veer which is a takeoff on the fullback slant. When the opposition pursues strongly we start our veer as we do our slant and veer it back to the in-side. Or, if their line is slanting and stopping the slant, we counter with this veer play.

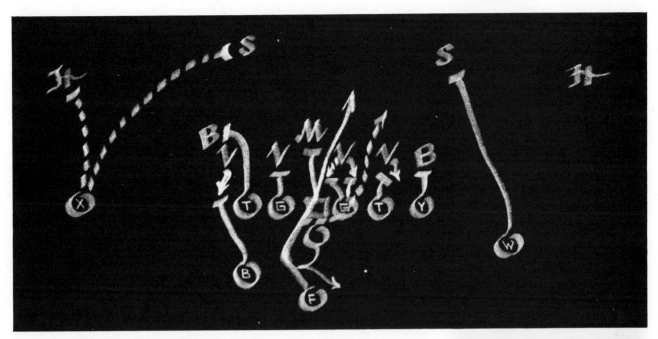

The flanker is usually in a near position 8 to 10 yards out and he releases toward the strong-side safety. The Y end drives out and cuts off the man over him. The right tackle has an important block. He drives the man over him, the defensive end or the first man to his outside, and must sustain that block. The right guard drives the man over him in the direction of that defensive man's charge. The center drives the middle linebacker who usually keys the fullback. The left guard drives and cuts off the man over him. The left tackle and left halfback work as a team as they do on the slant with do-dad blocking. The offside offensive tackle takes the defensive end on an inside charge. If that end goes to the outside, he looks for the weak-side linebacker and seals on him. The halfback do-dads with the offside tackle and he'll take the linebacker on the outside or the defensive end, whichever shows outside. The quarterback reverses to the fullback as on the slant and gives the ball to him as deep as possible. The fullback starts to slant to the left, takes two steps and drives toward his right tackle. He veers back toward the center, keying the block of the right guard. If the right guard drives his man to the outside the fullback veers directly up

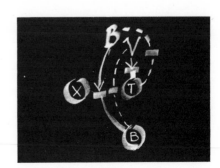

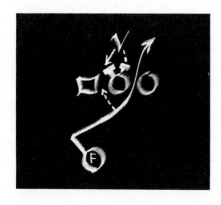

the middle. If the right guard has driven his man to the inside, the fullback veers back to the outside of the right guard's block and inside the right tackle's block. Again, this is a run-to-daylight play.

COACHING POINT: There is an option that the center and guard have. We call the blocking even and the center blocks to his right or to the onside. The right guard falls behind the center and blocks the middle linebacker. It is best run, however, with the straightaway drive blocking.

In the category of influence plays we can consider any play where the quarterback carries the ball an influence play. The quarterback as a passer naturally sets up the quarterback as a runner. There are various plays that he can use. In today's game it is not considered good form to have the quarterback run very much, but as long as you have a quarterback who has the potential for a long gain it's a very, very valuable weapon for the offense, and must make the defense play a little bit more honest.

QUARTERBACK AS A RUNNING BACK

The end of the bootleg: the quarterback has rolled into the end zone. This touchdown was the result of each man on that offensive team carrying out his assignment perfectly and fooling the defense.

Quarterback sneak

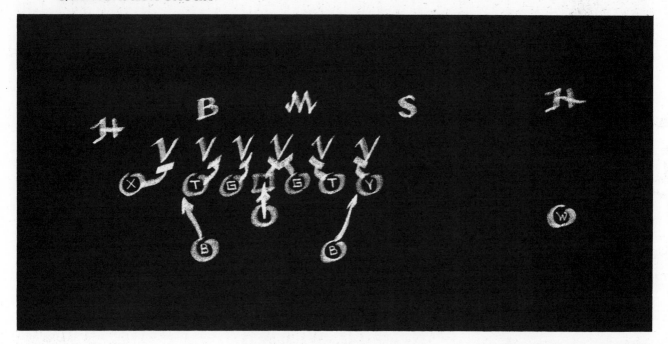

There is the quarterback sneak, familiar to everyone, which is simply a wedge play with the quarterback sneaking, usually for very short yardage. It is almost an impossible play to stop for less than the yard gain.

Quarterback draw

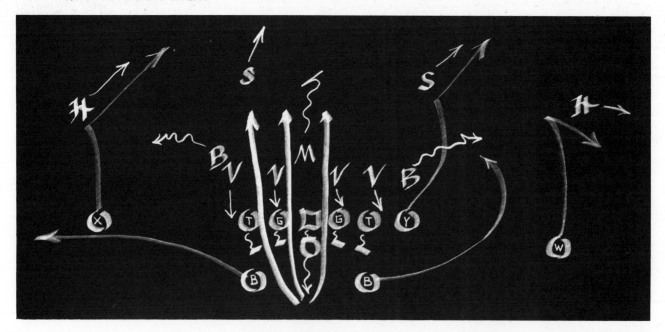

Then there is the quarterback draw which is not used to any great extent but is a very, very effective play. Usually one defensive lineman is assigned to stop the regular draw. There has to be a back left in the backfield that the quarterback can draw to or hand the ball off to. Now, if you send both backs out of there on pass patterns, there is the tendency of everybody on the defense to drop back and the pass rush from the front forward to come ahead full steam. Now the quarterback comes back, sets up a bit shorter than he usually does on a pass, and then he draws. In other words, he lets the linemen come in, the linebackers go back and then the quarterback pulls the ball down and carries the ball, usually up the middle for a good gain. This is a very effective play for good running quarterbacks and, properly called late in the game, can be a long gainer.

Roll-out pass

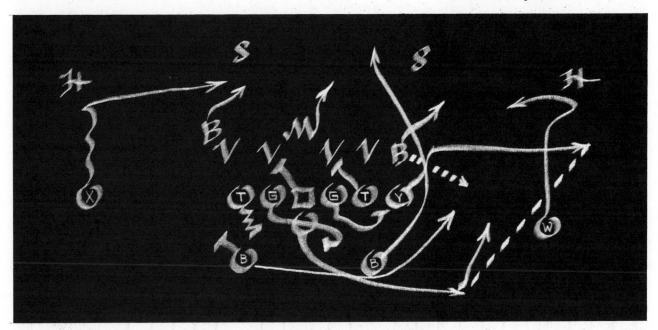

The roll-out pass is another type of quarterback action. It is different from the bootleg. In the bootleg the quarterback fakes to the backs and then sets up to the opposite side of the backs that he faked to. In the roll-out he follows those backs, using them as blockers if it's a run all the way, or using the backs as possible receivers.

For example, both backs go to the right, the quarterback fakes to these backs and he follows them and sets up. He can either set up or continue, but he has the same essential keys as he does in the bootleg. He keys the linebackers and if the defensive men go back he runs the ball, using his backs as blockers. If the defense forces, he throws the ball—for example, throwing the ball to the Y end out in the flat.

Bootleg

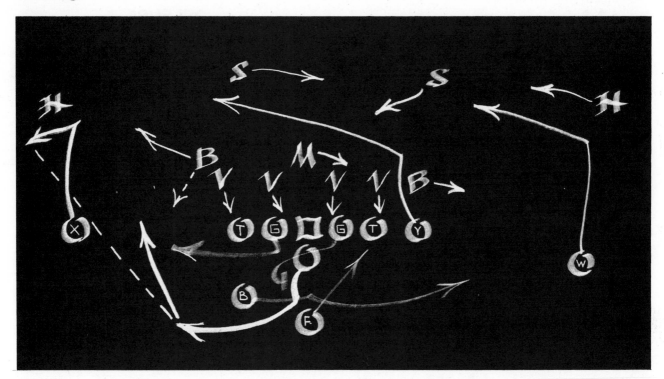

And then, of course, there's the bootleg play, and two of the great practitioners of that were Bob Waterfield of the Los Angeles Rams and Y. A. Tittle of the San Francisco 49ers and New York Giants. The bootleg is usually an option type of play where the quarterback has the option of either throwing the ball or running it, depending on what the defense does. You can have a weak-side bootleg in which the backs fake to the strong side and the quarterback fakes the ball to them and then sets up either inside the rush or outside the rush. The quarterback keys the defensive people, and if the defensive man rushes that means he'll throw the ball to an end who's usually running a square-out route or a turn-in route. If the linebacker drops on the weak side then the quarterback will, of course, run the ball. He usually has a blocker who's out in front of him protecting him or a lead blocker if he decides to run.

Up to now we have discussed the plays designed to move the ball down the field. Any one of them, of course, may break for a score. But now let's discuss plays that must score, the plays that make up the goal-line offense. Football really is two things: it is, first, getting the ball off your own goal line and, second, getting it across your opponent's goal line. To begin with, the basic goal-line defense is the 6–1 with the two outside linebackers usually down in a three-point stance and coming hard across the line of scrimmage.

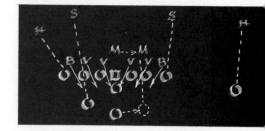

Quick trap

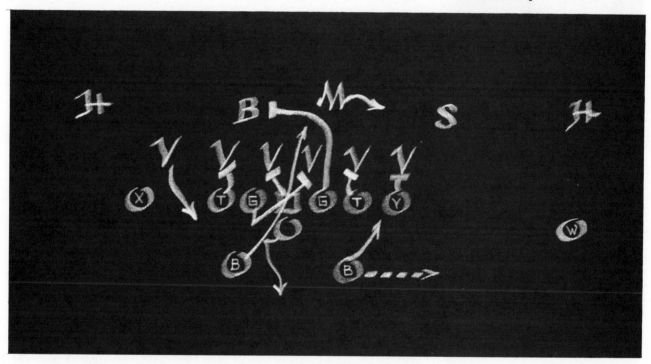

Now let's take a look at the quick trap. The quick trap, the lead goal-line play, is designed to split the two defensive tackles. Like all traps, it is very successful against penetrating defenses and usually when a team is in a goal-line defense, they'd better be penetrating if they want to stop anything.

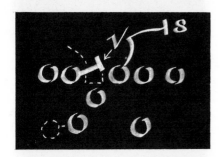

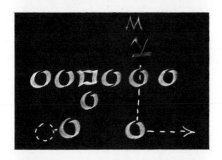

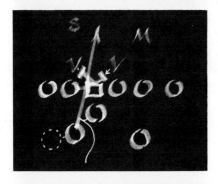

We ask the center to block back on the offside defensive tackle. He's got a real difficult block. There's not much room to operate in there, so we ask for a stand-off here and if he can get a stand-off he can do the job.

The man who must really make the move or must really move the defensive man is the offensive left guard, in this case, or the right guard, should the trap be coming from his side. That guard has got to have real quick action; he's got to come across flat; he's got to gain ground and he's got to drive that onside defensive tackle and seal that man from coming into the play. The offside guard on the trap going to the right releases outside that onside defensive tackle over him or the man that's to his inside, and comes across to block whoever is the strong-side linebacker. In this case, it is usually the safety man. Remember the strong-side linebacker is now on the line of scrimmage in a three-point stance and penetrating. So the strong-side safety comes up into that position and he becomes a linebacker on the goal-line defense.

The reason we like to run this from a Red formation, although it can be run from the Brown formation, is that usually the middle linebacker lines up in front of the fullback and keys on him. So we can send that fullback out on the flat to try to pull the middle linebacker out of there. He can move ahead to try to move the man directly over the tackle. We ignore this middle linebacker. We don't block him. The dangerous man who is keying the halfback, the ball carrier, is the safety man. The halfback comes into the hole quick and hard, and I mean he's got to come in quick and hard! In fact, we don't care if that back cheats up in there. We ask him to move up close. Many times he'll line up right behind the quarterback. He'll line up there just as close as he can so that he can get in the hole just as quick as he can, almost riding the back of the trapping guard.

A very important block is the one that the left tackle must make: a cutoff block on that defensive end. The tackle must make the cutoff block because if the man over him comes in hard, he can stop the play by driving into the hole vacated by the trapping guard and catch the ball carrier before he has reached the hole. So that offside tackle must sustain that block.

A very important point here is the action of the quarterback. He uses what we call a slice pivot. He opens up to the halfback who is coming right at him and he's got to open up wide enough to give the halfback a great deal of room. Many times, for example, the onside defensive tackle will close so hard because he recognizes trap immediately so that it's almost impossible for the pulling guard to move him; the back will then move outside of that block by the pulling guard and into the area vacated by the defensive tackle. He'll move outside of the trap when that happens and that's why the slice pivot is so important, because it gives that back the chance to read the block of the offensive guard and to be able to cut inside or outside of that block.

One year we made 16 touchdowns with this goal-line trap play.

This is Paul Hornung scoring on our quick trap on the goal line. The excellent blocks by the center (No. 51) and the guard (No. 63) open up that hole for him.

Onside cross-blocking play

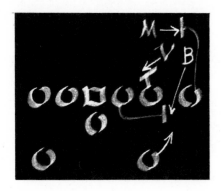

Now let's consider another goal-line play designed to take advantage of a linebacker who's coming across real hard. In fact, we invite him across. We call this play our onside cross-blocking play. The defensive strong-side linebacker usually comes across real hard on the snap of the ball on the goal line. We ask our Y end to take the same position as he does on the sweep. In fact, we want this to look like the sweep down on the goal line as best we can. We also want the middle linebacker to believe it is sweep because of the Red formation and because of the spread of the Y end, and we also want to influence the strong-side safety. That defensive player usually provides the rush from the outside with the strong-side linebacker taking the inside.

As the strong-side linebacker comes across, the Y end releases from his block, goes behind the linebacker and seals on the middle linebacker who is following the fullback as he would in a sweep. The defensive end in a goal-line situation

This is the result when every man on that offensive team does his job. The fullback (No. 31) has room enough to drive a truck through that hole and he scored.

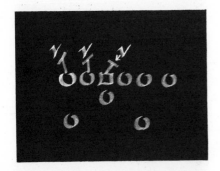

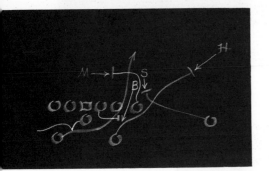

is closing hard across the face of the tackle toward the inside, so the offensive tackle has a comparatively easy block. The onside right guard pulls and traps.

That's why we call it a cross-block—it's a cross-block between the onside guard pulling for the trap and the Y end cutting across to block the middle linebacker—and he pulls hard and flat just as he does in the sweep, and he traps the strong-side linebacker who is coming across hard.

The center blocks back onside and he's got a comparatively easy cutoff block because of the closeness of the defensive tackle and the fact that most times they're in a gap defense so that tackle might be even coming toward him. There is a cutoff by the left guard inside and a cutoff by the left tackle inside on both the defensive offside end and defensive offside linebacker.

The fullback comes right at that strong-side linebacker and he puts on a great act so that he can make that linebacker think he's going to be blocking him inside as he does on the sweep. Then he goes on past that linebacker and releases out for the cornerback. The flanker takes the strong-side safety man, and the ball carrier, taking the ball from the quarterback, comes across and hits in between the block of the pulling guard trapping the strong-side linebacker and the offensive tackle who is taking the defensive end on a straight drive block.

COACHING POINT: The fullback actually sets up the linebacker for the block of the offensive guard who is pulling to kick him out. He goes right at that outside linebacker, making that linebacker think that he's going to take him in. That opens up that gap just a bit wider and then he continues on and blocks the defensive halfback as that guard kicks out to take the linebacker.

An additional goal-line play is one we refer to as the drive play, which goes to the strong side or onside to the strength of the formation. It is particularly good since from this formation, the Brown formation, we have been very successful in running the weak-side slant play to the fullback which breaks out to the outside of the weak-side linebacker. The middle linebacker is usually looking for that particular play when we go into the Brown formation. It's more or less a counterplay to the slant or veer play which works with it and is a strong-side play.

And we like this play because we get an extra blocker in that our fullback is the lead blocker. The fullback leads to the hole. He picks off anyone who comes into that hole—middle linebacker, outside linebacker, safety man–he drives the first man who crosses his path. And it is a drive play. The right guard drives on the man on him or the first man to his inside. The right offensive tackle, the onside tackle, drives the

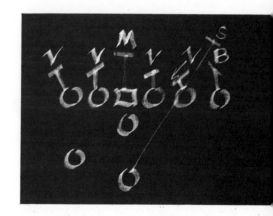

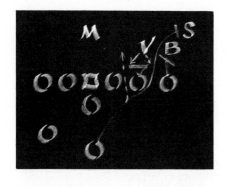

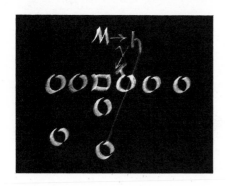

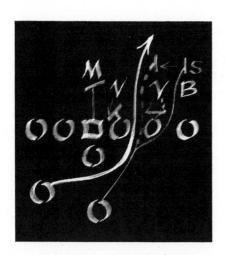

man over him. The Y end drives the man over him. The center tries to release through for the middle linebacker if he can, the left guard cuts off the man over him and the off-tackle or left tackle cuts off the defensive end over him. It's all solid blocking.

The fullback has a particular technique in this goal-line situation. If we were to run this play in the middle of the field, not in a particular short-yardage situation but at any other time, the fullback's technique is a little different than it is on the goal line or on a short-yardage situation. For example, in the middle of the field we ask the fullback to drive for the outside leg of the offensive right guard. And he will help the guard if the guard needs help in picking up on the block on the tackle against him. If the guard has him, the fullback would lead through the hole to pick up the middle linebacker or to help on the middle linebacker.

But on a goal line, since these defensive men are penetrating and they are coming in hard, there is a different technique used here.

Now the fullback leads to the offensive tackle's position. If the offensive tackle drives his man to the inside, the fullback would lead through the hole to the outside of that tackle's block and take the first man he happens to meet. If the tackle drives the defensive man out, the fullback will come inside that offensive tackle's block and pick the first man he sees. And, of course, the ball carrier just follows that fullback wherever he's going.

COACHING POINT: The quarterback must open up and give that ball carrier the ball just as quickly as he can. He doesn't want to wait too long. The longer he waits the more he will cut off the sight of the halfback; so he's got to open up and give the ball to the halfback just as quickly as he possibly can, and he uses an open pivot so he can give that halfback all the room and all the visual aid he needs to see the hole.

And the running back just follows the path of the full-back. If the fullback goes outside the block of the offensive tackle, he goes outside with him. If the fullback goes inside that block, he goes inside with him.

In a goal-line situation the assignments are the same; but because of the gap defense, the fullback keys the block of the tackle rather than the block of the guard.

SUMMARY

We have discussed and analyzed individual specific plays. Every coach, at every level, has his favorite plays. These have been mine. Remember, however, every play is designed for a purpose and for that purpose to be fulfilled every man must do his job on every play. Because, as we know, at any place, at any time, any play might go all the way. At the very least, every play is a stepping-stone to where all teams want to go. We all want to go to the end zone. That's the running game.

5
Defense Against the Run

As the running game is the heart of offensive football, so the defense against the run is the heart of defensive football. Defensive football is a game of reaction—reaction by the defense to the offense as it declares and tries to carry out its intention.

I have stated that it is defense more than anything else that wins championships. And of the two facets of defense, defense against the run and defense against the pass, the team that can force the offense to throw the ball more than it runs the ball, more often than not will win. In my nine years with the Packers in Green Bay we played in ten championship games—six NFL championships, two Western Conference play-offs and, of course, two Super Bowls. We lost only one of those ten championships—the first one in 1960 to the Philadelphia Eagles. In those ten championship games our defense has given up only three touchdowns to the run. The first one we gave up against the Eagles was the one that beat us. The next time a team scored on us running was in

January 1967 in the NFL championship game against Dallas when the Cowboys scored two touchdowns rushing. But it was our defense in the last minute and a half of the game that forced the interception that sealed the win for us.

A defense that cannot stop the run is not going to win very many football games, no matter how excellent its pass defense may be. Of course, you still have to have a good pass defense to be a winning team. In the final analysis, therefore, defense is play recognition, but that play recognition must be prefaced by the responsibilities of each man at each position.

Now, let us consider the positions and the responsibilities in the overall defenses against the runs, starting with the 4–3 inside.

4-3 INSIDE

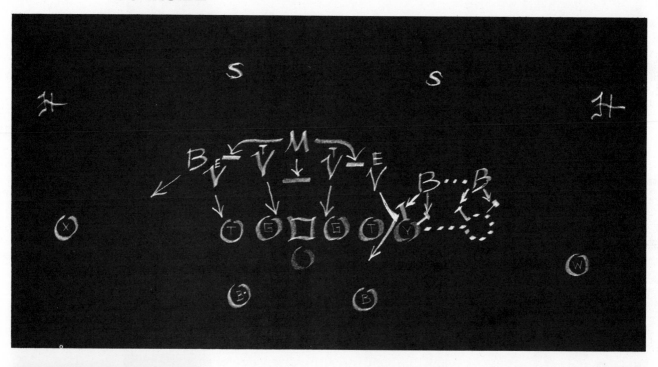

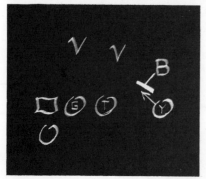

The strong-side linebacker. If the offensive end, the Y or tight end, is in a closed position 2 yards or less from his offensive tackle, the strong-side linebacker positions on the Y end's outside shoulder. If that Y end is in an open position—out 2 or more yards—the strong-side linebacker positions head-on over the Y end. The strong-side linebacker's initial move is to step into that end with his outside foot for his best chuck, to push that end off-stride. His primary responsibility is to the off-tackle hole. He will have help wide in the secondary. He

Here the strong-side linebacker, tackle and halfback stop the ball carrier.

One of the major responsibilities of all defenses is to contain. By that we mean to keep the offense within itself. Here you see the results of a good contain where the weak-side linebacker (No. 60) and the two defensive tackles have contained the scrambling quarterback.

keys that Y end. If the Y end goes down the line he goes down with him, pushing him off his block. Above all, he must not get hooked in by that Y end.

The strong-side defensive end positions on the outside shoulder of the offensive tackle. If the offensive Y end is in a closed position, that is, next to his offensive tackle, the strong-side defensive end will step into the Y end with his outside foot.

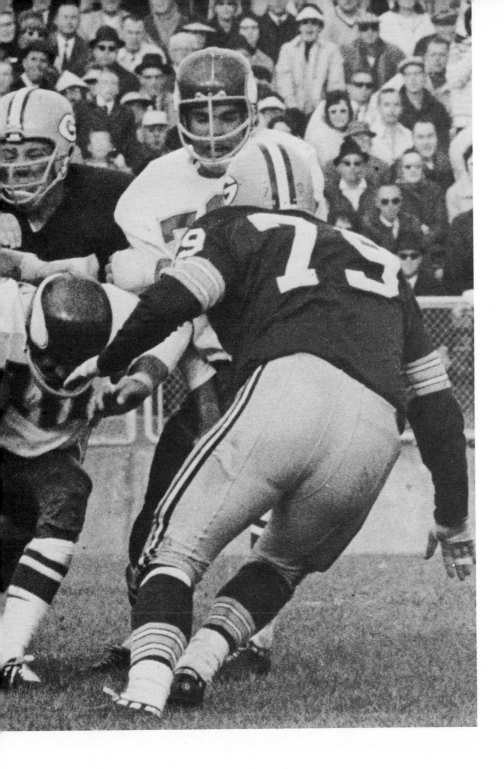

He reacts if that end blocks in by fighting across the face of that block by the Y end. If there is no block by the Y end he reacts to the tackle's move. He fights the pressure from either the end or the tackle to help either outside or inside. If the offensive tackle blocks down on the defensive tackle, the strong-side defensive end plays the trap.

The strong-side defensive tackle takes a position 3 feet off the

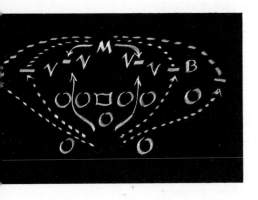

ball and head-on over the offensive guard and usually in a four-point stance. He steps with his inside foot to the inside shoulder of the offensive guard. He reacts to the block of the offensive guard. If there is none—in other words, if there is no block by that guard—he plays *trap*. He reads trap immediately and he looks for the trap blocker coming across. The strong-side defensive tackle's responsibility is to the inside. Let's put it another way: he must not get trapped; he must not be driven out by that offensive guard.

The middle linebacker takes a position head-up on the center, 1½ yards deep. He moves in the direction of the backfield action. He fills the hole inside the defensive tackles and reacts to the offensive tackles. The middle linebacker's first responsibility in this defense is the hole between the defensive end and the tackle on either side. His secondary responsibility is the off-tackle play and the end run.

The weak-side tackle's position, movement and responsibility are the same as that of the strong-side tackle—3 feet off the ball head-on over the guard and in a four-point stance. He steps with his inside foot to the inside shoulder of the guard and he reacts to that block. Again, this tackle must not be trapped. His responsibility is from the weak-side offensive tackle to the strong-side guard. He must not be trapped or be driven out by the weak-side guard.

The weak-side defensive end takes a position on the outside shoulder of the offensive tackle. When the offensive end is tight to his side he moves into the offensive tackle and reacts to his block. When the end is split to his side he works in or out with the linebacker on his side. When the end is tight he closes the inside; when the end is split he works with the linebacker and keys the tackle.

By keys I mean that if that offensive tackle blocks down on the defensive tackle, the defensive end reads trap. If that tackle sets as on a pass, he rushes the passer. If that tackle blocks down on him, the defensive end fights through the block, looking for an outside play.

The weak-side linebacker's position depends upon the defense called. He works with his weak-side defensive end. Against the split end he keys the offensive guard and the offensive tackle on the weak side for quick reactions. When the weak-side linebacker is on his end's hip he works inside-outside with that defensive end.

If the offensive tackle and guard pull to his side, he plays for the sweep if he has outside responsibility. If the offensive tackle sets as on a pass, he drops off into his area of responsibility, depending upon the pass defense called. If the guard pulls to his side and the offensive tackle blocks down on the defensive tackle, he reads trap on the defensive end and fills the hole.

4-3 OUTSIDE

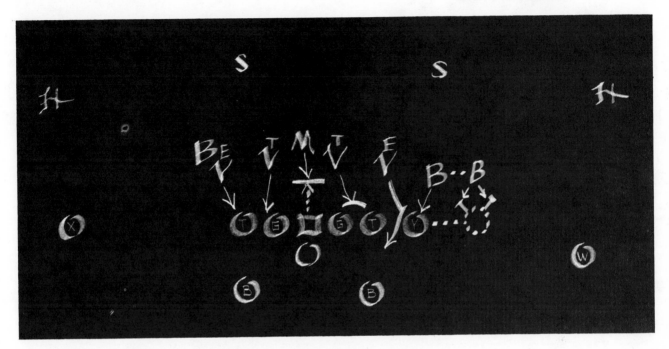

The strong-side linebacker's position is the same as it is in the 4–3 inside. When the Y end is close he is on the outside shoulder. When the Y end is open he is head-up on that end. He steps with his outside foot into the offensive end and reacts to the end's move. He keys the end and he helps the defensive end on the off-tackle run. He reacts to the end run, fighting through the blockers or forcing it back to the pursuit.
The strong-side defensive end plays 1 foot off the line versus a Y end who is tight or close. He steps into the end with his outside foot. He reacts to that end if the Y end blocks down on him. If not, he reacts to the tackle's move. His responsibility is the off-tackle hole; otherwise he fights the pressure and reacts as a football player.
The strong-side defensive tackle's position is the same as it is on a 4–3 inside, 3 feet off the ball, head-up on the guard

and in a four-point stance. He steps with his outside foot to a position where the guard cannot hook him and reacts to the guard's block. His hole responsibility is between the strong-side offensive guard and tackle.

The middle linebacker's position is the same as it is in the 4–3 inside, 1½ yards deep. He keys the center; he meets the center's charge, and he reacts to his block and plays the center's shoulder. His responsibility is between his two defensive tackles. He must not let the center or a folding guard block him out of the hole. If the center blocks down to either side on the defensive tackles, the middle linebacker fills that hole, looking for a guard folding behind the center, fighting off any blocks to plug up the hole.

The weak-side defensive tackle's position is the same as it is in a 4–3 inside, head-up on the guard, 3 feet off the ball and in a four-point stance. He steps with his outside foot to a position where the guard cannot hook him and reacts to the guard's block. His responsibility with a tight end to his side is the hole between the offensive guard and tackle. When the end is split, his charge is straight, reacting to the guard's block.

The weak-side defensive end's position is the same as it is in a 4–3 inside, on the outside shoulder of the offensive tackle. His initial move is the same as in the 4–3 inside, and except when the linebacker is on his hip, he works inside-outside with that linebacker.

The weak-side linebacker's position depends upon the pass coverage. As on the 4–3 inside, he works with his end when he is in a hip position. When on the end's hip he works inside-outside. Against a split end he keys the guard and tackle and forces the end run from the outside.

The weak-side linebacker drives past the blocker to get the ball carrier and make the tackle near the line of scrimmage.

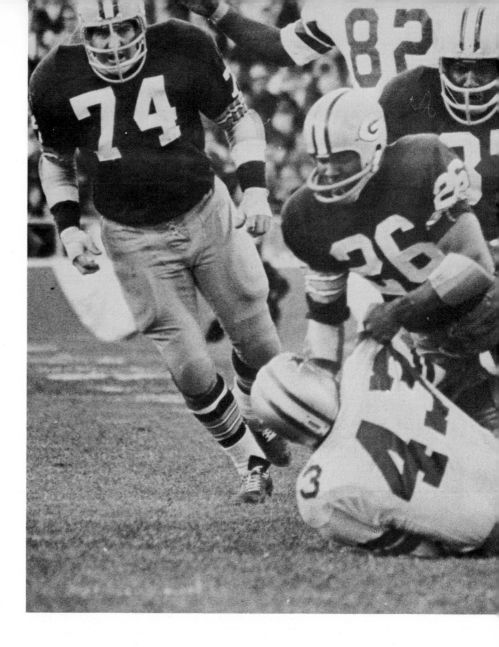

4-3 UNDER

If the balance defense, the 4–3 defense, does not hold up to the side where the offensive formation is strong, you may shift your linemen to that side. For example, the Brown formation is strongest to the weak side, that is, to the side away from the flanker. Therefore you would shift your linemen to that particular position. We call this the under-defense—the linemen shifted to the weak side of the formation and the linebackers shifted to the strong side.

The strong-side linebacker. In the 4–3 under, he takes a position the same as he does in the 4–3 inside and outside; in other words, when the tight or Y end is close, on the outside shoulder. When the tight end is open, he is head-up on that

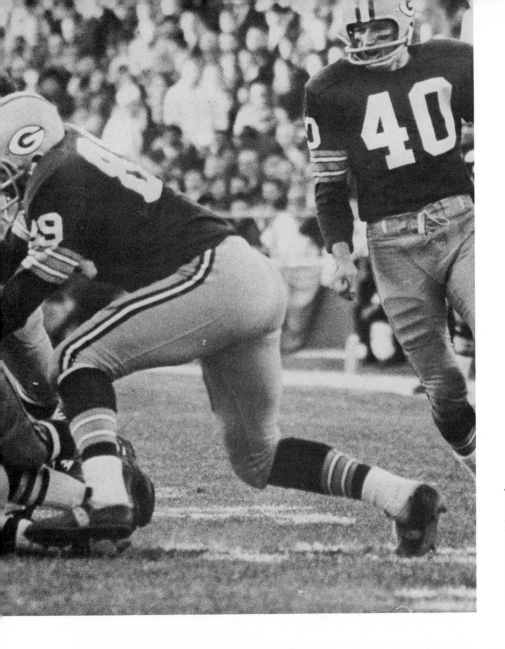

This picture shows what good defense is all about. The ball carrier has been tackled and the pursuit is there—five defenders against the lone runner. The strong-side halfback and the strong-side linebacker have made the tackle as their teammates converge.

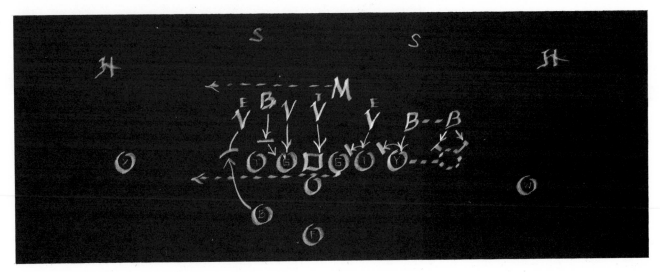

end. He steps with the outside foot into the offensive end and reacts to the end's move. He keys the Y end and he helps the defensive end in the off-tackle hole.

The strong-side defensive end positions on the outside shoulder of the offensive tackle. He steps into the tackle with his inside foot, reacts to the tackle's block and keys on the offensive guard. He may have a deal with the middle linebacker at any time.

The middle linebacker positions on the outside shoulder of the strong-side guard, 1½ yards deep and off the line. He keys the guard; he reacts to his move or to his block. He must not be hooked in by the guard and he may work with the strong-side defensive end. When I say he keys the guard, if the guard pulls across the formation or back to the weak side, he should go with him.

The strong-side defensive tackle takes a position on the strong-side shoulder of the center; that is, to the side in the formation that the tight or Y end is set. He charges straight into the center and reacts to the center's block and plays the ball. When a pass shows, he always rushes the passer to the side that the flanker is set on—to the strong side of the formation. He is also responsible for the draw.

The weak-side defensive tackle takes a position head-up on the offensive guard. He charges with his inside foot through the guard. His responsibility is to close the inside hole. He may work with the weak-side linebacker.

The weak-side linebacker takes a position on the outside hip of his defensive tackle. His responsibility is the hole between the defensive end and the tackle, and he may work with the defensive tackle.

The weak-side defensive end takes a position on the outside shoulder of the offensive tackle. He steps with his outside foot. His responsibility is to contain and play the near back's block; that is, the block of the back that is set to his side. He must not be blocked in by the tackle or by the back. He is responsible for the wide play.

That ball carrier has to expect punishment when he runs into those big defensive linemen.

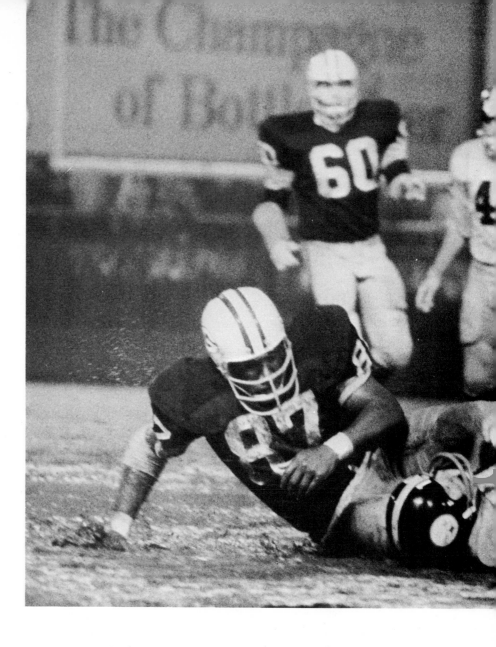

4-3 OVER   If the 4–3 defense, the even defense, does not hold up to the side where the offensive formation is strong, you may shift your linemen to that side. Therefore, against the Red formation, which is stronger to the side to which the flanker is set, you may shift your linemen to that side. We call this the over.

The strong-side linebacker. If the offensive tight or Y end is close, the strong-side linebacker takes a position on his outside shoulder. If the Y end is open, he takes a position head-up. His initial move is to step into the end with his outside foot for his best chuck. His primary responsibility is the off-tackle hole. He has secondary help wide.

The strong-side defensive end's position is outside the offensive strong-side tackle. He charges on a straight line to-

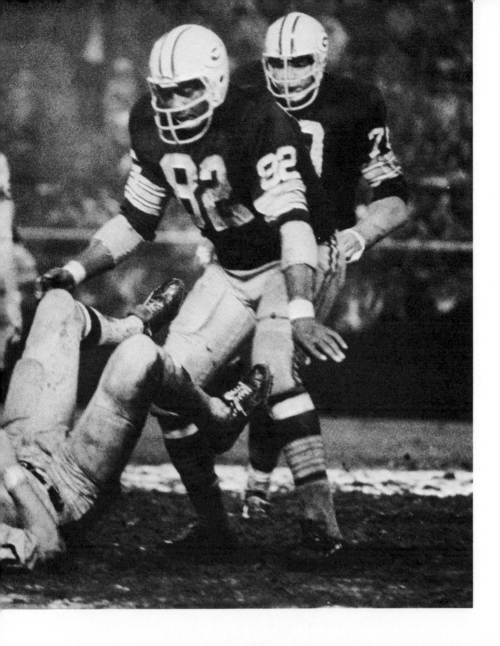

The two defensive ends meet at the same point—the quarterback. He had tried to scramble and was caught by both defensive men, containing the play.

ward the fullback. He charges close off the tail of the offensive tackle. He keys on the guards. If the guards pull, it gives him a pretty good key that the play is the sweep. His responsibility is to close the inside hole and react to the movement and the block of the offensive tackle.

The strong-side defensive tackle positions outside the guards. He charges on a sharp angle through the outside shoulder of the guard. His responsibility is to close the inside hole. He reacts to the movement or the block of the guard. He must not be hooked in by the guard.

The middle linebacker takes a position 1½ yards off the line on the outside shoulder of the weak-side guard. He keys the guard; if the guard pulls he goes with him. He reacts to the guard's move and to the guard's block.

The weak-side defensive tackle takes a position on the weak-side shoulder of the center. He charges straight into that center. He reacts to the center's block. He plays the ball. When pass shows, he always rushes to the weak side of the formation. He is responsible for the draw play also.

The weak-side defensive end takes a position on the outside shoulder of the weak-side tackle. When the end is tight to his side he moves into the offensive tackle and reacts to his block. When the end is split he works inside-outside with the linebacker on his side.

The weak-side linebacker's position is usually a hip position, when the end is split to his side. He keys the guard and the tackle for quick reactions, works inside-outside with the defensive end. He is responsible for the end runs.

DEFENSE AGAINST THE END RUN

A team that cannot keep its opponent from running to the outside is a team that has lost the control on which the defense against the running game is founded. So the defense must demolish every end run. As we know, the end run is basically a power play off tackle, and when the ball carrier turns the corner clean, even though the middle linebacker and offside defensive halfback and safety are moving, the angle of pursuit is so great that they cannot hold this play down. Therefore the defense must turn the end run back to the pursuit men—and early.

The end run is not difficult to stop. When the play is underway the outside linebacker, the defensive halfback, the safety and the defensive end are coordinated; and by coordinated I mean that it is predetermined, either by the overall defense or by an audible call from the halfback or the safety, which of the three types of end-run forces will be used. And regardless of the type of force that is used, there are three essentials to good defense against the end run. One: there must be a contain man. Two: there must be pursuit by the whole defense. Three: there must be a man to check for the play pass.

HALFBACK FORCE

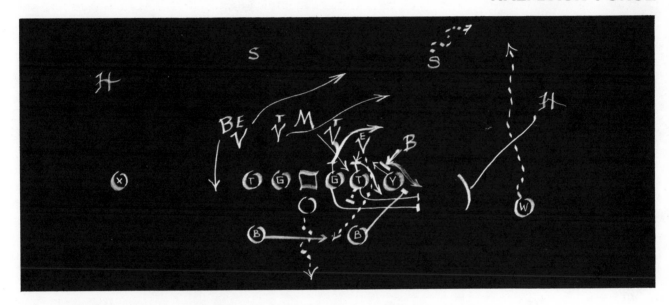

The halfback and safety force takes its name from the back who will make the force and contain the play. In the halfback force the position of the defensive halfback is about 5 yards deep and 1 yard off the outside shoulder of the wingback. This position will vary according to the pass defense that is predetermined. One other thing: usually, when the wingback is in close, the force will be by the halfback. In other words, if the wingback is very close to the Y end, the halfback is always the forcer, and then he must have only one key, which is the flow of the backfield. However, with the normal spread of the wingback, the defensive halfback's keys, when he is the force man, is first the Y end. If the Y end blocks down on the defensive end or another defensive player, the defensive

The strong-side halfback comes up to the line and forces the ball carrier (No. 40) back.

halfback knows right now it is run, and he will play it as such.

The defensive halfback's secondary keys are the near offensive tackle and the near offensive guard—the tackle and guard to his side. If they show run by aggressive blocking or by pulling, he again has the key of run. So he comes up to force from the outside. In other words, he comes up on an angle to the line of scrimmage to force the play from the outside back to the pursuit. How far he comes up depends, of course, upon how long it takes that play to develop. Sometimes he'll be almost in the backfield and what he must do is contain the play. He must force the runner back to the inside. He must force the runner back to the pursuit men who will be coming off the line of scrimmage.

The position of the strong-side safety man is that he lines up about 2 yards off the outside shoulders of the Y end, 5 to 7 yards deep. His key is also the Y end. If the Y end releases he plays pass. The safety's secondary key is again the offensive tackle and the offensive guard. If they show run, he covers behind the defensive halfback—he is the man who watches for the play-action pass or the option pass that comes off the run. He will have to pick up the wingback if the wingback were to go downfield on a play-action pass.

The strong-side linebacker, as we have discussed in the 4–3 defenses when the Y end is tight or in the closed position, is on the outside shoulder of the Y end. If the Y end is flexed or if the Y end is spread a bit, he plays head-up on the Y end. The linebacker steps into the Y end with the outside foot. Again, his key is the Y end. If the Y end blocks down then he must chuck him and at the same time pick up the keys of the offensive guard and tackle. The linebacker is responsible for the off-tackle hole. He must never be hooked by the Y end. If the Y end tries to hook him, the linebacker must fight to the outside.

The strong-side defensive end takes his position, the three-point stance with his inside foot advanced off the outside shoulder of the offensive tackle. The defensive end drives into that tackle on the snap of the ball. If the Y end blocks down on the defensive end that end fights to the outside. His next key is the tackle. If the tackle blocks down, the defensive end plays for trap. If the tackle sets for a pass the defensive end rushes the passer.

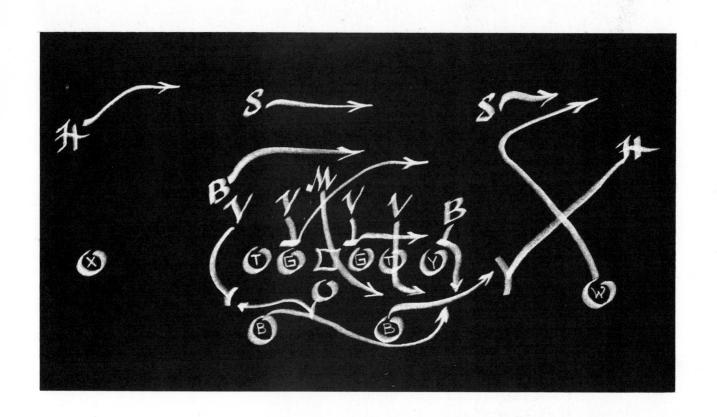

Here is what will happen in the halfback force. With the flow of the backfield and the blocking of the Y end, the strong-side defensive halfback will come up to force and be the contain man, and force the runner back to the inside. The strong-side safety man picks up the wingback and covers for the play-action pass. The strong-side linebacker fights to the outside and tries to penetrate around the block of the Y end. The strong-side defensive end hits and penetrates; the defensive tackle hits the guard over him and pursues from the outside. The middle linebacker cuts up wherever there's daylight to chase from behind. The weak-side defensive tackle hits his man and pulls to the back to pursue. The weak-side defensive end comes across the line of scrimmage and chases from the back. He is also a contain man against any reverses. The weak-side linebacker, as soon as he sees the flow, pursues from the outside. That's the way to contain a run!

The weak-side safety, of course, with the flow of the backs to the strong side, comes across into the center of the

SUMMARY

The ball carrier is not yet to the line of scrimmage and the force is there to meet him. There is the safety (No. 46), the linebacker (No. 58) and the middle linebacker (No. 66).

field and looks for any receivers who might be leaking downfield, and if none, goes up to help on the tackling. The weakside defensive halfback retreats slightly and also looks for anybody leaking downfield.

These defensive halfbacks have a great responsibility, but when you add the factor of playing against a Gale Sayers, then you really have pressure. Sayers may have been the purest natural runner I've ever seen. Hugh McElhenny was another, as was Jimmy Brown, but since we played the Bears more than the 49ers or Browns, Sayers was the greater problem. He killed us in 1965 in Chicago as the Bears beat us 31–10. In every game we played against them when they had Sayers, he was our single greatest defensive challenge.

In the 1967 game Sayers broke one for 43 yards and a touchdown, but a key defensive play in that game helped us win, 17–13, and clinch the central-division title early. The Bears were driving and in our territory. From the Red formation they ran a sweep with Sayers carrying. The defensive halfback Adderley forced quickly, the linebacker Robinson fought off the block of the fullback, and the middle linebacker Nitschke came behind the pulling guard. Adderley avoided the guard, tackled Sayers behind the line as Robinson and Nitschke hit him at the same time, causing a 5-yard loss and taking the steam out of their drive.

This is a good example of the defensive back fighting off the blocker to get to the ball carrier.

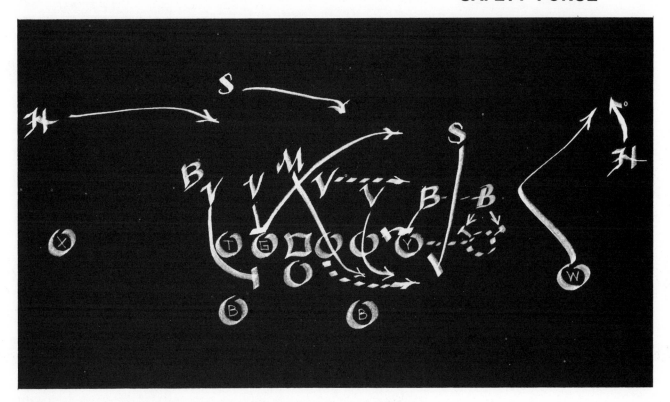

In the safety force the defensive halfback's position is approximately 5 yards deep and 1 yard outside the outside shoulder of the wingback. Of course, his position may vary according to the defense that is called. The defensive halfback's primary responsibility now, and his only key, is the wingback. His primary responsibility here is pass. He does not key into the backfield. He does not key the linemen but rather just keys the wingback.

The safety's position would be 5 to 7 yards deep, about 2 yards off the outside shoulder of the Y end, but since he is the force man he can cheat up a little. The reason he cheats up a little, since he is the force man, is that the one thing he does not want is to have a crack-back block on him by the wingback. With the defensive halfback playing deep for pass, if the wingback came off and caught that safety fairly deep and cracked back on him, then the safety would not be able to get up in time to contain, and the run could get to his outside.

So he will come up as close as possible, usually cheat up there a little so he can beat the crack-back block by the wingback.

COACHING POINT: What I mentioned earlier proves the point: the closer the flanker comes to the Y end, the more difficult it is for the safety to force, because it's easier for the flanker to crack back on the safety. So, usually, when the flanker takes a close position, the defense is forced to use a half-back force with the safety rotating back to cover pass.

When the wingback is flexed the safety's key to this force again is the Y end and, secondarily, the near offensive tackle and the near offensive guard. If the Y end releases, the safety plays pass and picks up the Y end, if that is his assignment. If the Y end blocks and the offensive guard and tackle show run either by pulling or by aggressive blocking, the safety will come up hard to the outside.

For example, if the offensive guard pulls to lead the running back to the outside, the safety will come up hard and fight that block by that guard, forcing the running back to the inside to the pursuit. He's got to turn the play back to the pursuit, that's his primary responsibility. If the runner breaks off quickly to the inside, then the safety man spins off the block of that guard and comes back in a pursuit angle.

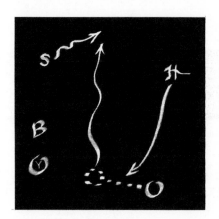 

When that ball carrier gets past the line of scrimmage the responsibilities of stopping him rest with the safeties and the defensive half-backs.

164

This is pursuit. The quarterback, trying to scramble out of the pocket, is being chased by the defensive end, and, because of the pass rush which forced the quarterback to pull the ball down, he is now a running back and fair game for those big defensive linemen.

The strong-side linebacker has exactly the same responsibility as he does on the halfback force. Again, when the Y end is tight he's on the outside shoulder. He steps into that end with his outside leg and chucks him. If the Y end is flexed or open, he plays him head-on. If the Y end blocks down, the linebacker closes the off-tackle hole. That's his primary responsibility: the off-tackle hole. Secondly, he will give outside help to the end run.

The strong-side defensive end has the same responsibility as he did in the halfback force. He lines up in a three-point stance with his outside foot up and he positions on the outside shoulder of the offensive tackle. Again, his key is to fight the block of the Y end; if the Y end blocks down on him he fights to the outside. If the Y end releases, the defensive end

keys the tackle. If the tackle blocks down, the defensive end plays trap. If the tackle sets for pass, the defensive end rushes the passer. The defense must feel the flow of the play. When the play starts and all these things happen these defensive men must read and feel that flow and the following happens.

Strong-side safety: come up and become the contain man.

Defensive halfback: drop back with the wingback to play pass.

Strong-side linebacker: chuck the right end and close for the off-tackle play; if the play goes to the outside, help on the run.

Defensive end: read run and crash in and pursue to the outside.

Defensive tackle: with the pull of the guard, chase from the outside.

Middle linebacker: come in behind the vacated hole of the pulling guard and chase from behind.

Weak-side defensive tackle: hit, fight off the block and pursue from the outside.

Weak-side defensive end: come across the line of scrimmage and become the contain man looking for reverses.

Weak-side safety and weak-side halfback: move over to the middle of the field, look for option passes or play-action passes.

THE LINEBACKER FORCE

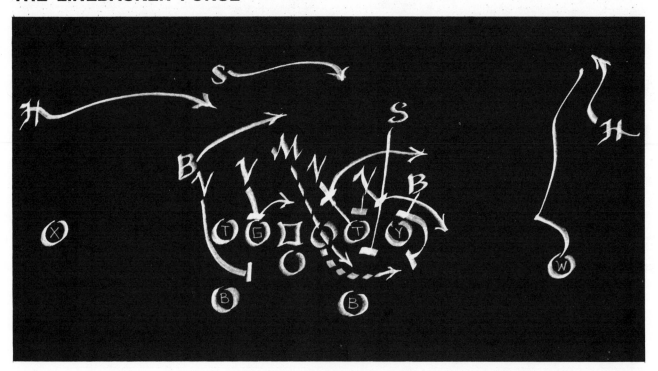

In the linebacker force of the end run the strong-side halfback's position is the same as it was on the halfback force and the safety force—5 yards deep and 1 yard outside the shoulder of the wingback. The position will vary according to what pass defense is called and, as in the safety force, the defensive halfback's only key is the wingback. He has no key inside. In other words, his primary responsibility is pass. If the wingback releases, the defensive halfback has got to cover for the pass.

The safety man in the other two defenses was 2 yards outside of the Y end and about 5 to 7 yards deep. Now he takes up the position with the same distance but directly over the Y end and his key is the Y end. If the Y end releases, the safety man plays pass. If the Y end blocks and the flow of the play comes toward him, the safety man will come up hard to force from the inside—inside the contain man who, in this case, is the linebacker in the strong-side linebacker force.

The linebacker plays the Y end or keys the Y end. If the Y end blocks and the flow comes to him, he immediately goes to the outside and contains. He penetrates to the outside immediately. His responsibility is the same as the halfback's and the safety's when they were the contain men—he forces everything back to the inside. If the play runs to the inside or shows to the inside, he spins off any blocks and pursues from the outside. The strong-side defensive end's responsibility remains the same as it was in the halfback and safety force. He reads the block of the Y end and the tackle. If the Y end blocks down, he fights out. If there is no block he reads the tackle. If the tackle blocks down on the defensive tackle, the defensive end reads trap. If the tackle comes at him he fights him. If the tackle sets as on a pass he rushes the passer.

The pursuit is the same; the defensive tackle strikes the blow and comes to the outside. The middle linebacker chases from behind and cuts into the backfield through the hole vacated by the pulling guard. The weak-side tackle strikes his blow and pursues from the outside. The weak-side defensive end comes across and chases from the back and is the contain man against any reverses. The weak-side linebacker chases and joins in the pursuit. The weak-side safety and halfback come over to the middle, always being conscious of option passes.

Another little maneuver you can use once in a while between the strong-side linebacker and the strong-side defensive end is what we sometimes call a tango maneuver—but only when you have experienced personnel particularly adept at reading and who are also very quick. This is called a tango—the linebacker and defensive end exchange responsibilities. In other words, on the snap of the ball the defensive end comes hard to the outside and is the force and contain man, and the linebacker moves behind him to cover on the inside. We call this a tango type of operation.

It can be very dangerous! If the Y end blocks down and hits that defensive end quickly before that defensive end can make penetration outside, he will shut off the defensive end and, with the linebacker coming to the inside on the snap of the ball, that Y end will take two men with one block. Then it's "Katie bar the door" because that end run will get to the outside. There is nothing there to stop it except the safety and that back will have a couple of blockers in front of him, so it's quite likely a good gainer.

The reason for making this move is that if the Y end goes to block down on the defensive end and the defensive end is quick enough and gets between the Y end and the tackle, he will be into that backfield.

What usually happens is that on an end run the offensive tackle will be blocking down on the guard. As he moves to block down, that linebacker coming on the snap of the ball will be into the backfield before the blocking can set up and often catch the back, just as he's getting the hand-off, for a big loss.

Remember the important points in all successful defensive play against the end run: 1) there must be a contain man to turn everything back to the pursuit; 2) there must be pursuit; 3) there must be a back who stays back to look for the option pass, 4) there must be angry gang tackling by everybody on that defensive team.

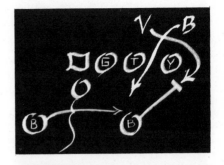

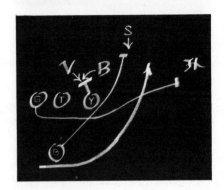

Here we see the result of the excellence of the proper force by the defense. All four of the force men—the strong-side halfback (No. 26), the strong-side linebacker (No. 89), the strong-side defensive end (No. 87) and the strong-side safety (No. 40)—are closing in on the ball carrier. They are forcing the play exactly as they should in the linebacker force, with the linebacker making the initial contact and the others in pursuit. In the bottom picture we see the result of the coordination among these four men.

6

Defensive Line Play

While it's the offense that gets the glory and the glamour, it is the defense that brings the championships to the team. Of the nine championships won by the Packers—division championships, league championships and Super Bowl titles —in only one game did we allow our opponents more than 20 points. In the rest of the games we held our opponents to 14 points or less. And in that NFL championship game, where we did give up 27 points against Dallas in 1966, it was the defense, with a minute and a half to go in the game, that stopped the Cowboys on our goal line and preserved the victory for us.

When I came to Green Bay in 1959, before we went to training camp we ran and reran the films of all the Packers' games of the previous two years. We graded every player and then we sat down to see what our primary needs were. Our conclusions were unanimous—we needed defensive help. There is nothing more demoralizing to a team than to watch the opposition run up and down the field on you, and, no matter how good your offense, if your defense can't stop anybody, believe me, you're not going to win any championships.

The characteristic most notable in the defense that we built in Green Bay was the mobility of the linebackers, the quickness of the defensive line and the speed and tackling ability of our defensive secondary. Our three linebackers formed the key to our ability to control the offensive teams because, with their size (averaging around 6'3" and 240 pounds) and quickness, they were big enough to come up to the line of scrimmage and stop those running backs; and quick enough and tall enough to drop back into those passing lanes, cover receivers and those backs coming out of the backfield, and cause the quarterback considerable trouble in finding his receiver.

Defensive football is a game of abandon, and you have to have the kind of players who will be able to play with abandon, the hell-for-leather types. Teaching defensive football is relatively easy because the basis of all defensive football is to eventually tackle either the ball carrier or the receiver, and tackling is easier to teach and keep tuned than blocking. That is simply because it's more natural. If a man is running down the street with everything you own, you won't let him get away. That's tackling!

But the defense also has its responsibilities and its keys, and just like the offense it has fundamentals that must be adhered to in order to be effective.

The defense may bend but must always contain. It must never break. The fundamentals of defense are **stance, attack, recognize, neutralize, escape, pursue and tackle.**

Defensive-line play, like everything else in football, begins with the basics, and the basic look of the defensive front four is concave, with the ends positioned on the line of scrimmage and the tackles playing off the ball.

We play our defensive tackles approximately 18 inches off the ball. This is particularly true in first and 10, second and long, and third and long yardage. Of course, on short yardage they've got to come up on the ball to stop the play for whatever yardage is necessary. I'm talking about third and 1, third and 2, or third and inches.

The reason we play the defensive tackles off the ball is that inside there, where the quarters are close among the offensive guards, the center and the defensive tackles, our defensive tackles have a little bit more room in which to react to the actions of the men they're playing over.

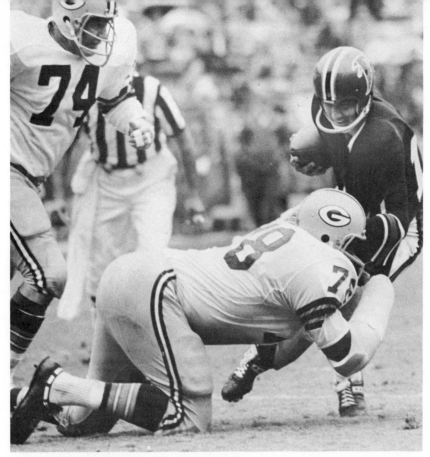

The quick penetration by the defensive tackle (No. 78) gets to the ball carrier as his teammate (No. 74) closes in to help.

Notice the number of Packers around the ball carrier. Eight players concentrating on stopping one man—that's pursuit.

Here is good penetration by the defensive tackles (Nos. 70 and 74). No. 70 is fighting through his blocker and No. 74 has beaten his man badly, is into the backfield and has a line on the ball carrier.

Also, another reason we keep them off the ball is that by playing off the ball it makes it more difficult for the center to get a good block on the middle linebacker. For example, on an inside charge by the defensive left tackle with the middle linebacker keying the fullback, the inside charge takes the defensive linemen into the center, and the middle linebacker, if the fullback goes to the left side, has outside responsibility and comes right off his defensive tackle's tail into the hole. Therefore, it's almost impossible for the center to make that block on the middle linebacker.

The same thing is true on the opposite side with an inside charge by the defensive right tackle and the fullback coming to the weak side. If the fullback is the middle linebacker's key, he will come right off the tail of his defensive tackle, again making it most difficult for the center to get to the middle linebacker. The defensive ends are positioned on the line of scrimmage on the outside shoulders of the offensive tackles in order to be able to gain contact with those tackles as quickly as possible.

To sum up then, the front four, as we do it, has the ends on the line so they can get to the offensive tackles as quickly as possible, and the defensive tackles are 18 inches off the ball, which gives them room to maneuver and also time to recognize the trap.

Once again as with all of football, with every position, the fundamentals and techniques of the defensive linemen begin with the stance. The stance of all defensive linemen is the three-point stance but less of a sprinter's stance than that of the offensive linemen. The defensive tackle also has more weight on his hands because, although the offensive lineman may have to pull and his weight is not completely committed to the front, the defensive man's first move is usually straight ahead or, at the most, a slight angle.

FUNDAMENTALS & TECHNIQUES OF DEFENSIVE-LINE PLAY

This is the stance of that defensive line. The tackles are off the ball and the ends are up tight.

On his initial charge, as the defensive tackle drives out of that stance, he must keep his feet under him and keep them moving. All of the power of his charge starts with his legs. Against running-play blocks and on his initial charge, the defensive lineman must control the offensive man. To break that offensive man's charge and then move him, the defensive lineman must first raise him. And to do this the defensive lineman employs a shoulder-and-forearm charge. Defensive linemen who are exceptionally strong in the arms and in the hands may also use a hand charge.

However, in the shoulder-and-forearm charge, the arm with the fist gripped is brought forward from the set position,

This is the shoulder-and-forearm charge by the defensive tackle (No. 74). He has made contact with the offensive lineman and raised him, and now will cut inside that blocker to go for the ball carrier or rush the passer.

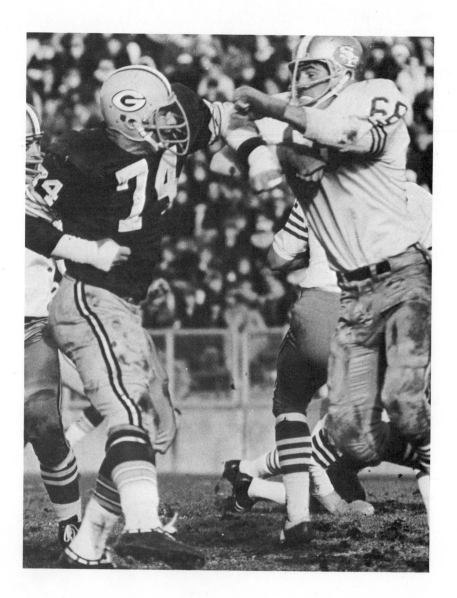

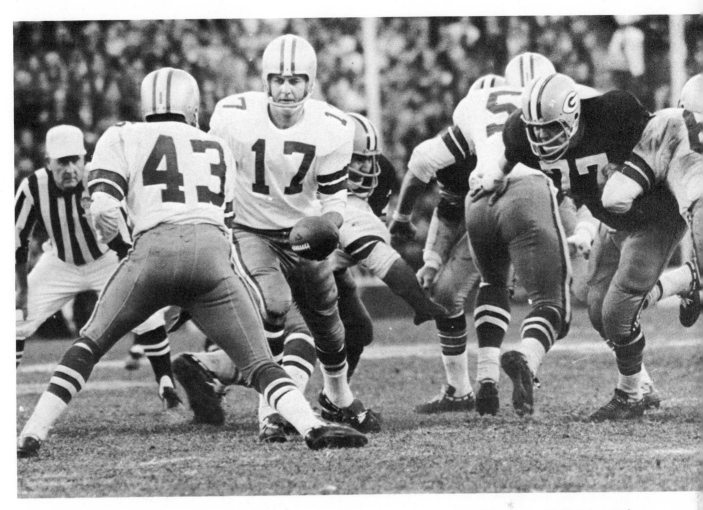

The defensive tackle (No. 77) has made good penetration, has beaten the blocker and is into the offensive backfield. Note that his left arm is pushing off the blocker as the quickness of his charge takes him to the ball carrier.

and as the defensive lineman hits the offensive lineman he lifts with that forearm. The offensive blocker's chest will be the target of the defensive lineman's arms and, on contact, that defensive man gets that forearm across and underneath and then lifts.

The shoulder and forearm used depend on the lineman's responsibility. If the lineman's responsibility is to his left, he uses his right shoulder and forearm, leaving the left arm free in case the back is already into that hole. If his responsibility is to his right, he leads with his left foot and uses his left shoulder and forearm. This leaves his right arm free.

As soon as the defensive man has broken the offensive man's initial charge and as soon as he has raised his opponent, the defensive man's hands are now brought into play because he must shed his man immediately.

If the pressure on the defensive man is from his right, he must fight out into that pressure. If the pressure upon the defensive man is to his left, he must look to his left and fight against that pressure. He must not, under any circumstances, go around the block.

For instance, for the defensive tackle being blocked down on by the Y end or tight end, the tackle, were he to roll around that block, would be out of the play. Rather, he must fight right through the face of that block and try to drive the blocker back into the path of the play.

COACHING POINT: All interior defensive linemen should always fight across or into the pressure of where the block is coming from. They should never roll around a block because by the time they do the play will be gone.

However, if the offensive lineman gets the block on the defensive player and drives him out, the next best move that the defensive man has is to spin out of the block, staying low and driving hard to try and get out and into the path of the ball carrier. He must, of course, first break the blocker's initial charge and then roll toward the play, never away from it.

In spinning, the inexperienced player has a tendency to stand up. If he does, the blocker will run him right out of there. The defensive player must spin low and continue to spin low to the hole. Remember, if at first he does not drive out low and hard to break the offensive man's charge and then spin low, he'll find himself blocked every time.

TACKLE'S RESPONSIBILITY AGAINST THE DRAW PLAY

Against the draw play some teams may hold someone on the line to play the draw, but it's not absolutely necessary. What I mean by holding someone on the line is that, on the snap of the ball, they will keep one of the four or five men on the

This is how to play the draw. The middle linebacker (No. 66), keying the fullback (No. 30), has him in his sights as one tackle waits for the ball carrier.

defensive front line back, always looking for the draw play. Actually, however, the tackles are expected to read draw and it is their responsibility.

When the offensive lineman playing over the defensive tackle sets as he does on a passing situation, the first reaction of the defensive man is to rush the passer. He charges at that offensive tackle, but he keeps his eyes on the quarterback, and as he's rushing the passer he must be conscious of any remaining backs that are in the backfield.

As he penetrates, a good experienced tackle will feel that offensive lineman trying to turn him toward an alley away from the area to which he is rushing, which is an unnatural

Here the defensive linemen are looking into the backfield and reading the blockers. You will notice the guard and tackle on the offense are pulling, but the middle linebacker is still keying the fullback (No. 43) and has not committed himself. The two defensive tackles are looking into the backfield and are starting to go with the flow of the play.

position for the offensive lineman. Normally that offensive lineman would not allow any penetration, or at least not without a good fight. A good experienced defensive lineman will feel that. He will feel the offensive line trying to get an inside position or an outside position to give the defensive tackle an alley in which to penetrate. The offensive lineman wants penetration. A good defensive tackle feels that. It comes with experience. Inexperienced teams usually must keep somebody back to play the draw play. Now, all that defensive tackle does, when he feels that offensive lineman giving him an alley or giving him that penetration, is stop his rush and fight back into the area he just vacated.

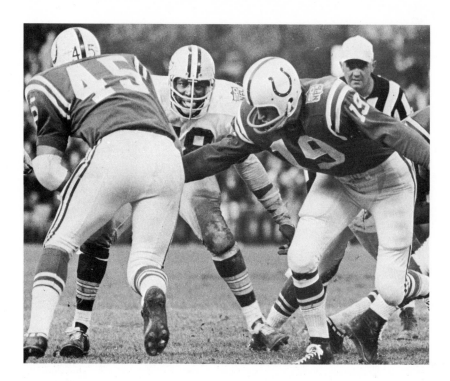

The quarterback has made the hand-off to the ball carrier, but the defensive tackle is there waiting. He was not fooled by the pull of the guard over him and he now has the ball carrier at his mercy.

DEFENSING THE QUICK TRAP

The main reason we keep the tackles 18 inches off the ball rather than right on the ball on the line of scrimmage is so that they can react quickly to the trap.

For example, if the offensive right guard playing over the defensive left tackle pulls to his left, the first thing that defensive tackle should think of is trap! As soon as that guard pulls, the defensive tackle's first reaction is trap! The defensive tackle on the other side can't read trap because he's fighting across. He's penetrating. He's busting in there. If the trap is coming from the right guard across on the defensive tackle, there's no way for that defensive tackle being trapped to read it. The man who must stop the trap is the defensive tackle who is uncovered for the moment.

So, what that defensive tackle does is fight right through the block of the center who's probably blocking down on him and drives the center right back into the trap hole. The defensive lineman who is being trapped, as soon as he feels he is trapped, must drop to all fours to try and plug up the play; but the man who must stop the trap, the man who is the key to stopping all trap blocks, is the defensive lineman who is uncovered.

By that I mean, when the guard in front of him pulls, the defensive tackle is momentarily uncovered until the center blocks down. He must fight through that block, driving that blocker back into the hole where the other defensive tackle is being trapped and where the ball carrier is headed.

Our defensive lines at Green Bay were never huge compared to some other teams in the NFL and we preferred quickness to size. One of the outstanding players in my nine years there and one who was on every one of my championship teams was Henry Jordan, No. 74, the defensive tackle. Henry did not have the great size; he was about 6'2" and 240 to 250 pounds. But he was extremely strong in the shoulders and in the hands and very, very quick. Before my first season began in Green Bay, I made a trade with the Cleveland Browns for Henry Jordan and gave up a fourth-round draft choice for him. Any time you can make a trade for one who becomes an all-pro defensive tackle or an all-pro anything—that is, indeed, a fortunate trade. His quickness was one of the things that made him such an outstanding pass rusher. In our 1967 Western Conference championship game against the Los Angeles Rams, when a lot of people had favored the Rams to beat us and some people were calling the Packers "old men," Henry got to Roman Gabriel, the Rams's quarterback, four

DEFENSIVE TACKLES AS PART OF THE PASS RUSH

Here is Henry Jordon (No. 74) getting to Roman Gabriel in our playoff game against the Rams. He got to Gabriel four or five times that day, playing one of his outstanding games in a great career.

or five times during the game. He had one of his great defensive efforts and was, to a large measure, responsible for our outstanding defensive success in that game. We held the Rams to seven points.

Rushing the passer

In rushing the passer, the defensive tackles move up on the ball rather than stay the 18 inches off it. Because they have such a small area in which to do their pass rush or to defeat their man, defensive tackles must beat them at the line of scrimmage or as close to it as possible. The defensive ends have a great deal more area in which to rush the passer than the tackles.

In defeating that man, once contact is made, feet and hands are ninety percent of the battle. Other things being equal between the offensive guard and the defensive tackle, the man who has the quick feet and moves his feet more effectively will win this hand-to-hand battle.

On the pass rush, it is most important for all of the defensive linemen to move on the snap of the ball so that whenever possible they can beat the offensive man to that pass set. Remember, the defensive lineman has a right to use his hands, and so he must bring his hands into play immediately upon launching his charge to grab the opponent by the shoulder pads or by the arm or whatever he can grab, and to pull past him.

Another technique that the defensive lineman uses in rushing the passer is that with that initial charge he raps his forearm against the helmet of the offensive tackle. Then, as the blocker brings his arms up to fight off that attack, the rusher drops or dips his shoulder underneath the raised arm or arms and charges past. Of course, as the blocker brings his arms down, he will sometimes grab the tackle and get called for holding.

I remember that Big Daddy Lipscomb, the great Baltimore defensive tackle, had a trick that, when he would rush the passer, he would put one arm up in the air and with the other hand he would reach out and tip the pass blocker's helmet down over the blocker's eyes, giving him quite an advantage. Not that it was legal, of course, but it was very seldom spotted and it was very effective.

The defensive linemen doing as they were coached—looking into the backfield immediately as they make contact with their opponents.

The defensive tackle has penetrated and forced the quarterback to pull the ball down.

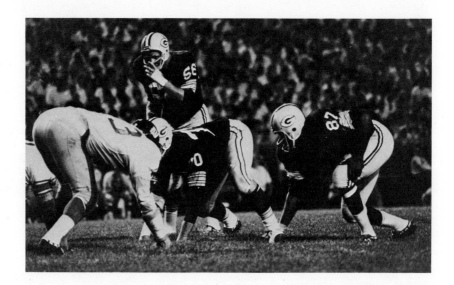

The stance of the defensive end is the sprinter's stance, a three-point stance, as shown by the defensive end (No. 87).

THE DEFENSIVE END

Defensive ends are the primary pass rushers in today's game of football. There is as much passing as there is running in professional football, and teams that do not get an effective pass rush are teams that are not going to win. Your pass rush has to come from all four defensive linemen, but if you can't get it from your defensive ends you are in very serious trouble.

The stance of the defensive end is slightly narrow and more of a sprinter's stance than that of the defensive tackle. This narrow stance permits the defensive end to move more quickly on the snap of the ball and to move better to either side.

The defensive end should remember that when the tackle opposite him sets as to pass-block, he must concentrate on that tackle on his initial charge. That charge will take him to the offensive lineman and, as he makes contact, the defensive end immediately looks into the backfield at the quarterback and, concentrating on the quarterback, uses his legs, feet, hands and head to get him to the quarterback. Once he has made contact with his opponent, he uses those hands to pull himself past the opponent, to discard the offensive tackle and open up the path to the quarterback.

The defensive lineman must never become stereotyped in his rush. However, one perfected move to the outside with a countermove to the inside is all he will need to go with such change-ups as blitzes and twists.

On an inside rush by the defensive end, success is based on the quickness of the charge and the ability of the defensive man to disguise his intent of going inside. The defensive end makes his initial charge exactly as he does on an outside rush—hard and right at the outside shoulder of the offensive tackle. After that first lead step, and when his hands have grabbed his opponent, the defensive end pulls by and across the opponent's face and takes an inside rush. Here, again, as in all defensive line play and in all of football, the hands and the feet determine who is going to win this battle. The quickness of foot of the defensive end will determine whether he gets the quarterback or not.

At Green Bay we were very fortunate to have one of the great defensive ends in the history of the game in Willie Davis. Willie came out of Grambling College and I traded for him with the Cleveland Browns because I thought he

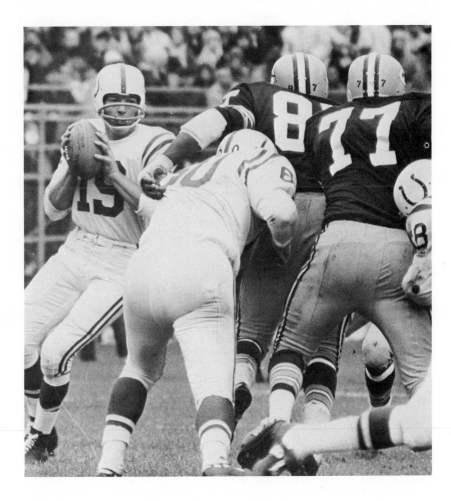

This is an inside rush by the defensive end (No. 87), beating his blocker and heading toward the quarterback.

would be better than what we had. In Willie we got a great one. For a big man, 6'3" and 240 pounds, he had great agility and terrific strength in the upper torso. It is this quickness and this strength that made him one of the great pass rushers. Very few offensive tackles could handle Willie one-on-one in a passing situation and this was a great help to our pass defense because it meant that they would have to keep a back in to assist that tackle, thereby releasing one of our linebackers to help out in the pass coverage.

In our first championship game against the New York Giants, they were so concerned about Willie's pass rush that they kept their fullback, Alex Webster, in the backfield most of the time to help block on Willie. This of course weakened the Giants' passing game and, since the pass was their major scoring threat, Willie's presence had a great deal to do with our success. Oftentimes the fan may not appreciate that a

Willie Davis (No. 87) doing his thing—rushing the quarterback. His quickness and strength made him one of the great pass rushers.

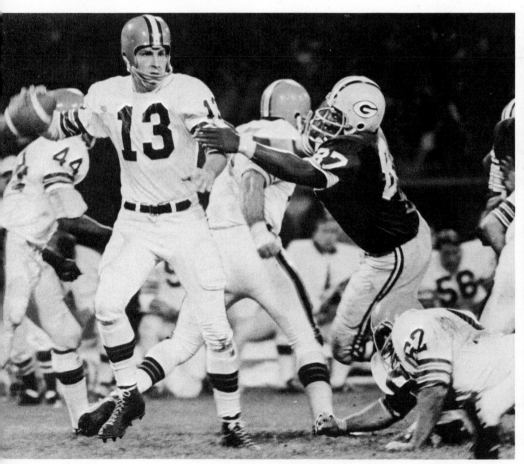

player like Davis does not have to get to the quarterback to help against the pass—his presence may make a team adjust, and with that adjustment comes another weakness. We had four interceptions that day.

In addition to his great pass rush Willie was a superb tackler and always at his best in the big games. In Super Bowl II he made eight unassisted tackles and got to the quarterback three or four times.

The successful pass rush is dependent upon 1) anticipation and quick recognition of the passing situation, 2) quickness and decisiveness in the initial move and, 3) the coordination of the hands, the feet and the head, with the shoulders forward to prevent the blocker from getting underneath the pass rusher.

SUMMARY

In addition, the rules of the team in the pass rush are the following: in driving for that passer the pass rushers must keep their eyes on the passer; they must squeeze the passer's area of operation; try to force the passer closer to another pass rusher; do not give the passer time to find a secondary receiver; force the quarterback out of his pocket —force him to throw on the move or force him to run. If the rush has not reached the passer, if they can't get that passer, the defensive men must get their hands up as he starts to throw so as to force the passer to throw the ball higher or to bat the ball down or, with the arms up, force him to pull it down and run with it. In other words, the pass rush is designed to do *two* fundamental things: 1) get to that passer and throw him for a loss, and 2) make that passer lose confidence in his pass protection and demoralize him and with him his team.

Keys for defensive linemen

On both the offensive and defensive teams all players have certain keys that tell them what the other is going to do. By keys I mean movement by the offensive or defensive people that will alert the opposition as to their intentions.

For example, when the running backs stay in the back-field as the quarterback drops back, and the backs set as if to pass-block, this tells the safety man that it is a pass play. Another key for the safety man is, when the offensive tackle sets to pass-block, he reads pass. The key for reading pass for the defensive tackles is that, when the men over them set for pass blocking, they know right now it is pass. So they make their initial charge against the offensive man and then look for the quarterback.

When the off-guard pulls away toward the back of the center, that is the key to that defensive tackle and the first thing he thinks of is trap! If the offensive tackle were to pull and go outside, that would be the key to the defensive end so he would go out with that offensive tackle looking for the pitchout and the sweep. If the offensive tackle or tight end playing next to the offensive tackle were to block down on the defensive end, that's a key to the defensive end. It tells him that the play is coming to the outside; therefore he's got to fight across the face to the blocker or spin out of there and get into the runner's path. The same thing with the defensive tackle: if the offensive tackle blocks down on him it means the play is going to his outside and he fights across the face of the offensive tackle trying to get into the runner's path.

To sum up: Defensive tackle—if the guard over you pulls, your key is to play the trap. The second key is to look for the sweep. Defensive end—if the tackle over you pulls to the outside, that key tells you it's going to be an outside pitchout or a sweep. Defensive end—if the Y end or tight end blocks down on you, it means an outside play. Ends and tackles—if the linemen over you set as on a pass, rush the passer, always looking for the draw.

The defensive tackle (No. 77) hits the quarterback just as the ball is released, and gives him a real shot.

This is containment. The tackles have the ball carrier as the middle linebacker comes up to put on the finishing touches.

Containment

The defense must bend but must never break, and it must always contain. Every defense must have a defensive perimeter in which the offense is contained. And each defensive formation should have a contain man on both sides of the formation. There must be a contain man on the strong side, the side to the flanker, and there must be a contain man on the weak side or the side away from the flanker.

The men who are the contain men will vary. For example, if on the weak side the defensive end has contain responsibilities or outside responsibilities then he must be the contain man. He must keep everything within him: he must make sure there are no reverses coming back, he must make sure that the quarterback pulling down the ball doesn't get outside the defensive perimeter. This frees that linebacker to go off in pursuit.

If the defensive linebacker is the contain man the defensive end can go off in pursuit. Now the linebacker has to wait somewhere on that outside perimeter so he can contain the offensive team within that area. Whoever is the contain man must keep the offense inside of themselves. The contain man can be either the defensive end, the outside linebacker, the defensive halfback or the safety. And when you are playing against scrambling quarterbacks it is very important on every play that the contain man know his responsibility and act accordingly.

One of the major developments in defensive football in recent years has been the tackle and end twist used on passing downs to rush the passer. This has been a very effective means of rushing the passer and one that, properly executed with quickness and precision, can be a marvelous addition to the defensive pass rush.

Stunts & twists

Tackle first twist

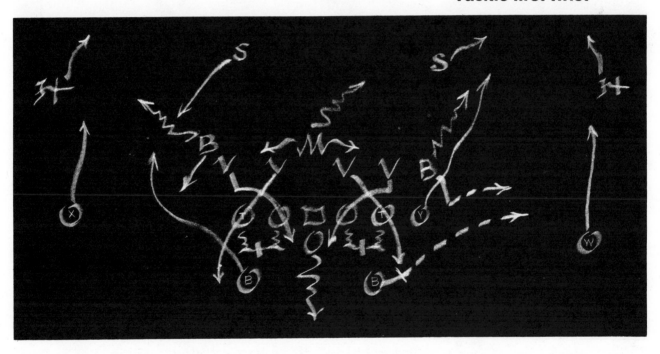

One method is to send the tackle first across the face of the offensive tackle. The defensive end, faking a drop step as if he's rushing to the outside, then comes up through the center in order to rush the passer. The purpose of this is obvious. As the defensive tackle drives across the face of the offensive tackle he draws the block of the offensive guard. The

defensive end first makes a slight jab step and a move into the offensive tackle to draw his block, then drop-steps and comes around the back of the offensive tackle. Usually these two offensive men, in trying to stay with the particular people they're supposed to block, run into each other and knock each other off, and it frees the defensive end for an uncluttered pass rush at the quarterback. And, of course, the responsibility for containment is now that of the tackle who is on the outside.

End first twist

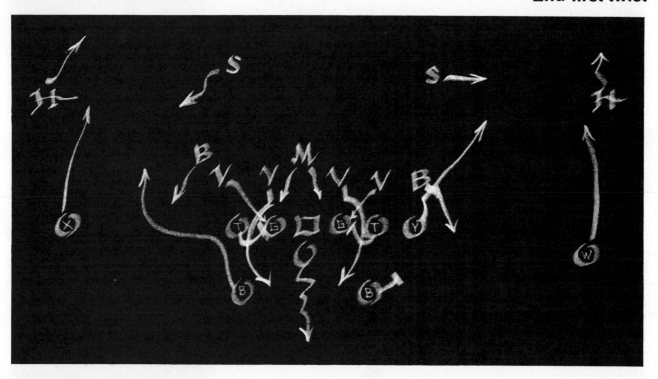

Another version of the tackle and end twist is to send the defensive end rather than the defensive tackle to the inside. This time the defensive end comes across the inside shoulder of the offensive guard and the tackle, first attempting to draw the block of the guard, drop-steps around the rushing end to rush the passer from the outside. This can be very, very disconcerting to blockers, and often what happens is that as the defensive end cuts quickly to the inside the offensive tackle goes with him. The offensive guard, as the defensive tackle fakes him, sets, and by the time he realizes that it's the twist the defensive end is on him, and then you

have a double-team block on the defensive end, but the defensive tackle is left alone coming to the outside to rush the passer.

Tackle & tackle twist

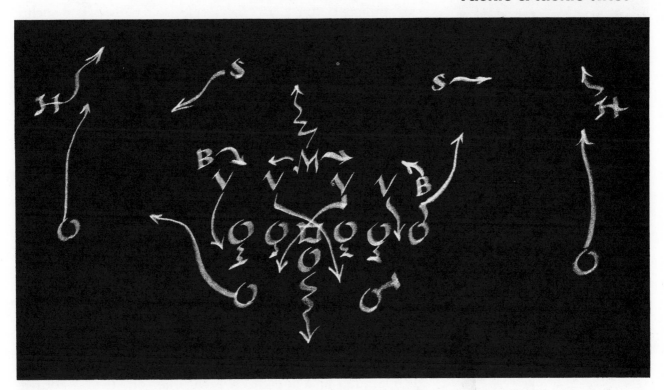

As between the defensive end and defensive tackle, where you can have an inside or an outside twist, so you can also have one with the two interior linemen, the defensive tackles. The two tackles line up directly over the offensive guards and with the snap of the ball one tackle will come across the face of the center for the offensive guard on the other side of the line; and cutting behind him will be his opposite number, the defensive tackle, coming in behind. Of course, if the offensive linemen stay man-to-man they will pick each other off and leave one of the tackles free to come in without any interference. The offensive linemen's only method of handling this is to area-block or switch-block.

When an offensive lineman sees the defensive tackle make an inside charge it is very difficult for him to let his man go to the other guard and wait. So this is a very effective defensive maneuver to rush the passer.

Tackle twist with
middle linebacker

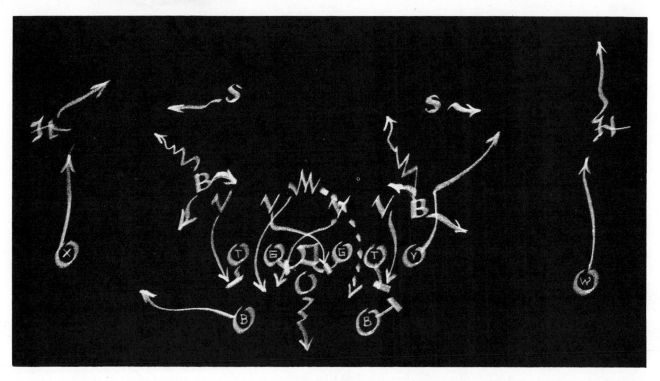

Good offensive linemen will be able to handle the tackle twist if they are experienced and are able to wait and hold their ground and not knock each other off. If you add the middle linebacker to the twist, however, you create a very serious problem for the offensive blockers. For example, assume an inside charge by the defensive tackle across the face of the guard, and an inside rush by the middle linebacker across the face of the center, both going to their left. The two of them will take their men into the offensive guard. Now the defensive left tackle will wait, and as those two men cross in front of him he will cut behind them, giving him a free run at the quarterback. To stop this, the center must recognize the twist as soon as that linebacker commits, and drop off and be ready to pick up the tackle as he comes around. That requires a great deal of experience and ability.

That tackle twist with the linebacker can be worked to either side and is an effective method of rushing the passer. It is also an effective method for disrupting the pass-blocking and making the offensive team lose confidence in its ability to handle these stunts and twists.

Pursuit

The heart of a defense is pursuit. Pursuit is dedication. Pursuit is persistence. Pursuit is getting to the ball carrier by taking the shortest course, and when you get there you get there in an angry mood. It is every man's responsibility to pursue until that whistle blows, and when that pursuit has been good and the play ends you can count your team colors around that ball carrier.

This is where the pass rushers should always meet—at the quarterback. Here the two defensive linemen (No. 77 and 82) have broken past their blockers and now the quarterback is theirs.

Tackling

As the offensive man is taught to drive through his opponent with his block, so the defensive man must learn to drive through the ball carrier with his tackle.

Tackling begins with the basic football position: feet spread, eyes on the opponent. The tackler must drive through his opponent, feet pumping, and lift. There are too many arm tacklers in football today. Players stick out an arm and expect a 220-pound back to fall over. And this makes for those 1,000-yard runners. The tackler must get his head and

shoulders into the ball carrier. He cannot stop him with just an arm. And after he's stung a ball carrier a couple of times with really solid tackling he'll find that ball carrier isn't that anxious to come at him. As with the ball carrier who wants to sting a defensive man, so the defensive man should really want to lay the wood to a ball carrier when he has a chance to tackle him.

In the open field the tackler must be very concerned that he does not launch his tackle too soon. The back with room to maneuver will move around it. He must position himself so that he forces the back toward the sideline or toward another tackler.

SUMMARY   These are the eight pillars of defensive line play: Stance, attack, recognize, neutralize, escape, contain, pursue and tackle.

Willie Davis is a dedicated professional who made his own personal commitment to excellence to become the best defensive end I ever coached, and one of the greatest of all time.

7
Linebackers and Defensive Backs

The second line of the defense is the linebackers—the men. Often they become the celebrated stars of the defense, but as the glory comes their way so do the responsibilities. Of all of the defensive men the linebackers have the most difficult assignments. They are a focal point of the defense against the run and an integral part of the defense against the pass. We expect the linebacker to be strong enough to fight off the blocks of those big offensive linemen and quick enough to get to that ball carrier. He must also learn patience and be patient enough to wait and read, and alert enough to understand his keys, recognize the run and close the hole.

He must also be fast enough, once he reads pass, to be able to cover the tight ends and the backs coming out of the backfield or, in the case of zone defenses, to drop back into his area and to be able to cover any receiver who comes in there, and break up the pass or intercept it.

The basic difference between the defensive linemen and linebackers is that on the snap of the ball the lineman acts and then diagnoses; the linebacker, on the snap of the ball, diagnoses and then acts. The linebacker never guesses but rather waits for his key. It is far better for him to be a little hesitant than it is to react too quickly and do the wrong thing. Of course, this requires knowledge, confidence and self-control, and when you find people who have those qualities you're very, very fortunate and your defense is going to be a good defense.

Today, the heroes of defense are those middle linebackers, and they have lent a great deal of glamour to pro football. Names like Ray Nitschke, Joe Schmidt, Sam Huff, Dick Butkus and all the rest have become household words. I can remember the days when the newspapermen who occasionally covered a pro-football game didn't know the name of any defensive player, and so a great deal of credit for the glamorization of the middle linebacker belongs to Paul Brown, one of the great coaches in the history of football.

In the late '40s and early '50s the offenses were controlled by a defense called an Eagle defense, so-named because of the excellent use made of it by the Philadelphia Eagles. It was a five-man defensive line up front.

Paul Brown's Cleveland Browns had dominated the rival All-American Conference in its four years of existence and when that conference folded the Browns, along with the 49ers and the Colts, came into the NFL. The first big game of that 1950 season was between the defending NFL title team, the Philadelphia Eagles, and the newcomers, the Cleveland Browns.

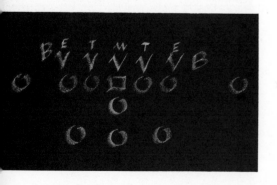

The Eagle defense was an odd-man defensive line featuring a five-man front, with the middle guard playing head-on over the center, the defensive tackles playing over the offensive guards and the defensive ends playing on the outside shoulders of the offensive tackles. This helped to force all runs to the inside, where that middle guard was waiting. And he was usually about 280 to 310 pounds, strong and tough.

So, during the game, the Browns on offense would very subtly shift the guards an extra foot or so away from the center. Now this widened the gap between the defensive

Here the middle linebacker is looking into the backfield for his key. He
then goes on to make the tackle before the back gets outside.

tackle and the middle guard over the center. If that defensive
tackle stayed in on the shift the offensive tackle now moved
out and widened the gap even more between the defensive
tackle and the defensive end, and also gave that offensive
tackle a better angle in which to block on the defensive
tackle, so the effect was to put that defensive tackle in a
position where he couldn't be right.

So now the Browns ran straight at that hole which
would develop on either side of that big middle guard. If
the defensive tackles moved into the gap, the offensive
guards had a great angle with which to block on those
tackles, and this is where the Browns's running game attacked. During the season other teams attacked any Eagle
defenses that were used and it forced defensive adjustments.

This changed the whole game for the defensive team.
The defensive middle guard became a middle linebacker.
The defensive tackles had to become much more mobile be-
cause, in addition to size and strength, they needed that speed

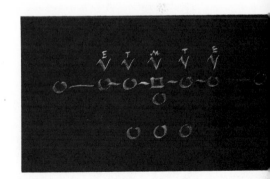

to be able to handle the power rushes inside and also pursue the outside runs as well as rushing the passer. Now the defensive ends became the primary pass rushers, and a premium was placed on speed and agility as well as strength.

But more than anyone, that middle guard went from a giant of about 300 pounds to a middle linebacker of 230 to 240 pounds. Now he had to be much more mobile, for he was a free-lancer. It gave him the opportunity for fame because he is out there in the open where he can be seen by the fans, taking those shots at the ball carriers after the defensive line strips the runners of blockers, and it has made Sunday heroes of the Schmidts, Nitschkes, Huffs and the rest.

It also changed the game for the offensive center, too, because now the emphasis had to be on his agility and not on his size. Instead of being required to move a monster playing him head-on, the center blocks to either side. These onside blocks on the side to which the play is going are not usually the type requiring the moving of a huge man. They are cut-off blocks, where the blocker just injects himself between the defensive man and the play.

It was Paul Brown then who started to break up the Eagle defense and move defensive football into a 4–3 defense. So people playing middle linebacker today can thank Paul Brown for having a great deal to do to create their position.

That final score, in 1950, was Cleveland 35, Philadelphia 10. The Browns went on to win the NFL title. About eighteen years later that score would be repeated in a place called Los Angeles and the teams would be Green Bay and Kansas City, and the game would be called Super Bowl I.

POSITIONING OF LINEBACKERS

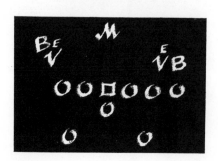

The three linebackers are positioned with the strong-side linebacker in a two-point stance, the football position, facing the Y or tight end and concentrating on him. The weak-side linebacker is in what we refer to as a hip position. I mean by that he's 1 yard deep and 1 yard outside the defensive end. The middle linebacker is directly over the ball, facing the quarterback 2½ to 4 yards off that ball. This is the familiar 4–3 defense.

In an odd defense we mean that one of the defensive linemen is playing over the offensive center. For example, if the lineman shifted to the strength of the formation, to the wingback side, the defensive tackle would take a position over the center. The two defensive linemen would move out into the gaps and the middle linebacker would compensate for that shift by taking a weak position, probably over the guard or almost over the guard. That's what we call the 4–3 over to the strong side.

4–3 over defense

Now, in the 4–3 under, which is also an odd defense, the tackle would shift to the head of the center, moving the other tackle and defensive end out into the gaps, and the middle linebacker would compensate for that movement of the defensive linemen by assuming a position to the strength of the formation or to the side of the flanker by lining up over the guard.

4–3 under defense

Coordination between linebackers & defensive linemen

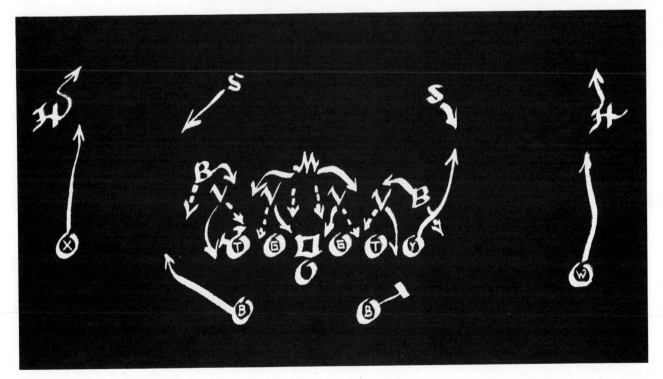

All defenses have their own little coordinations between individuals on the team. In this case, there is a coordination between the middle linebacker and the two defensive tackles, just as there is a coordination on the outside between the outside linebacker and defensive end, and the outside linebacker, defensive end and cornerbacks. So, basically, defensive football is a team defense with small teams within the whole team working together. There is coordination between the middle linebacker and the two defensive tackles forming a triangle in the middle of the defense.

For example, on an inside charge by the defensive tackles the middle linebacker has outside responsibility, usually in a hole that's outside of the defensive tackles, and his key is to follow the flow of the backfield to the left, if that is its first move, and to fill the hole to that side.

If it's an outside charge by the defensive tackles the middle linebacker's responsibility would be the inside hole. He would have a secondary key in this case. If the center's set is as on a pass the middle linebacker would move out of there and immediately go his pass coverage. If the center were to block down to either side, the middle linebacker would fill that hole vacated by the center immediately because he would know that either the fullback or the halfback is coming in there. If the center were to drive out on him he would meet that charge, trying to force the center back into the hole to close the gap.

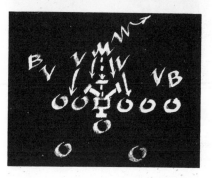

This was a key stop in our playoff game against the Colts. The two linebackers stopped the ball carrier just short of a first down in the overtime period, forcing a field-goal attempt from a longer distance.

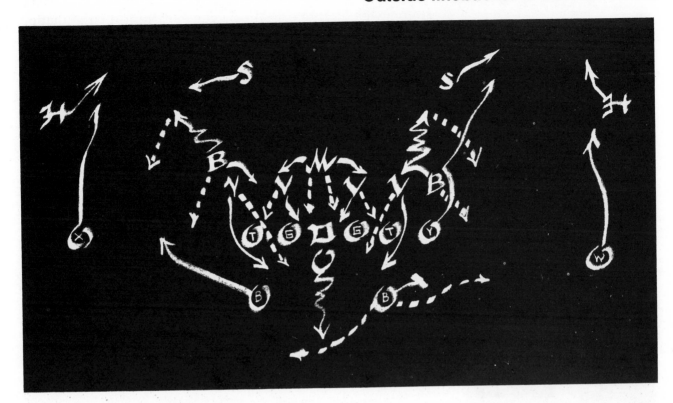

Just as there is a coordination on the inside between the tackles and the middle linebacker, there is a coordination on the outside between the defensive end and the outside linebacker as far as responsibility is concerned. For example, with the defensive end having outside responsibility, the first responsibility of the outside linebacker is to the hole to his inside. With the end having inside responsibility the first responsibility of the linebacker is to the outside on running plays.

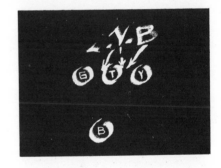

If it is a pass and the defensive end has the outside rush, the first move of the linebacker would be to the inside and as soon as he recognized pass he would come to his pass coverage. If, however, the end had inside responsibility on the pass rush the end would continue to the inside. This means that the outside linebacker would be the contain man on, for instance, a quarterback who would roll out because the outside linebacker's responsibility would be to the outside. Whoever has the outside responsibility is the contain man. He would drop to his pass coverage as soon as he recognized pass, but he still has the contain responsibility.

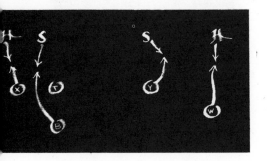

BLITZES

In addition to their responsibility in a normal or basic defense, the linebackers become the spearhead of the defense in what I believe is one of the most dramatic maneuvers in football, the blitz. The blitz can be effective against both the run and the pass and, properly called and executed, may change the whole course of a game, destroying the offense's preconceived plans and with them its morale by hurrying the throw of the passer or dropping the passer or the runner for a big loss.

Before we discuss blitzes let me emphasize that no matter whether we're having a one-man, two-man or three-man blitz the defensive secondary, when a blitz is called, takes its men man-to-man. In other words, the cornerback will be on the wingback, the weak-side cornerback will be on the split end, the strong-side safety will cover the tight or Y end, and the weak-side safety will cover the halfback coming out of the backfield. They're on their men man-to-man whenever there is a blitz.

Blitz by weak-side linebacker

On an inside blitz by the weak-side linebacker, the weak-side defensive end or the man he's working with is now the contain man and the pass rusher from the outside.

The key for the two remaining linebackers, that is, the middle linebacker and the strong-side linebacker, is the action of the fullback. If the fullback blocks to either side both the remaining linebackers go to their respective hook zones for pass defense. The middle linebacker goes to a weak zone looking for delays or for anybody coming into that area, and the strong-side linebacker goes to the strong-side hook zone to help underneath for the safety man, and that linebacker is also looking for delays from the fullback.

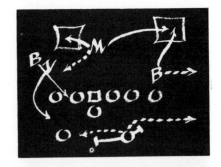

If the fullback flares to the strong side, the strong-side linebacker is to take him man-to-man and cover him wherever he goes. The middle linebacker now moves to the strong-side hook zone.

If the fullback flares to the weak side, the strong-side linebacker moves to the hook zone and the middle linebacker covers that fullback man-to-man.

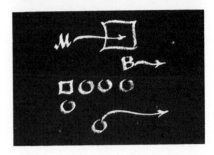

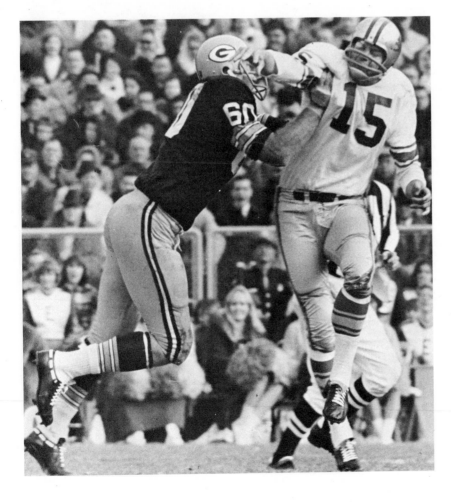

Here is a good blitz by the linebacker (No. 60), getting the quarterback just as he released the ball and forcing an incompletion.

Strong-side blitzing linebacker

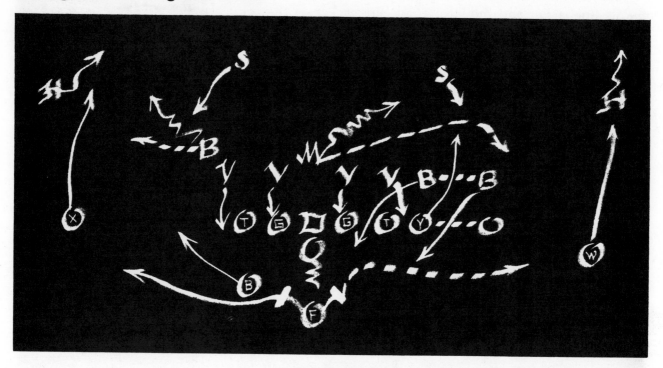

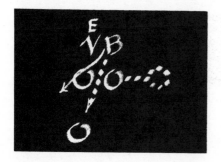

In the blitz by the strong-side linebacker, the strong-side linebacker usually works in coordination with the strong-side defensive end. His blitz can come from the outside or it can come from inside that defensive end. Where he blitzes from usually depends upon the split of the Y end or the tight end. If the Y end is split out he'll probably blitz from the outside. If the Y end is in tight, he'll probably blitz inside the defensive end. Of course, the purpose is to draw the block of that offensive tackle on the defensive end and then release the linebacker inside. The fullback is usually looking for the blitz from the outside, so sometimes that strong-side linebacker can get inside that protection. He can also blitz inside both the defensive end and the defensive tackle. That's another phase of the strong-side linebacker blitz.

And in all of those the deep secondary is man-to-man on the offensive ends and the halfback. The key for the remaining linebackers is, again, the fullback. If the fullback blocks to either side the middle linebacker goes to a strong-side hook zone looking for delays and helping on the underneath patterns for the strong-side safety, and the weak-side linebacker comes to the weak-side zone looking for delays into his area.

If the fullback flares strong the middle linebacker has him man-to-man and the weak-side linebacker moves into his hook zone. If the fullback flares weak the weak-side linebacker has him man-to-man and the middle linebacker moves into the hook zone on the strong side.

Of course, in all of these blitzes there is a contain man on either side, and it is the linebacker's responsibility as a contain man to keep a roll-out quarterback inside that defensive perimeter even on a blitz. For instance, if the blitz were to be from the weak side, and it was an inside blitz, it would be the responsibility of the weak-side defensive end to be the contain man, and the defensive end on the strong side would be the contain man there, keeping the quarterback from rolling out.

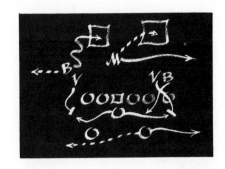

Middle-linebacker blitz

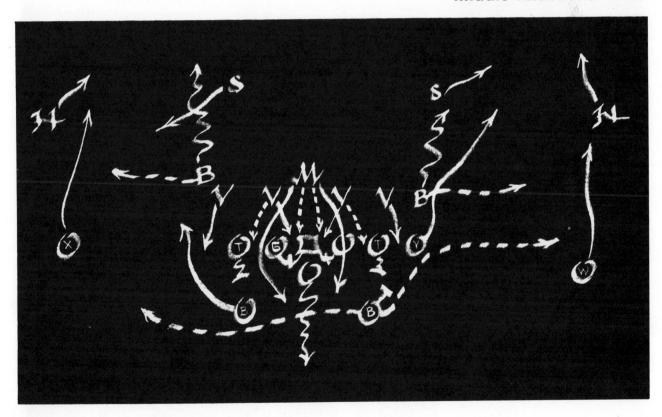

The second line of your defense is the linebackers, and here one of them is tackling the ball carrier as the other comes up to help.

In the blitz by the middle linebacker the blitz is usually in coordination with one of the defensive tackles. For example, the middle linebacker can blitz to the strong side with the defensive tackle taking the inside, or he can blitz to the weak side with the weak-side defensive tackle taking the inside. Or he could blitz right up the middle with both defensive tackles taking the outside.

In the middle-linebacker blitz, the two remaining linebackers, the strong-side linebacker and the weak-side linebacker, now still key the fullback as they do in all the blitzes. On a block by the fullback both go to a hook zone. On a fan-pass route by the fullback they cover him man-to-man on the side he comes on, and the other linebacker goes to his hook zone. If he goes toward the weak side the weak-side linebacker takes him man-to-man and the strong-side linebacker goes to the hook zone.

The middle linebacker on a blitz has hit the quarterback, knocking him off his feet, and then makes the tackle.

Sometimes we'll have a combination of more than one line-backer blitzing. Sometimes all three linebackers will be blitzing at once. For example, the weak-side linebacker and the middle linebacker are blitzing at the same time. The middle linebacker still blitzes in coordination with the defensive tackles either to the right or to the left. The weak-side line-backer can blitz either to the inside or to the outside. With the middle linebacker blitzing and the weak-side linebacker blitzing, if the fullback were to flare out to the weak side, the fullback would be uncovered. To protect against this, in any combination blitz, the defensive ends are responsible for covering the fullback in the flat.

So, usually, when the middle linebacker is blitzing, and the weak-side linebacker is blitzing, if the fullback were to come out the defensive end would cover him.

The same thing holds true if the strong-side linebacker and the middle linebacker are blitzing. The defensive end would have to be on the outside if the fullback came to the strong side and the strong-side linebacker was in the blitz with the middle linebacker. The defensive end would then have to cover the fullback if he came out as in a fan-pass route.

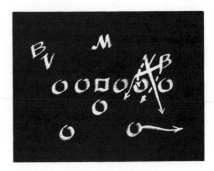

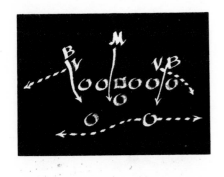

The blitz by the middle linebacker (No. 66) caught the runner for a big loss behind the line of scrimmage. The defensive end (No. 87) comes in to help on the tackle. Oftentimes the blitz is very effective against the run.

The same thing holds true with the three-man blitz: middle linebacker, strong-side linebacker and weak-side linebacker. Now, if the fullback goes strong he's covered by the strong-side defensive end. If the fullback goes weak he's covered by the weak-side defensive end.

The blitz is often as effective against the run as against the pass, and many times will do more to disrupt the running game than it will to disrupt the passing game. But, blitzing is of itself a change of pace in the defense and an exciting move, but teams that live by the blitz die by it because good defensive teams blitz only sparingly and only when they think it's most judicious. Our offense would always rather play a team that blitzed a lot because, in blitzing, if you don't get to the quarterback you leave yourself very exposed in the secondary.

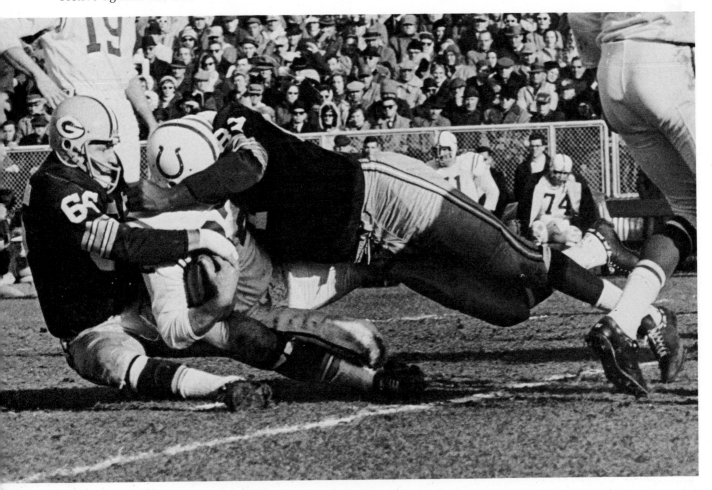

This is the position of the strong-side linebacker playing over the tight end. Note the concentration by the linebacker and the excellent position of the hands and forearms getting ready to chuck that tight end.

There's another responsibility for the outside linebacker who plays over the tight or Y end. On running plays he must keep that offensive Y end or tight end from blocking down on the defensive end, and to do so when the Y end goes to the inside the strong-side linebacker has to push him off the block and then be in a position to close the off-tackle play or to close on the outside should it be a pitchout.

On a pass play the strong-side linebacker has to chuck him and keep him off rhythm. That's all we ask him to do. In other words, we want that strong-side linebacker to hit that tight end as hard as he can—chuck him—and then release him. If the Y end were to release quickly and do everything on rhythm, the passing game would be a simple operation. We tell that strong-side linebacker to chuck him and to hit him hard to keep him off rhythm. The strong-side linebacker has two different chucks: one when the man goes to the inside and one when the man goes to the outside. To the inside he drives him down the line of scrimmage. He just pushes him right into the line to throw off his rhythm and then the strong-side linebacker goes back into his pass-coverage, looking for anyone coming into his area.

Linebacker over the Y end

On a release to the outside, when the Y end is trying to get to the outside of the strong-side linebacker, that linebacker will drive him and push him out toward the sidelines just as far as he can push him and then go back into his own hook zone.

When that linebacker drops back in his hook zone he becomes, of course, a defensive back, and he is required to play the receiver and the men he's responsible for just as any defensive back. Those linebackers have to have the speed and agility and the hands to be able to cover those strong tight ends as they come out and those quick backs who are also good receivers. It is a difficult job, but when they're doing that job right that pass defense is solid. In addition to their defensive responsibilities in stopping the run and being effective on the pass defense, it is the linebackers more than any other individuals on the football team who are responsible for stopping the long gain by the run. The defensive linemen will strip the blockers and, if possible, make the tackle, but it is the linebackers who must get that back at the line of scrimmage or as close to it as possible. The linebacker must never allow himself to be cut down. He must play off those blockers until he can get his shot at the halfback. And once he gets his shot he has to connect. He has to nail him, to make that tackle.

DEFENSIVE BACKS

The last line of your defense, the defensive backfield—the corner men and the safety men—are a very special breed of football player with very special assignments. We want them to have speed, agility, brains and toughness, too. And their basic assignments are, first, against the pass, and second, against the run. Primarily their assignment against the run is in turning wide plays to the inside.

These defensive backs are extraordinary athletes and they must have the capacity to accept an occasional defeat. When a lineman is beaten it is seldom seen in the stands but when a defensive back is beaten it's right out there in the open where everyone can see it. Defensive backs must be of such a temperament that they do not become flustered when a man beats them. They must be like a baseball pitcher who knows that once in a while someone is going to hit a home run off him. When that happens, the defensive back must not be bothered; instead, he must make that receiver pay, and he does that by tackling that receiver so hard when that receiver catches the ball that the next time that man comes out he's going to be looking for that defensive back.

Good defensive coverage by the defensive halfback (No. 26) and the linebacker (No. 60) leads to an interception by that back.

It is a lonely job. A defensive back knows where his help is coming from against every formation and in every defense but basically it's still man-to-man; it's him against his opponent. Even as his defeats are out in the open, so are his victories—including the interception that can turn the ball over to his team and may even turn the ball game around.

FUNDAMENTAL TECHNIQUES OF DEFENSIVE BACKS

The alignment of the defensive cornerback is 1 to 2 yards outside of the receiver's outside shoulder, 4 to 7 yards deep. The depth of the cornerback is designated by the overall defense that is called.

The outside foot is forward, weight evenly distributed upon both feet or upon the balls of the feet, knees flexed in a basketball stance, concentrating upon the receiver.

As the offensive end comes down the field the defensive back back-pedals, keeping his shoulders parallel to the line of scrimmage with his weight evenly distributed, and using his arms to assist the ease of movement. As the defensive man back-pedals he gains a position 1 yard outside and 2 yards off the receiver, never allowing the receiver to gain a head-and-head position with him.

When the receiver has made his break the defensive man must push himself to stay in step with that receiver, and he should still maintain a position on that receiver so that if the receiver were to change direction that receiver would make contact with that defensive back and actually have to run over him in order to get to the ball.

Once the defensive back has made his break and is in stride with the receiver he should look through the receiver and to the ball going past the receiver, either to knock the ball down or to intercept it.

Cornerbacks must have speed and should be excellent athletes who can cover a good receiver man-to-man.

Safety man

The physical requirements for the safety man do not have to be as high as they are for the cornerbacks. Some speed may be sacrificed in the player who has the capacity and the willingness to acquire the knowledge necessary to play safety. Basically, the safety is responsible for covering the halfbacks and the tight ends and helping out on the deep receivers.

Good pass coverage and a good rush cause this incompletion.

Primary functions of the secondary

The defensive secondary has two primary functions. One is to contain or to force the end run and the other, of course, is defense against the pass. In containing or forcing the end run the strong side, or side to which the flanker is, it is usually predetermined that the halfback will force or the safety will force. One of these two men will usually force and contain the end run and bring it back to the inside, back to the pursuit.

Another way of determining who is to do the force is the split of the flanker from the Y end. The wider the split calls for the safety man to force. The closer the position of the flanker to the Y end usually calls for the halfback to contain or to force, turning the end run back to the inside.

On the weak side, with the weak-side defensive halfback and the weak-side safety the same rule of thumb applies. With the wide split by the X end it is usually the safety man's position to force. With the close split by the X or split end usually the weak-side halfback will force. This is also predetermined. They usually use a code word— a very simple code word will be "you" or "me."

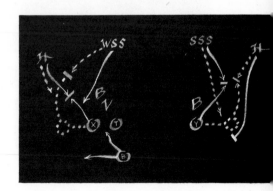

Defensive men's keys

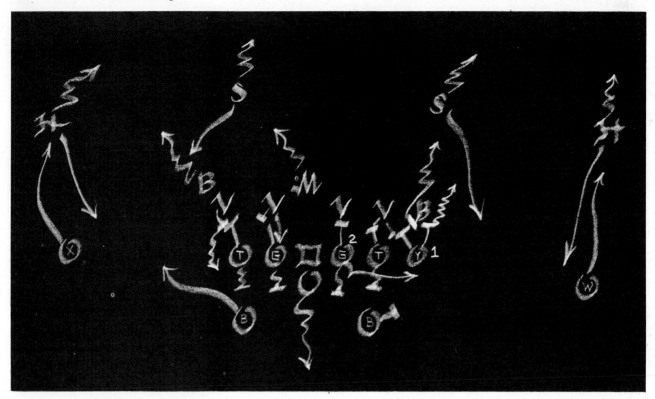

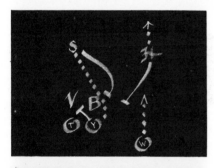

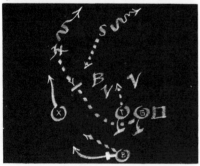

Both the strong-side halfback and the strong-side safety key the tight or Y end to determine whether it's run or pass. The Y end is their key as to run or pass. If the Y end blocks in then the force man must go up immediately to contain and turn the end run back in. If it is the safety man he comes up on the outside to turn the run back in. If it is the halfback who has the same key of the Y end he comes up on the outside to turn it back into the pursuit.

On the weak side the key as to run or pass for the weak-side safety and the weak-side defensive halfback is the weak-side offensive tackle. If the weak-side offensive tackle comes downfield they know immediately it's run. If he sets for pass, they know now—right now—it's pass. So that is their key and, again, it is predetermined who is to do the forcing for the end run.

The extraordinary versatility of the offense in today's game places a great burden on the linebackers and defensive backs. Size, speed, intelligence and experience are the basic requirements for those defensive players, and after that comes the little extra—desire—that separates the great ones

The outside linebacker (No. 58) forces the play and makes the tackle on that runner.

from the good ones. They all are good, otherwise they would not be in this league, but the great ones have that ability to come up with the big play at the right time. And making the big play is not just a sometimes thing—the great ones do it throughout their careers.

We never lost to the Cleveland Browns while I was at Green Bay and, although we did not play them that often, they were always a powerful team, and we did meet in key games, including the 1965 National Football League championship. The Browns had Jimmy Brown, one of the great runners of all time, plus a good passing game and excellent defense. Our defense never let Jimmy Brown run wild, and one of the reasons was the play of Ray Nitschke. Jim Brown was his responsibility and, in that championship game, Nitschke made the defensive play to stop Cleveland and seal the championship for us. It was late in the third quarter, we were ahead, but a Cleveland touchdown would give them the lead and the momentum. They were driving and on our 40-yard line when they threw a circle pass to Brown down on the goal line. Nitschke, keying Brown, went all the way with him and batted the ball out of Brown's arms. It was a great play and seemed to take the spirit out of the Browns. We won, 23–12. Jimmy Brown never had a 100-yard day against the Packers.

In the 1966 NFL title game, Dave Robinson made the play that stopped Dallas on our 2-yard line with time almost gone. We had a 34–27 lead and there should have been no problem. But we blew an extra point and let a Dallas fumble get away when four of our men played footsie with the loose ball. After a pass-interference call, Dallas had the ball on our 1- or 2-yard line, fourth down. The Cowboys' quarterback, Don Meredith, called a rollout with the option to pass or run. It was a great call because he had blockers in front of him and, if our defense forced hard, he could lob the ball into the end zone to a receiver; and if the defense dropped back, he could pull the ball down and follow his blockers into the end zone. He only needed 2 yards.

The man who had to make the play for us was the linebacker. He did. Dave Robinson, as he was taught to do, analyzed before reacting and, reading rollout, fought through the blocker protecting Meredith and then chased Meredith with his hands up high, screening him off from his receivers, and when Dave got to him he tried to pin both arms and forced Meredith to throw the ball up for grabs. We intercepted and that was that.

Here the strong-side linebacker (No. 89, Dave Robinson) has made the interception and is headed downfield. You will notice that his defensive teammates have started the downfield blocking that oftentimes breaks a linebacker or defensive back for a touchdown.

Under the most intense pressure, the linebacker did it perfectly—analyzed, reacted to the keys, pursued, forced the poor throw that led to the interception that sealed the victory.

I have never been one to have our linebackers blitz a great deal. I feel that the less you blitz, the more effective the blitz is for you because of the element of surprise. In Super Bowl I the blitz and the play of our all-pro safety Willie Wood helped to break the ball game open.

We were leading at halftime by only 14–10 and I told the defense to stop being so cautious and go after the Chiefs's offense. Early in the third quarter, with Kansas City having the ball near midfield, on third and 5 we called our first blitz. We blitzed the strong-side linebacker, Dave Robinson, and the weak-side linebacker, Lee Roy Caffey, and got a great rush from tackle Henry Jordan. The blitz caught the Chiefs's quarterback and his blockers, and forced a bad throw. In fact, the passer was hit as he tried to escape and Willie Wood cut in front of the receiver and intercepted, ran the ball to their 5, from where we scored on the next play. That made it 21–10 and it was all over.

The pressure of championship play is the most intense a football player ever experiences. The great ones perform like champions, coming up with the big play when they have to, despite the pressure.

8

Passing, Pass Receiving and Pass Blocking

One of the most exciting plays in football is the long pass for the touchdown. It is right out there in the open where everyone can see and appreciate the science and artistry that are combined in the successful pass play. In the game as we play it, the passer—once he has taken the ball in the center-quarterback exchange—has approximately 3.5 seconds, sometimes less, to drop back, scan the field, step into the pass pocket, pick his receiver, set himself and throw. In that small interval of time the receiver must free himself beyond the line of scrimmage, run his route, break clear, spot the ball and catch it. Perfection in this is the product of practice and persistence.

Of all the people on your ball club—and you are involved with all of them—there is no other one with whom you spend as much time as you do with your quarterback. If this is a game through which you find self-expression—and if it isn't you don't belong in it—then the quarterback is the primary extension of yourself and he is your greatest challenge and also can be your greatest satisfaction.

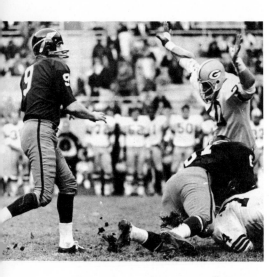

This is Sonny Jurgensen throwing against the Green Bay Packers in 1968. I was general manager of the Packers then. When I came to Washington I found Jurgensen to be an exceptional quarterback.

In my years in pro football I have been blessed with three outstanding men to play quarterback for me, Charlie Conerly of the New York Giants, Sonny Jurgensen of the Washington Redskins and, of course, Bart Starr.

Conerly possessed exceptional poise. He was a master at getting rid of the ball under pressure, and when his receivers were covered he had that rare knack of throwing it just a little off target so that it could not be intercepted or called intentional grounding. The fans, who didn't know what Charlie was doing, used to boo him unmercifully, but he threw for few interceptions and he seldom had to eat the ball. I have never coached a football player who had more courage.

Sonny Jurgensen possesses maybe the best arm in all of football and it has been a shame that he's never had the personnel around him to supplement his great artistry. I have never seen anyone who could throw as many different passes —long, short, over the middle, sidelines, whatever you want —as effectively as Sonny Jurgensen.

And Bart Starr is the greatest quarterback who ever played football. Starr is the greatest because he won the most championships. It's as simple as that. Isn't winning the job of the quarterback?

In the toughest kind of competition, championship games, Starr completed sixty percent of his passes and had only two interceptions. In the six NFL championship games of which he won five, and the two Super Bowl games of which he won both, he threw for fourteen touchdowns, over 1,500 yards, and had only two interceptions in 192 attempts. He completed 113 passes in those eight games.

There are many great quarterbacks, and I don't mean to be disparaging of any of them when I say Bart Starr is the greatest. But if we're in this game to win, then he is the best quarterback to ever play because he won the most championships.

But it wasn't easy for him, and when I first joined this team the opinions of the Packers and the rest of the NFL was that Starr would never make it. That shows you how wrong the experts can be. They said he couldn't throw well enough and wasn't tough enough, that he had no confidence in himself and that no one had confidence in him. But after looking at those films over and over before the first team meeting, I knew he had the ability, the arm, the ball-handling techniques and the intelligence, but what I didn't know was what kind of inner strength he had and how much confidence he had. He proved that to me and to all of football.

Drafting a quarterback

Because of the enormous load he must carry and the way we play the game you spend more time with your quarterback and his back-up man than you do with any of the other players on the team. Without a good quarterback you just don't operate. And so every year each club is looking for some promising college senior, not to replace its present quarterback, because few can make it that first year, but for the future.

Since in the T-formation he handles the ball on every play, and because so much of the pro attack has to do with passing, a quarterback must have sure hands and be an excellent passer. His I.Q. must be above average, because he must not only be able to absorb the coach's game plan each week but he must have a thorough knowledge of what everyone does on every play, and he must know the opponent, the qualities and characteristics of each individual on the other team. That's not an easy chore and quite often quarterbacks who have all of the ability physically to throw and handle the ball can't handle the complicated defenses that are thrown at them in today's game.

The quarterback should be strong physically and be able to take the punishment when those 270-pounders unload on him. He should also have enough height to see his receivers over those opposing linemen. Each year it seems those defensive linemen get taller and taller and those defensive backs get quicker and quicker and the quarterback's job gets tougher and tougher.

A quarterback must have great poise, too, and he must not be panicked by what the defense does or what his own offense fails to do. He must know the characteristic fakes

The quarterback calls the play in the huddle. The effectiveness of his selection will be tested in the next few seconds.

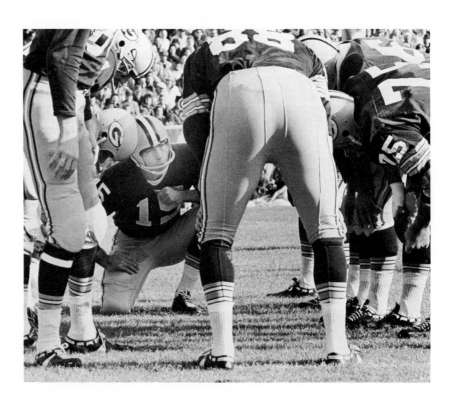

Even with the defensive player hitting him, the quarterback is continuing with his follow-through.

and patterns of his ends and backs, and anticipate the break before the receiver makes it. Then there are those times when, by the nature of its rush, the defense overextends and leaves itself open to a run. So the quarterback who can run has a great advantage. However, one of the common tendencies you find in a rookie quarterback or even a second- or third-year man is that as soon as he sees an opening he will pull the ball down and run. We don't draft quarterbacks for their running ability. We draft them for their ability to throw the ball and to run the offense. Some quarterbacks have been very successful as runners—Fran Tarkington, Frankie Albert, Bob Waterfield, Bobby Layne, Otto Graham—but primarily they are still passers.

When you go to the draft each year, if you can find all of this in one man you have found a very special person, and each year you try. Although you have more knowledge about the college quarterback than you do about anyone else you draft, the first-year quarterback, because of the complex intricacies of playing the position, is still the biggest question mark of all the players you draft.

The great difference between the college game and the pro game is that they do not emphasize the pass as we do. There is no way that they possibly could. They don't have the time to put in an intricate passing attack or to find a combination of a passer and a receiver that work together over a period of years. What generally happens is that you will have a good passer with adequate receivers for a couple of years. Then that good passer will get a great receiver for one year, but then the passer will graduate and the receiver will be there without a good passer for the next two years; so it isn't to be expected that the college teams can pass the ball like the pro teams. I have known college coaches who have been in the business for ten, fifteen or twenty years who say that they have never had more than one or two superior passers in those years and, more often than that, when the superior passer was there they didn't have the great receiver.

PASSING
As in every phase of football, success in passing is founded on fundamentals, and in the passing game they begin with the mechanics of passing.

In positioning behind the center the quarterback assumes a relaxed stance, a relaxed position. His knees are slightly flexed, his feet are on a straight line spread to about the width of the shoulders. The arms are extended but not rigid, elbows in close to the body. The upper part of the body is slightly erect. Actually it is the fundamental football position.

When the center snap is properly executed the ball will arrive in the quarterback's hands with the laces across the underside of the fingers of the passing hand. After the quarterback has taken the snap, and brought the ball to his midsection, he starts his retreat, raising the ball with both hands to shoulder height. He must not turn his back on the line of scrimmage.

He retreats, instead, in a three-quarter-turn position as he goes back 9 yards before stepping up 2 or more yards into the pass pocket. Remember, the quarterback brings the ball immediately to his midsection, and he must get away from the center as quickly as possible.

One of the secrets of great passers is their ability to get away from the line of scrimmage and drop back quickly. This gives them a longer time to scan downfield and look for the receivers. This is why a quarterback like Namath, in addition to Starr and Jurgensen and the others, is so effective—because of the quickness with which he drops back.

The quarterback raises the ball to his shoulder height and uses short jabbing steps to get back. At the end of that retreat, his right foot is the brake against that rear movement and then he pushes off that foot to come back into the pocket.

Another method of retreat for the quarterback is the straight drop back. Some quarterbacks prefer this method. All he does is take the snap and back directly up, keeping his shoulders parallel to the line of scrimmage, and look downfield with a full facing of the defense.

The reason that the quarterback retreats in a three-quarter-turn position or straight back is that he must be scanning downfield during the retreat. He must be reading the defense and picking out his primary and secondary receivers, and it would be almost impossible for him to do this if he turned completely around, retreated and then turned back and tried to read the defense.

Scanning the defense as you retreat is a mark of an experienced quarterback. Often quarterbacks, particularly rookies, make up their minds before they drop back whom they're going to throw to, and as they drop back they look for their primary target and that's all they're interested in. Then they wind up, throw it and are very surprised when it's intercepted. The quarterback must be able to look for his primary, secondary and even third receivers as he's coming back.

The right foot is the brake against that quarterback's rear movement as he sets up. Now he is ready to step into the pocket.

PLAY-ACTION PASSES

Up to now we have discussed, in the passing game, the quarterback's drop either as a three-quarter turn, keeping his eyes on the defense, or a straight drop with a complete facing by the quarterback into the defense, scanning all the way. There are, of course, other methods, and one of these is the play-action pass where we fake the run and then throw. In this action the quarterback, the running backs and the offensive line simulate run and it develops into a pass.

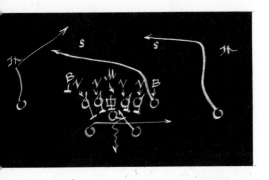

For example, where the fullback will come in hard toward the middle and the halfback will come across, the quarterback turns to the fullback, makes the fake to him and then drops back into the passing situation. Now, in order to be effective, the quarterback has got to make this look as much like the run as he possibly can. So his action is exactly as it would be on the run. He actually will turn his back on the defense. Of course, the offensive linemen must also carry out their simulation run. Their blocking must be semiaggressive. They must drive out at the defensive men over them and then retreat. Drive and then retreat. What they're trying to do is to make the linebackers play run so that the wingback, the Y end and the X end will get behind them. The linebackers sometimes shut off the routes of the receivers on a straight passing situation, but if you simulate run you hold those linebackers so that those receivers can get outside.

We use this kind of play, naturally, in a running situation. We fake run when the whole defense expects run. We fake run and then throw. The easiest thing really to defend against is the pass in a passing situation. Second and long, third and long—that's easy. The most difficult thing to defend against is a pass in a running situation.

The linemen are simulating run with drive blocks by guards 63 and 64 as the quarterback fakes to the fullback on this play-action pass.

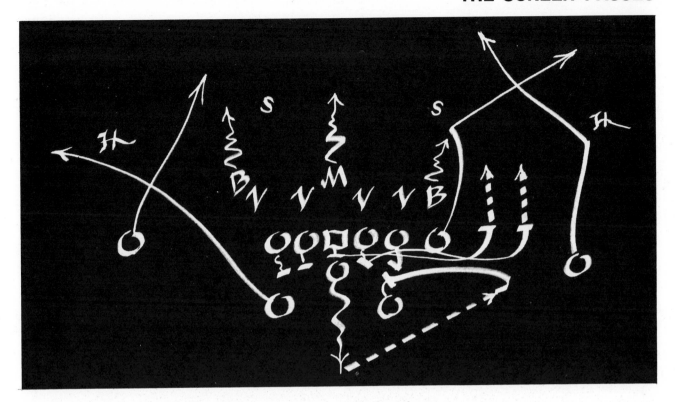

We have been discussing the play-action pass in which a run is simulated and a pass develops. The screen pass is another play in which the quarterback must practice deception. This is a situation where the defense expects pass. When the quarterback drops to his regular passing position, using either a three-quarter turn or a straight drop back, he wants the defensive men to drop back, the linebackers in particular. All the receivers drive off the line of scrimmage, down the field hard, simulating deep pass all the way. The linebackers go back to cover their lanes. The linemen set, just as they do on pass. The backs set just as they do on pass. The quarterback drops back to a position 8 or 9 yards exactly as he would on his normal pass play and looks downfield, allowing the defensive people to come in. He wants these people to get in, as deep as possible, and then he retreats a little more into a deeper position. Meanwhile, the blockers are releasing and move out into the flat with the back, in this case the receiver, following them out. The quarterback throws a delayed-action type of pass out to that back in the flat.

Scrambling　　When throwing from the pass pocket, however, the quarterback will learn that the pocket is not always a stable barrier. It will sag and give at one point and expand at another. Therefore the quarterback must have that quick-footed action to move in any direction, and he must be able to feel, to sense, where that pocket will sag or break before it does. And, sometimes, there's no pocket at all and there's no disgrace in eating the ball.

There are times when the quarterback cannot throw the ball, either because his pass protection breaks down or because all his receivers are covered. He has a choice now of pulling the ball down and running with it if he can; sometimes he can't because all the running lanes are clogged and he's forced to eat the ball and take his loss.

Sometimes there is just no pocket and there are no receivers open, and you have to run for your life.

The other thing he can do, of course, is throw the ball away so he'll not be caught for a loss. And he must either throw it out of bounds or he must throw it into an area where there is no defender. It is never a desperate act, really, but it is a calculated act. And it's also quite an art to be able to throw that ball in an area where it can't be caught by either your receiver or their defender. Many of the great quarterbacks have mastered that art and I remember seeing Bart Starr one time put it right into the tuba section of the Packers' band on the sidelines and the defense screamed that it was intentional grounding, but there was a receiver nearby and the referee didn't call it.

Each year in that draft we try to find a quarterback, but so does everyone else. When we get one and we bring him to camp everybody is looking at him the first day of practice. We want to find out if he can really throw. We have a passing drill with the centers, the quarterbacks and the receivers making their various moves. One year our new boy was there with Starr and back-up quarterback Zeke Bratkowski, and everybody else on that practice field was sneaking a look to see if he could throw because everybody knows how important this is to the whole team.

So Bart threw and Zeke threw and then the new boy took his first snap from center, and with all of us watching he steps back toward where the pocket would be and he lets it go. And he was very impressive; he could throw the long ball, he led his receivers well, his actions were fluid and he exuded the confidence a quarterback must have.

Later at the Five O'Clock club with the coaches, I said, "We have a natural here—the kid has the touch." He did not have great coaching in college and he had some minor faults. He carried the ball low and it took him too much time to get it into passing position, and on the short passes he had a tendency to throw the ball down. We worked with him on these things in camp and we started to spot-play him in our pre-season games, and when he looked excellent we thought we had come up with a real find.

Then the bubble burst. We tried him late in the regular league game and he lost all his poise under pressure. He forgot the game plan he knew letter-perfect and he couldn't

THE MECHANICS OF PASSING

find his receivers and he lost the quickness he had exhibited in practice and he threw an interception. Of course, the team lost all confidence in him. He simply could not move the club. What leadership qualities he seemed to have were missing in action. I remember one veteran quarterback who lost them, too, when he began to believe that his receivers were dropping the ball on purpose as a plot to persecute him.

So when you go into that draft and you draft that quarterback and you bring him to camp, you never know; he can look great and the mechanics can be perfect, but under pressure—that's when you can tell whether you've got one or not.

Even in practice, as on the playing field during the games, the concentration and dedication of Bart Starr are evident.

The quarterback's grip on the ball will vary depending upon the size of his hand. Usually there are two or three fingers on the laces of the ball. The index finger is toward the rear of the ball but actually points at the target when the ball is thrown. There should be no pressure of the palm on the ball, but rather the pressure should be in the fingers of the throwing hand. Actually, there should be a space between the ball and the palm.

The quarterback's action, as he receives the ball from the center, is to bring the ball either chest-high or shoulder-high and control it with both hands. In fact, he keeps both hands on the ball until the actual throwing action begins. As he sights his target the ball is raised above the ear. The ball is pointed not toward the target but away from it on a 45° angle and the elbow is pointed down. That's what gives the spiral action to the ball.

As he throws, the quarterback steps over the front foot and, with a right-handed passer, it is the left foot. That left foot is pointed directly at the target and he throws over that foot just as a baseball pitcher would.

Quarterback's grip

The passer is completing the forward movement of the arm, even though under great pressure in this Super Bowl game.

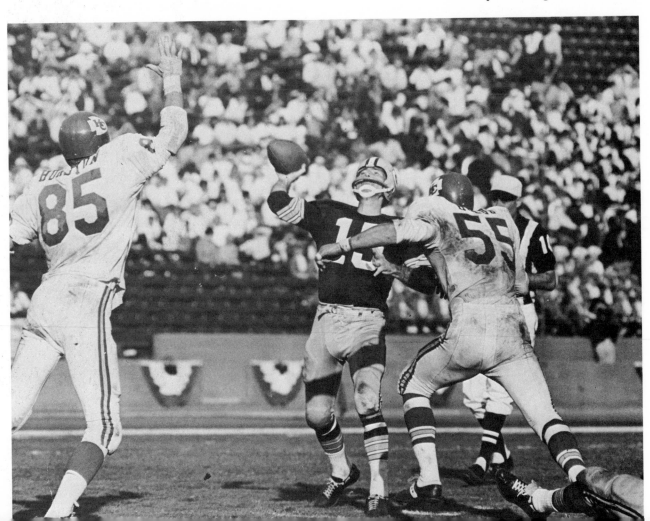

SUMMARY As the quarterback drops back from the line of scrimmage he holds the ball in both hands. The fingers of the passing hand are spread, two fingers on the laces and the index finger near the tip of the ball. The ball has already been brought up to shoulder-height. When he has picked out his receiver the quarterback brings the ball up directly behind his ear with the elbow pointed almost directly away from his target. The left foot is pointed in the direction he is going to throw, the left arm is out as a stabilizer; the quarterback moves into the throw, releases the ball and follows through over the forward leg.

Speed of the pass As a general rule, the ball should be thrown crisply at all times, no matter what route the receiver is running. This is especially true when the ball is thrown to a receiver who is in front of a defender or when a defender is close behind the receiver. For example, on a route which we might call an acute type of route where the defender is behind the receiver, or a turn-in or a comeback sideline type of route where the

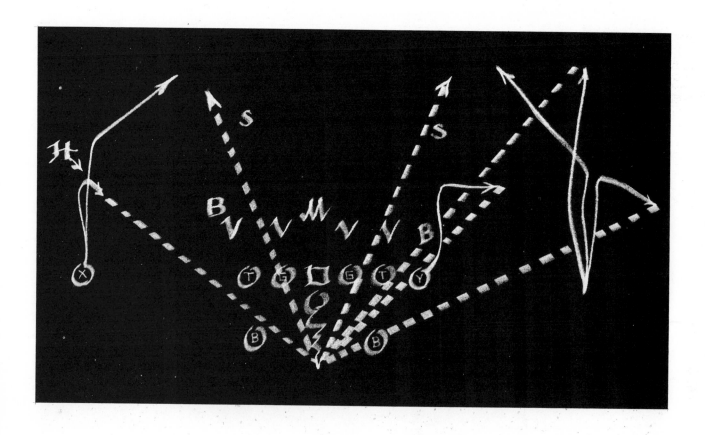

ball is thrown back to the receiver, then the ball is thrown on a flat trajectory and thrown crisply and hard, and about chest-high to the receiver. The instruction to the receiver is to always come back to the ball to catch it.

Of course, you have another type of pass which is thrown on the fly route where the receiver runs a fly pattern, a sideline type of pattern, a deep pattern. Now the ball is thrown in a high looping action to keep it in the air so that the receiver can run underneath it.

In throwing the ball to the post pattern to either side, the passer must remember that, when thrown by a right-handed passer, the ball will rotate in a clockwise type of action. So, when throwing to the right side, the pass thrown from the quarterback to the receiver on a post pattern on the right side has a tendency to drift into the receiver. As a result, the quarterback gives this receiver a pretty good lead because he knows the ball will drift back to him.

In throwing to the left side on the post pattern the ball, in a clockwise action, will drift away from the receiver so the quarterback doesn't lead him as much as when he throws to the right post.

The center & the quarterback

We have talked about the center as a blocker in the offensive line. But, all offensive football begins with the snap of the ball from the center. Many fans do not pay much attention to the exchange between the center and the quarterback, but it is vital to the success of the offense on every single play. A split-second hesitancy by the center can put his whole offensive team offside, and if the snap to the quarterback is not sharp there might be a fumble.

In today's defenses there is a great deal of emphasis on the odd-man line, by that I mean where there is a man head-on over the center. These men are usually huge defensive tackles, weighing anywhere from 260 to 300 pounds, and also very quick and strong. So the center's responsibility is complicated in that he not only must snap the ball to the quarterback to start the offense but often has to handle head-on a man who outweighs him by 20 to 40 pounds. In an even-man line, of course, there is nobody over him so, on passing plays, most often he will snap the ball and then drop back as a blocker.

The center has the defensive tackle over him in this odd-man defense. If this were a pass play the center's first move would be to slam that defensive man, and then drop back, hit and retreat, hit and retreat.

Center-quarterback exchange

The center's stance is the offensive stance with the feet spread to the shoulders' width, with the toes of the right foot opposite the arch of the left foot. As the center takes his position over the ball, which is before him with the laces up, his head is slightly behind the ball because the center can be offside too. He places his right hand on the ball with only the thumb touching the front end of the laces and the other fingers under the ball. He places his left hand on top of the back end of the ball and it merely rests there.

The snap is executed with only the right hand and arm, but placing the left hand on the ball will insure better balance. The snap or delivery of the ball is made with a natural and simple pendulum swing that never changes. The arm is straight and comes back hard and fast, following the same path every time. As the locked arm passes the right knee the center will find that this pendulum swing produces a natural quarter turn of the ball and presents it with the laces in perfect position for the quarterback's grip.

It may not seem important, but that snap must be done with such split-second timing that we have spent hours working on nothing but that. I remember the hours we spent arguing about that center-quarterback exchange in the coach's office at West Point. We were trying to determine the difference between the time required to snap the ball to the quarterback with the full wrist turn, as they were doing at the Point, as against the quarter turn, which I was recommending. I felt that the ball would be presented in a better position to be handled for passing and handing off. One of us would be the quarterback and another the center and a third had a ruler and a piece of chalk. He'd stand the ruler upright on the desk and hold the chalk at a certain height. When the quarterback said, "Hut!" the center would snap the ball and the third man would drop the chalk. If the chalk hit the desk before the snap of the ball into the quarterback's hands, he'd raise the chalk slightly on the next try. As it turned out, the quarter turn was faster than the full wrist turn. It was only a fraction of a second faster, but that's what we deal with in this game. On the snap signal the center starts his pass motion, every lineman starts his motion, and every back starts his motion, except for the quarterback who must wait until he gets the ball. Obviously any substantial time loss there will defeat you, so even that—that fraction of a second— makes a difference.

When that snap is executed correctly the ball always arrives in the quarterback's hand with the laces under the second joints of the fingers of his passing hand. He doesn't have to seek the laces. This is particularly important when the play is a quick pass. All the quarterback has to do is to raise the ball and throw.

In the snap the essentials are uniformity and speed. The center must not lift his tail with the snap, for if he does he will force the quarterback's hands up and lose the target. The perfect snap is always identified by that "pop" as the ball strikes the quarterback's hands. The practice field, of course, is where we perfect that timing of the snap and the charge of the offensive line where the team learns to come off that ball on the snap as one man. This is the cadence drill.

Two types of cadence are used in football—the rhythmic and the nonrhythmic. For example, in the rhythmic cadence hut! hut! hut! there is a set length of time between each hut. In the nonrhythmic cadence there is no set length of time, and an example would be, hut-hut—hut!

We prefer the nonrhythmic cadence and the reason we do is that it prevents anticipation of the snap count by our offensive line. In other words, it allows our line to get off the ball as a unit, and it also prevents anticipation by the defensive line of our snap count. The quarterback can call that snap at any time in the nonrhythmic cadence. He can hold it for that last count until the defense is on the verge of making a mistake. For example, on three it would be hut! hut!, and he can sit there and watch the defensive line and at the opportune moment he can give that third hut! which is snap the ball, and that offensive line is off as one man.

The quarterback, in calling his signals, must make sure that everyone hears him. This is especially important on an audible, where he is changing the play at the line of scrimmage, and his voice must be heard by all of his teammates, especially the receivers, split wide to either side.

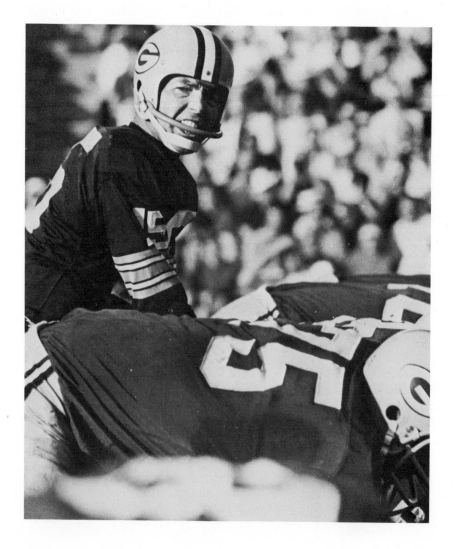

The quarterback's hands should be placed thumb to thumb to receive the ball from the center with the right thumb extended slightly beyond the point of the left thumb, with the right hand upward and spread, and with the left hand outward with the wrist cocked slightly to the right. There should be strong pressure on the center's tail so that he can feel the position of the hands for the snap. And on that snap the quarterback rides the center forward. There is hard pressure of the quarterback's thumb against the other thumb because when the ball hits the bottom of the hand there is a reflex action in which the underneath hand, the left hand, will snap under the ball and cradle it.

SUMMARY: THE MECHANICS OF PASSING

On a pass play the successful delivery of the ball to the receiver is determined before the ball leaves the quarterback's hands. It is dependent upon the correct snap by the center to the quarterback. It is dependent upon the quarterback making the correct drop back. It is dependent upon the quarterback scanning the field as he drops back in a three-quarter turn, or straight drop back, reading the defense, picking his receiver, setting himself properly, stepping up into the pocket, striding with the lead foot pointing at the target, cocking the arm, releasing the ball and following through. After that, it is up to the pass receiver.

THE PASS RECEIVER

Ten other men combine all their efforts to get the ball to him and he must catch it. At Green Bay we were fortunate to have three great outside receivers in Boyd Dowler, Max McGee and Carroll Dale. None of them ever had blinding speed but all were expert at reading the defenses and running their routes, and since our passing game is built upon the ability of our receivers and quarterbacks to coordinate and read the defenses, we did not depend upon speed-burners.

When you go into the draft and pick a receiver, like a quarterback or any other player, there are a couple of things that you have to find out when you get him in that first inter-squad game. You have to test a receiver's desire. Timid ends or flankers won't block those big bully linebackers, but when you see one who will put his nose in there every time and take his licks, you know you've got a good one. One test is to throw to him across the middle where those defensive backs get a good shot at him, and after he gets knocked down watch how he gets up and comes back to the huddle. Another test is to throw that down-and-in pattern and watch and see if he shies away or if he's kind of looking out of the corner of his eyes for that defensive back coming up. If he's concentrating on the ball and catches it, you know you've got a good one.

We've built our passing game around the ability of our quarterback and our receivers and our backs to recognize the pass defenses that are being used against them. This recognition of the defense is difficult to teach, so it is difficult to learn, because the receivers must spot it on the first step across the line of scrimmage and at the same time the defense, remember, is trying to disguise its intentions. Although you'll see the same defense over and over you will probably never see the same situation twice. You have to give your receivers those basic defenses and your own formations and you tell them how to run their routes; and you try, on the blackboard and on the practice field, to set up the different situations and how the enemy personnel will play it. You never get that defensive back in exactly the same position though, and then your receiver has to think of that signal and of how to escape the linebacker who will be knocking his timing off and how to get out into the pattern and what he is going to do against that defensive back.

We have timed this over the years and we know that receivers must make their open interval between 2.5 seconds and 4 seconds after the snap of the ball. Since the quarterback usually has only about 3.5 seconds, all your receiver has got is about 1.5 seconds before the ball is there, and your quarterback must also anticipate. But there's something about a great receiver who knows how to get open. Fakes can be taught, but it isn't just that; it's a feel the receiver has about the defensive man; it's the way the receiver makes his fakes. Fakes can be taught but that feeling comes from experience.

Receiver's fundamentals

The catch is the end product. What goes into its production starts with the basic fundamentals. In this case, it is the receiver's stance.

The stance is a sprinter's stance because the receiver is first a runner, then a blocker. The tail is up, the head relaxed, the rear foot is about 18 inches behind the front foot. His head is up and he looks downfield at the man he's going to run his pattern on. The weight is forward because the player has no need to go to either side, and he drives off the rear foot straight ahead on his toes and always aims at the outside leg of the man covering him.

Coaching Point: It is inexcusable for an offensive receiver to be offside. He knows the snap count, he is watching the ball and even if the crowd noise drowns out the quarterback's signal he should never leave the line of scrimmage until the ball is snapped. There is no reason for a receiver to ever be offside.

This is the receiver's stance: weight forward on the hand, feet spaced in the sprinter's stance, head up, looking in toward the ball, waiting for it to be snapped.

On short and medium passes the receiver's purpose is to start moving the defensive man back. On the snap signal he comes off the line of scrimmage at almost full speed to get that covering man to react immediately. The receiver's stride should be natural and, though he may vary his speed to throw off the defensive back, he should never change his stride.

The practice field is where those receivers perfect that stride and their fakes and their ability to catch the ball, and we were fortunate in Green Bay that our receivers had the chance to practice against one of the finest defensive teams in all of football. That helped them and it also helped our quarterback and conversely it also helped our defense.

Of course, getting there isn't always easy. The receiver must expect to run into rough going on the way out because he's going to be hit by those linebackers if they can get to him and by those defensive backs—which is perfectly legal since they can bump or push the receiver until the ball is put in the air. But he must survive and still run his routes

Here are excellent examples of the receiver concentrating on the ball. In one he has already been hit, but his eyes are on the ball and he is ignoring the defensive man as he brings it in to him. In the other he is up in the air, thumbs together, fingers spread, concentrating as he's about to be hit by that defender.

and make the catch. All of the pass patterns, all of the pass blocking, all of the precision that goes into the passing game are for nothing if the receiver does not catch the ball. The first rule is: once the receiver has made his move and spots the ball he must never take his eyes off the ball. In other words, he must look at it all the way into his hands. He must not be distracted by anything. And, even though he knows he's going to get hit, he must concentrate on that ball. The receiver should also remember one other thing: if the ball is thrown to him and he doesn't catch it, he's going to get hit by that defensive man anyway, so he might just as well catch it.

The receiver must learn to ignore the hands of the defensive men who are between the ball and himself, just as the catcher in baseball ignores the swing of the bat as he crouches behind the plate. The catch itself should always be made with the hands, and the receiver must never depend upon his body as a backstop or backboard. The arms and hands must be relaxed, and a receiver must not grab at the ball. How many times have we seen a receiver anxious to catch the ball stick his hands out as it is coming at him, and now the hands and the arms are stiff as boards and the ball bounces off.

When the ball is coming straight at the receiver at chest height or higher the catch is made with the hands together, the thumb tips pressing together and the hands cupped. When it is coming at him below the chest he catches it with the little fingers together. When he is catching a ball that is going away from him, say on a post pattern, his elbows are together and his hands are held with the small fingers touching, cupping the hands with the palms in toward him. Now, if the thumbs are held together when the ball is out to the side, in holding the thumbs together the receiver's inside arm is raised, blocking his vision so he cannot keep his eye on the ball all the way.

On passes that are leading the receiver and forcing him to extend himself the receiver should, whenever possible, run under the ball and not leap for it. A man whose feet leave the ground cannot cover the ground. This is a habit that most of the receivers bring with them from college. They've got to run under the ball rather than leap for it.

Techniques of catching

Here you see the receiver, out in the flat, catching the ball with his little fingers together.

Another point is that, when the receiver has made his break and the ball is slow in coming to him, he must come back to meet the ball. Otherwise, a defender could possibly move in front of him and reach over to block the ball or even intercept it. The receiver must also remember that when the ball is slow in getting to him he has to use his body as a shield between the ball and a defender.

The receiver has come back to meet the ball and has jumped in the air to put himself between the defender and the ball, shielding it from the defender.

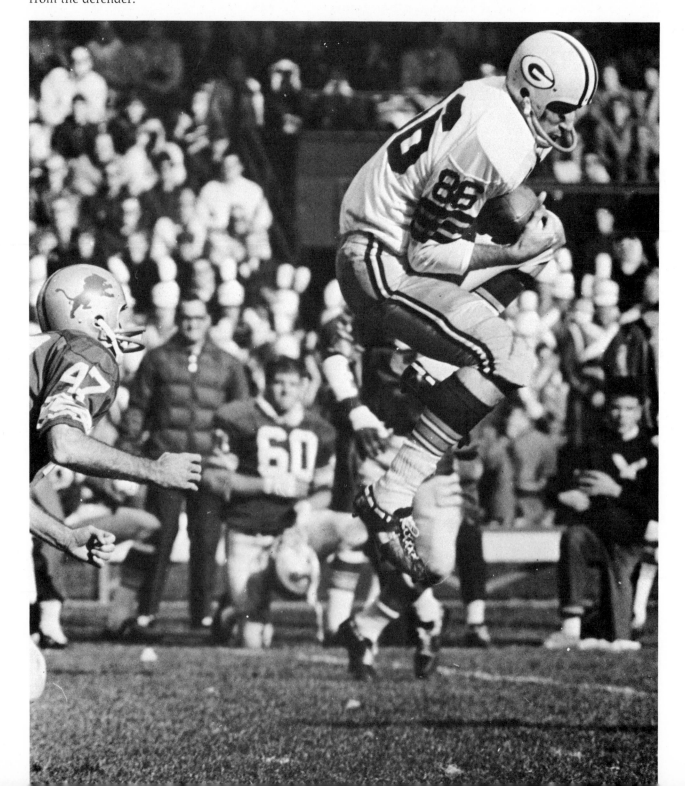

Naturally, all passes are not going to be thrown perfectly, but the responsibility of the receiver remains the same: to get to that ball and to catch it.

All of our receivers have the same names for each of the routes they run, and the designation is called by the quarterback in the huddle. For example, a Y wing turn in means that the Y end and the wingback run turn-in maneuvers. The split end will run a maneuver that is already part of that play and is not called in the huddle.

There is no secret to perfection in the passing game—it's just hard work and concentration. You work at it just as you do all phases of the game. Those receivers run those routes over and over and over. The blackboard is where it is explained, and if they don't understand it there they'll never execute it properly in a game. But on the practice field against the defense is where they learn it and where they come to believe in it. Over and over they run those patterns and over and over you tell them their keys against each defense until it becomes automatic, and all the receivers and the backs and the quarterbacks are on the same wavelength. Then you do it over again and again and again.

Once the receiver catches the ball he becomes a running back. Now we ask of him the same determination, the same second effort and the same commitment to excellence that we ask of any running back or anyone. This is the receiver's reward—his payment for all the routes he ran and never saw the ball, for the bruising he took getting out there to run the routes. And now he can turn a game or even a season around.

Max McGee helped turn Super Bowl I around with some magnificent catches. For many years with the Packers, Max had been our leading receiver, but that season he had not played much. In fact he had caught only four passes. One of them, however, was the last touchdown against the Cowboys in the NFL title game that gave us the winning margin.

Boyd Dowler, our starting receiver, was hurt on the first play from scrimmage in the Super Bowl, and Max went in to replace him. He caught seven passes, two for touchdowns, and was one of the stars of the game for us.

Routes of the pass receivers

Max McGee is going into the end zone after catching Bart Starr's first touchdown pass in Super Bowl I. McGee had a great game, catching seven passes and scoring two touchdowns, turning in one of the fine performances of his career.

The unsung soldiers of the successful pass play are the pass blockers. Football is a game of aggression and forward movement, but the pass blocker is called upon to perform a maneuver that contains a contradiction. The pass blocker must be aggressive and yet he must retreat—hit and retreat, hit and retreat, hit and retreat. It is not easy, but the rewards are great when the pass blocking is properly executed.

The most difficult thing we have to teach our offensive linemen is pass protection. When they come to us from college their experience is limited by the fact that seventy-five percent of the passes thrown in college evolve out of their running game and they use an aggressive type of block up front. We use drop-back protection, either man-to-man or area, to form that pocket, and it is not easy to teach that upright, ground-giving but still tenacious blocking we demand. To the aggressive types who play this game the concept of retreat is strange and unnatural, but we want an aggressive retreat, and I tell them all the same thing: "This is a personal battle between you and your opponent."

Like so many of our running plays, the pass protection that we use is based upon whether the defensive line is even or odd. On an even-man set the two offensive guards are covered. There are two linemen over the offensive guards and the center is uncovered by a lineman. In an odd-man situation, the center is covered by a lineman, the lineman is right on the center's head.

The first thing the offensive line must know is whether the defense is in an even or odd defense, and the center will usually call the particular blocking assignments.

The rule for the tackle is to take the man over him or, if there is no one over him, then the first man to his outside. That's on the even setup. The same rule holds true, by the way, on the odd defense. That is, the tackle takes the man over him or, if none, the first lineman to his outside.

The guards on an even defense take the man over them; in an odd setup, the first man to their outside position; if none, that is, no man or lineman over him and nobody to his outside, then the uncovered guard will take the middle linebacker wherever he goes.

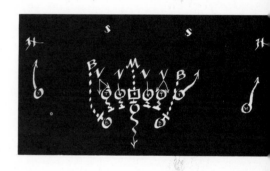

If the middle linebacker were to blitz inside, the guard would have to come over and get him. If the middle linebacker were to blitz outside, then the guard would have to come out to get him. If the middle linebacker were to blitz directly over him, then of course the guard could take him. If the middle linebacker did not blitz but went back into the pass defense, the guard would be a fill man in this situation and would help anywhere that he possibly could. If, for example, anyone broke away from one of the other blockers, the guard would be in a position to help out.

The center, on an odd setup, has the man over him. On an even setup he does not have a man over him and his responsibility is the middle linebacker on the blitz. The middle linebacker with the blitz left, the center has to move out to take him. If the blitz is to the right, then he'd have to move out in the same position to take him. If the middle linebacker is over him, then he would take him on directly. If the middle linebacker went back in the pass defense, the center would simply set and fill. In this case the same rule that was applied to the guard is applied to the center who is uncovered.

Here you see the center (No. 57) picking up the blitzing middle linebacker as the quarterback is about to throw.

The center would fill and help anyplace that he could. If anyone broke away he would be out there to help.

I think it's important to realize that the uncovered man—by that I mean the uncovered offensive lineman—is always the fill man. Either of the guards or the center, the one with no one over him, is the fill man.

The two remaining backs are positioned to block on either of the outside linebackers if they should blitz, the strong-side or weak-side linebackers. The backs therefore take a pass-blocking position on this assignment, picking up any linebacker that comes. If no one blitzes, the backs also fill and help out.

So if the middle linebacker and neither of the outside linebackers should blitz, we now have a secondary line of protection composed of the center and the two backs. They then form a perimeter in the backfield. Of course, your first perimeter, as always, should be your offensive linemen.

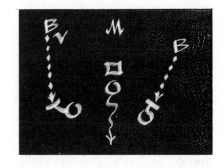

BLOCKING TECHNIQUES ON PASS PROTECTION

In discussing those offensive linemen and their pass-blocking responsibility, let's begin with the offensive tackles. Of all the pass blockers, the offensive tackles are responsible for the most territory and, therefore, must be extremely mobile and agile.

When the tackle comes off the line he must open up and position himself so that his head is lined up right in the middle of his man, usually the defensive end, as he concentrates on that man's belt buckle. On contact, the offensive tackle brings his arms and shoulders up in order to force his opponent's hands away from his jersey and his shoulder pads. The tackle hits and retreats, hits and retreats, always keeping the pumping action of his legs up and never allowing the man to get a firm hold on him.

On an inside charge by the defensive man, the set by the offensive tackle is the same as on an outside charge, and as the defensive man moves to the inside, the blocker goes with the move. He drives his head into the chest and pinches the defensive man with his outside shoulder, driving him down the line. Remember that on the inside move by the defensive man, the blocker must always get his head in front of the rusher and pinch him with the outside shoulder.

The quarterback has finished his throw but the guard continues to block for him.

The guards

Compared with the tackle, the guard's area of responsibility is not as large, but because he battles in relatively close quarters it is even more of a head-on street fight. Again the offensive guard must hit and retreat, hit and retreat, hit and retreat. He gives ground even more grudgingly than the tackle and, again, everything starts with his feet.

In the retreat the guard must keep those feet moving. He must never be caught flat-footed, and that is the same as with the offensive tackle. When the guard comes off the ball he sets to the inside, feet pumping, giving the pass rusher only one way to go—the outside. The blocker, the offensive guard, must keep his eyes right on the opponent's belt buckle. On contact, he explodes, arms and shoulders up, head driving into the defensive man's numbers, feet continuously pumping.

The pass blocker, whoever he is, must never give up the inside route because that's the shortest way to the quarterback.

The second type of pass block that the guards must master, and one that is very effective against an extremely aggressive opponent who prefers a strong head-on charge, is the cut block. The guard, for example, will explode with his head into his opponent's numbers. He sets and with his forearm breaks the defensive man's hold on his jersey or shoulder pads; then he throws his head and shoulders across the legs of his driving opponent.

As we know, against an odd-man line the center will have a man over him so his technique for pass blocking differs in this situation. Since he has to make the snap to the quarterback (and it would be awkward for him to make that snap and drop back), the center will use an aggressive technique. As he centers the ball he drives out at the man over him and then, rising with his man, he hits and retreats, hits and retreats.

Against an even defense, when the center has no one over him, his responsibility is to act as the fill man and to pick up any blitzing linebackers. When he picks up the linebacker his technique is the same as that of any pass blocker. The middle linebacker will be coming like a runaway freight train, so the center must be poised, must hit hard and give ground grudgingly, just like everyone else.

The linebackers, of course, do not always come at the center head-on. The linebacker may have a deal with one of his interior linemen in which the tackle would take an inside rush and the middle linebacker go to the outside. This is intended, obviously, to disrupt the offensive blocking. If the center does not spot this and retreats quickly, this particular blitzing maneuver may well succeed.

The center

This is perfect pass protection. The quarterback completes his motion and the defensive ends are still way on the outside. The center has knocked his man down and is looking for somebody else.

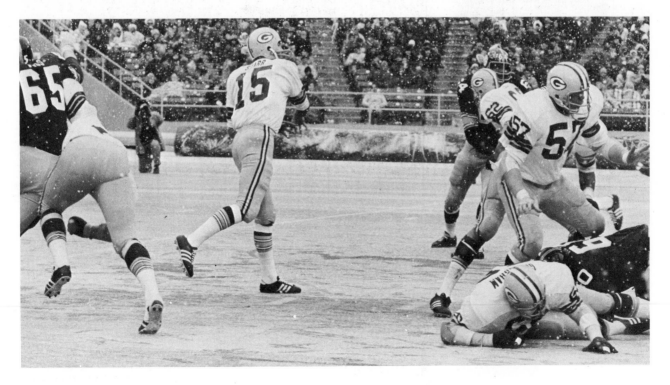

SUMMARY

The offensive tackle must keep those legs pumping and feet moving. Everything starts with the feet. The tackle drives his helmet into the numbers and brings his arms and shoulders up, breaking that hold. He will wheel that man to the outside and beyond the quarterback. On an inside rush, the offensive tackle will get his helmet in front of the pass rusher, pinch with his outside shoulder and drive the defensive player down the line.

The offensive guards must also keep those feet moving and never be caught flat-footed. The guard's battle is man-to-man. He must drive the helmet into the chest of the defensive man. Hit and retreat, hit and retreat—and never give up that inside route to the quarterback.

The center, against an odd-man line and with that man over him, will first slam that man and then pass-block. Against an even defense and with no one over him, the center then becomes the fill man. He will, of course, pick up the blitzers. If no one blitzes he then area-blocks.

Here is an excellent illustration of the pass pocket forming. All the linemen have made contact, with the center (No. 57) looking to help out on anybody who may break through. The back (No. 25) is going out in the pattern as the quarterback drops back, looking downfield and reading the defense.

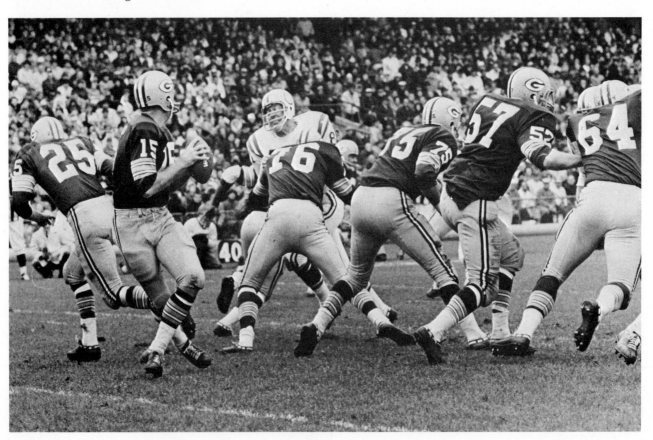

The pass pocket starts to form as the fullback (No. 33) goes out, first keying the linebacker.

What we have just discussed was the blocking assignments on the three-man pass patterns. Obviously not all passes are the same and many times we send out a fourth man. In this particular case, let's discuss the fullback's role going out into his pass pattern, either in a flare operation or a circle operation or into the flat.

    You must understand that all of the linemen have the same blocking responsibility they had in the three-man pass pattern. It does not change. I might say here that the simplest way we could present this to the team, the better, and the less change we have to make, the better.

    We have to send the fullback out for many reasons. When the fullback is out, the blocking rules of everyone else remain the same. The center, the guard, all blocking remains the same. The uncovered man is the fill man in exactly the same way as in the three-man pass, offensive guards have the same rules, as do the tackles. The remaining back has the same rule where he has the weak-side linebacker—if he should blitz. Now, if the fullback goes out and if the strong-side linebacker were to blitz, you would say, "Who is to take him?" "Who will stop that blitz?"

BACKS IN THE PASS PATTERN

Here is another illustration of the check release by the fullback. No. 33 is starting out in the pattern but his eyes are on the linebacker. If that linebacker comes he'll move to take him; if he doesn't, the fullback will continue out in the pattern. The quarterback is also reading the fullback because he knows if the fullback stops to block that a blitz is on.

Well, we have what we call a check release—a check release by our fullback. It's just a momentary check and it takes a fraction of a second for the fullback to realize that the linebacker is or is not going to blitz. In order to be a good blitzer, the linebacker has got to come right on the snap of the ball. The fullback knows this, so if the linebacker does not come on the snap of the ball the fullback will run his route.

For example, consider what we call a fan-circle route or a fan-flat route, where the fullback goes out into the flat or over by the sidelines and then turns upfield. Before he goes out he checks momentarily; if the linebacker does blitz, the fullback does not go out. The fullback takes him if the linebacker blitzes. If the linebacker drops off into the pass defense, the fullback runs his route. You've got to understand the reason we're sending the fullback out: to move that line-

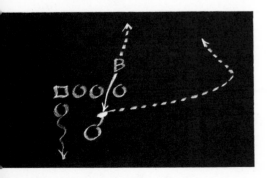

backer. That's the reason he's going out. On the flare route we want the linebacker to go out with him. On a circle route, we want the linebacker to cover him. Well, if the linebacker blitzes, he's taking himself out of the pass defense and, therefore, there's no reason for the fullback to go out, so he stays in and blocks.

There are times when we would send both of the backs out in a pass pattern and the same pass-blocking rules apply to the linemen. The same rules apply to the three-man pass, the same rules as for the fan pass.

There is one little change, however. The uncovered man, who in the odd-man line would be one of the guards, is now responsible for the weak-side linebacker. In the even-man

BACKS DIVIDE

In this sequence we see the result of the back going downfield on a backs-divide pattern. He is covered by a linebacker and a safety, but splits the two men and is now in perfect position to catch the ball. His concentration on the ball is perfect as he catches it and takes it into the end zone.

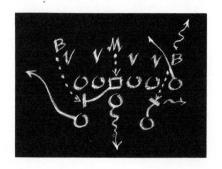

setup the uncovered man would be the center. He would be responsible for the weak-side linebacker. Another way of doing it is to block the center weak and pull the guard out for the weak-side linebacker. Either of those two ways works very, very well.

Now, when both backs are out, the fullback has the same rule. He's still responsible for that linebacker if he blitzes. If he doesn't blitz, the fullback is out in his pattern, either a flare or circle route.

The halfback, regardless of whether the weak-side linebacker blitzes or not, is out in his pattern. That's a must. He must come out of there with speed because of his many long routes down the field. This back is the speed-burner in most passing attacks. He is a good receiver; therefore, we want him out right now.

The one man who is not covered is the middle linebacker. What happens if he were to blitz? If he were to blitz,

what happens to the passer? Well, it's obvious, of course, that the passer is going to get knocked down by the middle linebacker. So now we cover that blitz by always releasing the Y end, the tight end, to the inside. When both of the backs are out in the pattern we always release the tight end to the inside, looking right now for the ball.

The Y end's key is the middle linebacker. If the middle linebacker blitzes he knows he's going to get the ball right now because the quarterback always keys the middle linebacker. This is what we call a backs-divide pass. If the middle linebacker blitzes, the quarterback immediately throws the ball to the Y end.

Our backs-divide pattern has been a bread-and-butter passing play for us for years. When Ron Kramer was playing tight end Bart would, with the blitz of the middle linebacker, dump the ball off to Kramer. You could almost feel sorry for those defensive backs who had to tackle him. He had great size—6'4" and 250 pounds for an end—and when he got up a head of steam in the secondary he was awesome. And with all his size, he was a great blocker.

In our 1966 championship game at Dallas our first touchdown was scored off a backs-divide. Elijah Pitts ran a circle route downfield and beat the linebacker, Bart hit him in the open and he took it the rest of the way, running over the safety on the 2-yard line to score.

The fullback (No. 31), after taking the fake from the quarterback, has moved into the line to pick up the defensive tackle. There is an excellent pass block by the guard.

In protecting the passer on play-action passes, that is, where we fake a run and then throw, the faking back or the back who fakes into the middle (and we always have one faking into the middle) is responsible for the middle linebacker. It's of primary importance for the faking back to remember that he must get the middle linebacker if he blitzes. The fake is secondary as far as this particular action is concerned.

For example, either in a draw fake or any other kind of fake, where the fullback in this case is faking into the middle, his first responsibility is the middle linebacker. If the middle linebacker were to blitz, he'd have to take him. If the middle linebacker were to blitz in another position, he'd have to break off his fake and get him. It is the back's responsibility to pick up the middle linebacker in whatever area that middle linebacker blitzes.

The back who is faking across is responsible for the outside linebacker if he were to blitz. Usually, as the back is coming across, the linebacker who is blitzing will stop because he'll go out to cover that back. One of the two linemen —the offensive guard or the center—is responsible for the weak-side linebacker. Now, it could be the center who is uncovered and is coming out, or it could be the center blocking back on the defensive tackle and the guard coming out. Either way is excellent. That's play-pass blocking. The other linemen have the same rule as they have for the three-man pass blocking, same rules odd and even. One thing you should remember: there is more of an aggressive block by the linemen to the side of the fake. They fire out and then drop back. Of course, one of these two particular men who are pulling out must show pass right away, but that's usually immaterial. The play-action pass is particularly effective in first-down or short-yardage situations where the defense would logically expect a run.

We have scored many touchdowns throwing off of play-action passes. As discussed, we usually have the fullback faking up the middle. In our championship game at Dallas our fourth touchdown was scored on such a play, and our X end, or split end, Boyd Dowler scored it, but at great hurt to himself. We were on the Cowboys' 16-yard line, second and 9. Some four plays earlier in the drive, on the first play after Dallas

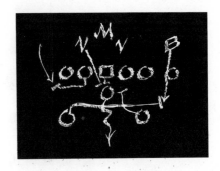

PLAY-ACTION PASS BLOCKING

had scored a field goal, Starr hit Carroll Dale for a long gainer, 43 yards to the Dallas 31. Now, with the defense looking for the run, and a controlled offense because we were in field-goal range, Starr faked to Taylor up the middle and Dowler ran a quick route and came across the middle, in front of the defensive halfback and beyond the middle linebacker who had been held in the middle by Taylor's fake. Starr pumped, stepped into the pocket and threw a bullet that

Dowler caught on his fingertips as he went into the end zone. I saw the officials signal for touchdown and the next thing I saw were Dowler's legs high in the air and his feet pointing at the sky. He had taken a shot in the end zone, summersaulted, and then landed on his bad shoulder. His teammates helped him off the field and he did not play any more in that game. Dowler did not lose the ball when he landed on his head.

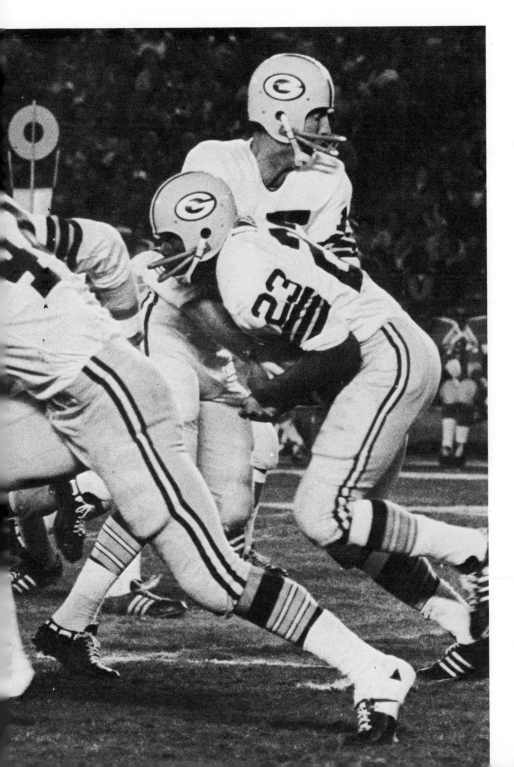

Here is the play-action pass. Note the offensive linemen as they drive out on the men over them, and the halfback (No. 44) drives toward the line as the other back (No. 23) fakes the hand-off. The quarterback has put the ball into his stomach and is now taking the ball away as he rolls out to the right.

BLOCKING STUNTS & TWISTS

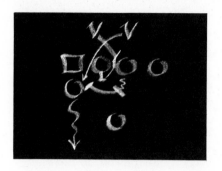

Up to now, in discussing pass blocking, we have assumed that the defensive linemen would rush the passer in a normal, straight manner. That is, tackles over the guards, ends over the tackles. However, there are other methods, other effective means of rushing the passer, usually used to confuse the blocking pattern or the blocking technique of the offensive line. I am referring particularly to the twist—twists in which the defensive tackle and the defensive end work as a unit. One of those twists is what we refer to as a tackle-first twist. I mean by that, the defensive tackle is the first one to show, the defensive tackle is the first one to penetrate, with the defensive end coming behind.

In this particular type of twist, the offensive tackle in setting, since he does set deep, sees that end loop and can come behind the offensive guard's block to pick up the end as he rushes up the middle. This is still a man-to-man set-up: it is guard on tackle and tackle on end.

Blocking tackle-first twist

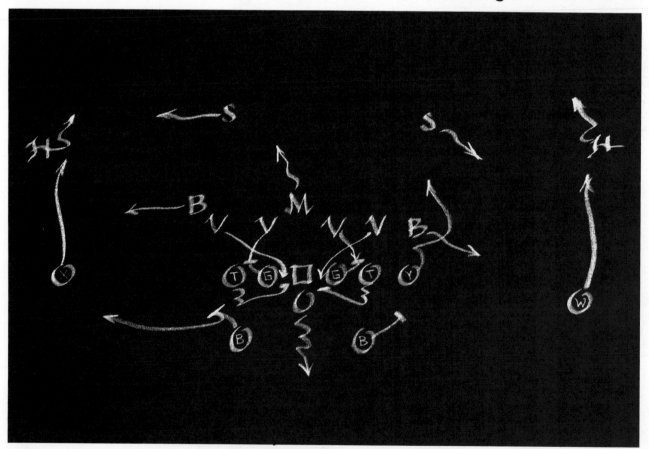

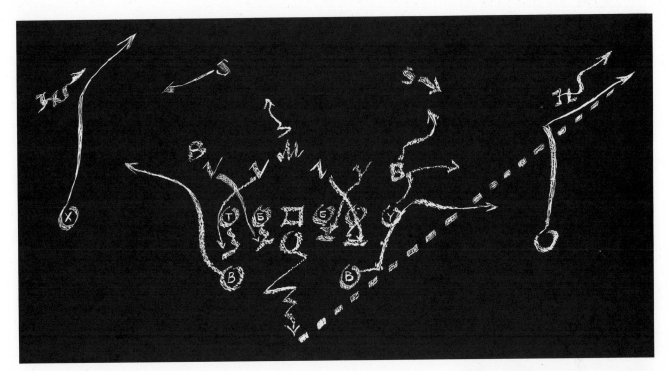

Blocking end-first twist

In the other twist, which we refer to as an end-first twist, we mean that the end is the first one to show and the first one to penetrate. This poses a different problem. The defensive end penetrates to the inside, and the offensive tackle, in setting deep, cannot get back to him quickly enough. So, as the defensive end goes in front of the defensive tackle and as the offensive guard sets to block, we could have a collision course if the offensive blockers try to stay man-to-man. In this particular twist, we area-block or we switch-block. I mean by that, as the tackle sets and he sees the defensive end go to the inside, he looks for the defensive tackle coming around and holds his position. The guard, when the defensive tackle drops off the line to go outside, has nothing to do anyway, so he sets and, of course, it's a simple matter for him to pick up the defensive end as he comes inside.

There are two twists again—tackle-first twist with the defensive end looping behind the defensive tackle in which we block man-to-man or stay man-to-man. In the other twist, the end-first twist, in which the defensive end comes first, the defensive end is the first one to penetrate with the defensive tackle looping behind him; and in this one we area-block or we switch-block.

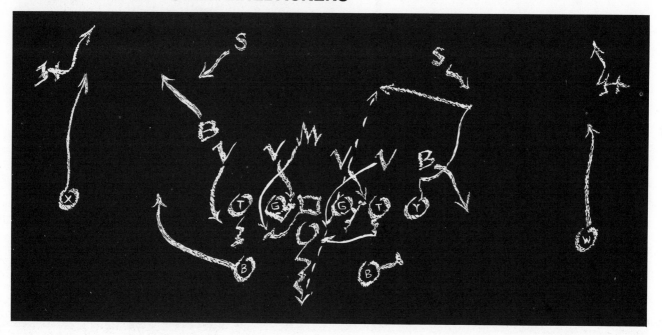

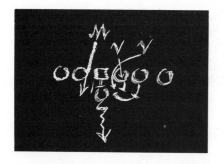

None of these twists is particularly effective by itself. However, when the twists are coordinated with the blitz they pose another problem. For example, on the tackle-first twist with the tackle going first, and the end looping up the center, the center if he has no one over him is the fill man, so he is in a position to help on the end coming up the center. However, with the blitz, the middle linebacker, for example, blitzing over the guard, would pull the center over to pick him up. Now, unless the offensive tackle can get over to pick up the defensive end on the blitz up the middle, the defensive end will really have a free run at the quarterback.

Whether it's a normal charge or a more sophisticated maneuver, it is still the pass blocking that makes the passing game go. The pass play, when it succeeds, may mean a quick score, but it never means an easy one. Touchdowns by passing are credited to quarterbacks and receivers, but the credit should be shared by everyone. At least, everyone who put on a pass block and made it stick.

Jerry Kramer, along with Fuzzy Thurston (No. 63), gave the Packers many great years as our offensive guards, blocking for the passer and for the runners.

9

The Passing Game

Nothing, of course, is more spectacular and nothing puts points up on that scoreboard faster than the big bomb. The passing game, however, is more than the big bomb. It consists of intelligent route running and a quarterback who has the experience and intelligence to read the defenses and the courage to hold the ball in the pocket until the right moment.

Our passing game is built around the fundamental proposition that our receivers and quarterback must be able to read the defenses that are thrown at them on the snap of the ball. Our passing game is also based on the success of our running game, and many of our pass plays are designed to look like the beginning of a running play.

Teaching recognition of the defenses is difficult because today's defenses are so sophisticated. When I first came to Green Bay the pass plays I put in took considerable time to assimilate but, with experience, our passing efficiency has increased to the point where Bart Starr has become the most efficient passer in the history of pro football.

We have achieved that excellent balance between the run and the pass that all teams strive for. In the early years we were more of a running team because we had Paul Hornung and Jim Taylor. Later we passed a little bit more because those defenses were always conscious of our running ability and that helped our passing game. In the 1966 championship game against the Cowboys, all but one of our five touchdowns came from pass plays. Later, in Super Bowl I, three came from the run and two from the pass.

Our receivers and our backs must all be able to read their keys on every pass play. The Y end usually keys the middle linebacker and the strong-side safety. The flanker usually keys the strong-side linebacker, the strong-side safety and the strong-side halfback. The split end keys the linebacker on his side, the weak-side safety and the cornerback playing over him. The backs key the linebackers. On the snap of the ball the quarterback, depending on the play called, will key two or more of these defenders. For example, on our backs-divide play, the following keys are used: with the snap of the ball the quarterback and the Y end key the middle linebacker, the fullback keys the strong-side linebacker, the split end keys the weak-side safety, the flanker keys the cornerback and the strong-side safety, and the halfback has no key but is out in the pattern, going deep.

Here is the beginning of the backs-divide play. The quarterback is back-pedaling, keying the middle linebacker, and the backs are starting out of the backfield. Notice the pocket starting to form in front of the quarterback.

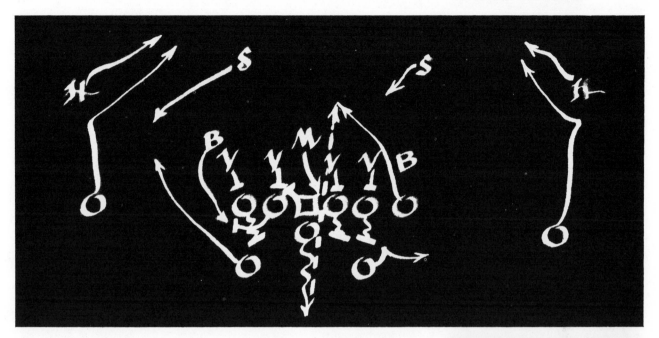

Now what happens is that, if the middle linebacker blitzes, the quarterback sees that immediately, and throws a quick pass over the middle to the Y end who, also keying that middle linebacker, knows that on the blitz the quarterback will dump the ball to him. If that linebacker were to drop off into pass coverage, the quarterback now looks to the strong-side safety. If that safety comes up on the tight end, the quarterback looks for the flanker on a post pattern because he knows that the defense is in a man-to-man defense. The flanker also has the key of the strong-side safety, and as that safety goes up to cover the Y end the flanker cuts to the post, looking for the ball. If that strong-side safety drops deep to cover behind the cornerback—this tells the flanker and the quarterback that it is zone and the quarterback looks for the flanker to break off his post pattern and come underneath to the space between the strong-side safety and the strong-side linebacker. If the zone is rotating to the strong side, the quarterback, keying the middle linebacker, would see this and would throw to the Y end, who would come open under the weak-side safety, between the middle linebacker and the weak-side linebacker. Remember, the weak-side linebacker is covering our halfback coming out of the backfield and the weak-side cornerback is on the split end as he comes into the zone.

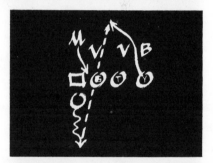

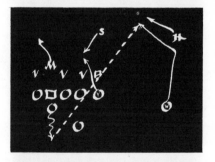

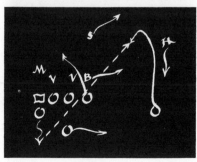

To be able to read the keys properly as the receivers are running their routes and those defensive men are trying to get to him, a quarterback needs not only courage but intelligence. Our passing game, as well as our running game, requires intelligence on the part of all the players, especially the quarterback. Bart Starr is the smartest quarterback I ever saw play this game, and he was so well prepared and disciplined that I almost never had to send in plays from the sideline. Our backs and receivers were also very smart, and that is why we won so many championships. Physical ability abounds on every team in the NFL. It is those teams that have the mental discipline and intelligence that react best under the pressure of championship competition. We lost one championship game because we were not mentally prepared to be champions. That never happened again.

I have discussed the coordination and timing we demand between the quarterback and receivers. We also demand absolute discipline in the running of the routes by the receivers. But first we demand complete familiarity with the pass defense which will determine the play called and the routes run by the receivers.

I want to cover the weaknesses of the different pass defenses, for it is on a team's ability to exploit those weaknesses that its success with the passing game will depend.

Remember, in all pass defenses the linebackers play a key role. But they must be concerned with the run as well as the pass, and that is why the play-action passes have grown so much in popularity. Also, not many linebackers can stay with those backs for more than a few yards after they get out into the pass pattern. So, in discussing the weaknesses of the pass defenses that are used today, remember that the linebackers can be controlled by the action of the backs.

Weaknesses of different pass defenses

Bart Starr is the smartest quarterback I ever coached and the most intelligent I ever saw play football. He was exceptional at following the game plan and at calling the right play at the right time. He may be the best "third down" quarterback to have ever played football.

Man-to-man defenses

In the man-to-man defense, a great burden is put upon the cornerbacks and the strong-side safety. We can control the weak-side safety with the action of the weak-side offensive halfback by either flaring the halfback out to the sidelines or sending him on a circle route over the middle.

The weakness of the man-to-man defense is that it is very difficult to control the post moves by the X end, the Y end and the flanker. Both of the cornerbacks, weak and strong, and the strong-side safety realize that there is no help to the inside because of the movement of the offensive halfback. Therefore, they have to be very careful and cover those particular offensive men both inside and outside, leaving them wide open for either post moves or for a fake of the post move, and then running a corner pattern.

Combination pass defenses

The weakness of the combination pass defense, which means that the defense combines two men to cover one man, is that the strong-side linebacker can be controlled. He has one major coaching point, as in a man-to-man pass defense. To help the coverage deep the strong-side linebacker is told to chuck the Y end real hard to prevent him from getting off on rhythm to the inside. However, in doing so the strong-side linebacker has to stay with that Y end for a few seconds, which makes it very difficult for him to cover a fullback who would flare out wide and come down the field hard.

That's one of the weaknesses and, of course, the other is that when you combine two men on one receiver you leave someone else open. For example, if there are two safeties covering the Y end, this Y end can hold both of these safeties, leaving the post area open to either the X end or to the wingback.

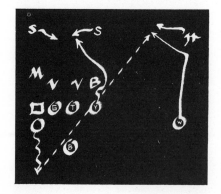

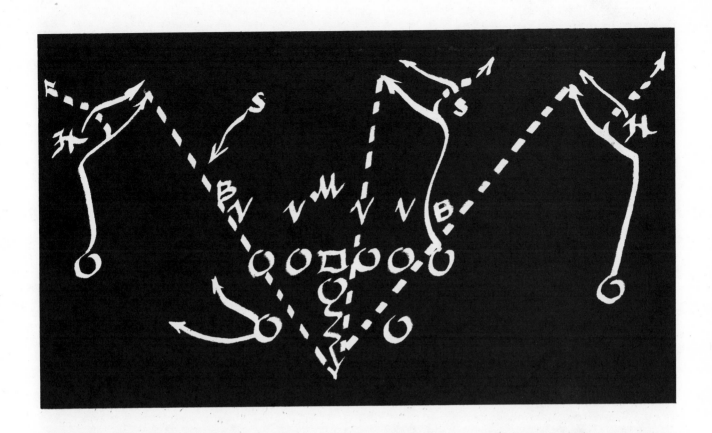

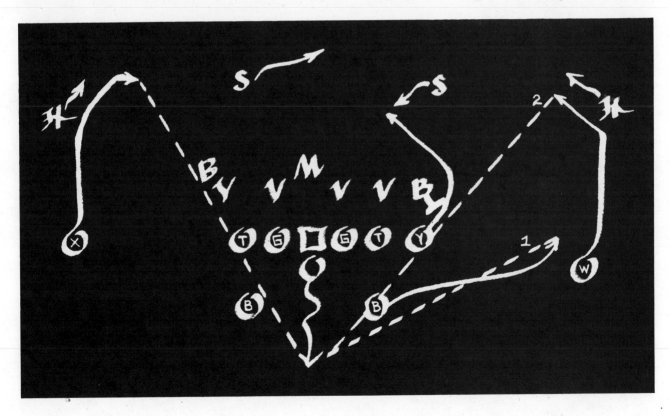

Zone defenses

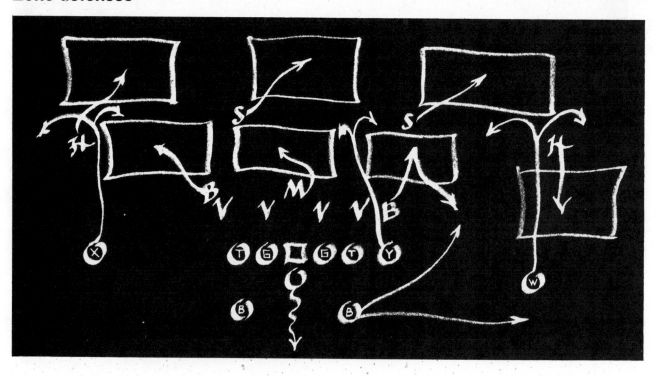

There are many weaknesses in the zone defense. The movement of the defensive men is as follows: with the snap of the ball the middle linebacker goes to a weak-side hook zone, the weak-side linebacker goes to the flat zone, the strong-side linebacker goes to the hook zone on his side with the defensive halfback coming up to cover the short flat zone, the safety going deep to cover the deep zone, the weak-side safety coming over to the middle to cover the middle

In this title game against the Giants the tight end, Ron Kramer (No. 88), has split the zone between the weak-side safety and the middle linebacker. Catching the ball, he turns upfield, leaving the defenders in his wake as he goes into the end zone.

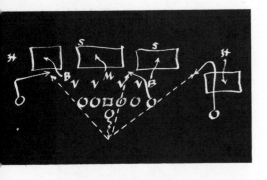

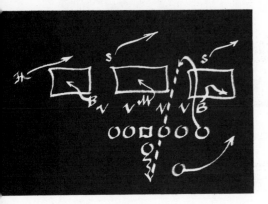

zone, and the weak-side halfback dropping deep to cover the outside deep zone. Well, that's great coverage for the deep pass and actually very seldom should a pass be completed for a touchdown against that pass defense.

However, there are many, many weaknesses in the zone. It is obvious that the big weakness with this defense is underneath the linebackers. With the middle linebacker going weak, and the weak-side linebacker going weak in the flat zone, and the strong-side linebacker dropping off deep, there is a great weakness underneath all of the linebackers, especially over the middle. In other words, a short passing game really picks the zone apart.

There is a weakness behind the strong-side linebacker, for example, and under the strong-side safety who has gone deep to the sidelines.

There is a weakness over the middle beyond the strong-side linebacker, past the defensive halfback and outside the linebacker. We can hold that strong-side linebacker by bringing the fullback out in a circle route, holding the linebacker up so that he has to cover that fullback, and that opens it up for the Y end to do a turn-in underneath the weak-side safety in the middle. There is a big hole in that area. There are many, many holes in the zone. And it takes a good quarterback and good receivers to know when to break off their routes and turn in against the zone.

There is also a hole if you bring your fullback out and you hold the defensive halfback. The safety has already gone deep and the Y end can run a sideline pattern, a short corner pattern, just beyond the defensive halfback and underneath the strong-side safety.

Free-safety defense

In the free-safety defense, with the snap of the ball, the weak-side safety comes to the center of the field and covers the middle zone. You can control the action of the weak-side linebacker who's instructed to drop off to the right by having the halfback flare out toward the weak-side linebacker. Then if you move your fullback out to the right, since the strong-side linebacker and middle linebacker are coached to go to the strong-side zone, they will follow that fullback going out there, and this leaves a tremendous hole right over the center where the middle linebacker and strong-side linebacker have vacated and, of course, you would pass to your split end or X end in that area.

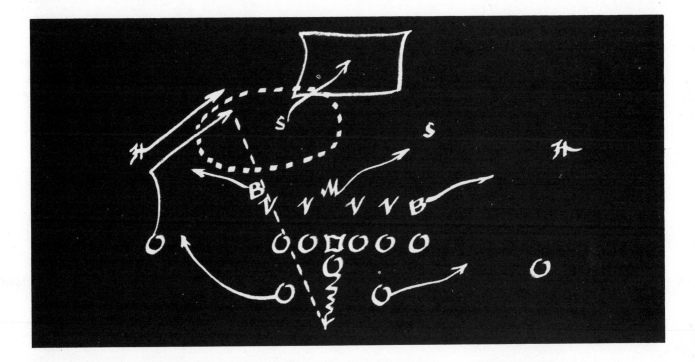

SUMMARY

The weakness of the man-to-man pass defense is that it puts a great deal of pressure on the cornerbacks and strong safety, and the best passes thrown against that defense are those requiring post patterns by the receivers.

In the combination defense the great weakness is that in order to cover one man with two men you leave yourself open for flares by the fullback and screens to the halfback, and for post patterns by the flanker on the strong side.

The weakness of the zone defense is the short passing game, throwing underneath the linebackers or throwing over the halfback between that halfback and the safeties, throwing to the side and over the middle underneath the linebackers.

And the weakness of the free-safety defense is that by having your backs flare out of the backfield, one going weak and one strong, you open up the underneath for the X end to run a short post pattern over the middle.

The mark of a great quarterback
—concentrating on passing the ball
as the rush swirls around him.

The 2-minute drill

I have spoken throughout of the mental discipline and mental toughness required to win. Nowhere is that more apparent than in those last minutes before the end of the ball game, or before the end of the half. Great quarterbacks and great teams are at their best here. Watching a team fighting the clock and the opponent as it drives downfield for the winning score is one of the most dramatic moments in a football game and in all of sport. It also tears the guts out of a coach.

We spend a lot of time on this drill in all of our prac-

tices. We'll put the ball on the 35-yard line and give the offense about 1½ to 2 minutes, and tell them to take it all the way. Now they are practicing it against our defense, which has its own pride and also knows all the plays. And sometimes the defense will hold but most of the time the offense will make it.

The advantage in the 2-minute drill is with the offense. First, the offense knows the plays that it will use against that particular team, and it also knows the defenses that team will employ in the 2-minute period. The defense does not want to call a time-out and, after each play, when you line up without a huddle at the line of scrimmage and start again, the defense tends, after three or four of these plays, to become confused. Most of your plays are pass plays that are short and hard to defend, usually sideline patterns that get the receiver out-of-bounds, stopping the clock. A team that is well poised, disciplined and thoroughly coached can handle a tough situation like this.

Today many teams have adopted a "prevent defense" to stop the offense in this 2-minute situation. I'm not a believer in that. A good, smart quarterback should be able to beat a prevent defense because he has less pressure from the front four now, because it's a front three. And if you give these good quarterbacks time, they'll beat you.

Here the tight end, cutting in front of the linebacker, has taken the ball over the middle from the quarterback. It is plays like this that work so well in the 2-minute drill and so effectively bring the ball down the field.

The prevent defense also admits a weakness to your defensive team. They are a coordinated body of eleven men who have played together all through the game and helped you get the lead. Then a fifth defensive back is substituted for a lineman. Now that unit is broken up for what I consider an unnecessary man. In the late-going, the smart quarterbacks know they have only one chance to score, and they know that a long pass will not be the answer. The short passing game is, and with more time to throw, even against an extra defensive back, that passing game will work.

I've often felt, watching my team in the 2-minute drill, that it could play a whole game without ever needing a huddle. I know it's never been done but I know we could. That would really shake up that defense.

Audibles

Today's defenses, in all of football—high school, college or pro—are so good that the offensive team must have a good system of audibles or automatics or check-offs. With the modern shifting defenses, the team that cannot execute properly after an audible is called is in deep trouble. Again, this requires intelligence on the part of all the players.

There are a number of systems used today to call audibles. One is to have a "live" color. Let's say the live color is green. As the team lines up, the quarterback calls out red, or blue, or white. This tells the team that the play called in the huddle is the play that will be run, so the snap number and everything stays the same. However, if the quarterback says "green," this immediately tells the team that the next numbers are the new play. Some teams have a rule that, with every automatic, the snap number is reduced by one—if it was three, with the audible the snap is now two. I do not care for this because it adds an additional factor that the backs and the linemen must remember.

The system I prefer is to repeat the snap number. For instance, let's say the call in the huddle had been "48 on 3," and the quarterback came to the line and called out "2–67." Since he did not repeat the snap number, the play called in the huddle is still on. But if he had come to the line and said "3–29," this would have told everyone that the new play is "29" and the snap count is still "3." The types of plays that we most often audible to are quick-hitting running plays, like trap plays, and passes.

THE PASS PLAYS

Here are some pass plays that have been successful for my team against all of these defenses and in all of the championship games that we have played, and the first one I'd like to explain is the fullback wide X and Y wing trail.

Fullback wide X & Y wing trail

The line blocking is normal pass blocking. The fullback runs a flat route, and he runs his pattern through the flat, and his purpose is to pull that strong-side linebacker into the flat and to stop him from dropping deep underneath. When the fullback reaches the sidelines, as he often does on all flat routes, he will turn upfield.

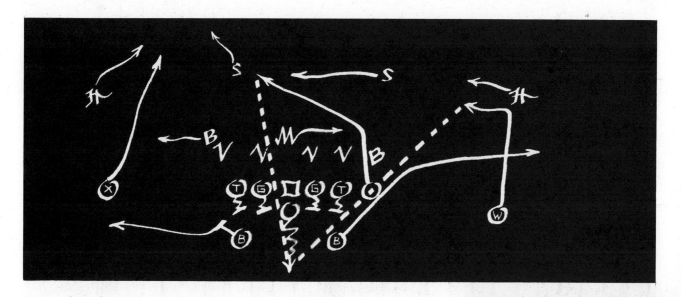

The halfback checks the weak-side linebacker for blitz. If there is none he runs a wide pattern to pull the weak-side linebacker with him so that the weak-side linebacker cannot drop back and get underneath the Y end.

The split end splits to 7 yards. He's the first-named receiver and he goes deep, running almost a split between the weak-side halfback and the safety. His object is to occupy both of them, to pull both of them out of the area so that the Y end may come open.

The Y end goes 3 to 4 yards downfield with an inside release on the strong-side linebacker, and runs an over pattern, crossing over to the other side of the field. He may go either underneath or behind the middle linebacker, but deepening his route so that in the area beyond his offensive tackle he should be 8 to 10 yards deep. The Y end will usually come open immediately after he passes the middle linebacker. If he has not come open then he will come open very late way across the field.

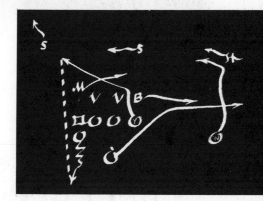

The wingback splits 10 to 15 yards. He proceeds straight upfield approximately 15 yards and then runs a trail pattern, running directly across the field parallel to the line of scrimmage.

Against the man-to-man coverage the wingback is the receiver most always open, because as the Y end goes across the field he takes the strong-side safety with him. The fullback pulls the strong-side linebacker out and the hole opens for the wingback.

As the quarterback drops back he keys the middle line-backer and the strong-side safety. The quarterback drops 8 to 10 yards. The first receiver he looks for is the Y end. He looks for that Y end as he passes the middle linebacker, and if the Y end is not open he looks for the wingback on the trail. The split end will not come open unless there is a blitz.

In the breakdown of the fullback wide X and Y wing trail, I mentioned that if a team blitzed the split end would

come open. That is what happened in our first game against the Dallas Cowboys for the NFL championship. Our last and eventual winning touchdown was scored on this play. Boyd Dowler had just scored our fourth touchdown but was injured by the tackle as he went into the end zone. He was replaced by Max McGee. With about 10 minutes left in the game we went the length of the field with Starr completing two or three long third-down plays.

In today's game the Y end is not only a blocker and receiver but, because of his size and strength, more often than not an excellent runner. Here you see the tight end (No. 81), after catching the ball, being tackled and, because of his size, he just throws that tackler off and heads downfield.

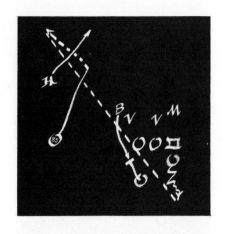

It was third and 19 on the Dallas 28 when we lined up in the Red formation. With the snap of the ball, Jimmy Taylor, keying the strong-side linebacker, went out into the flat, Starr keyed the middle linebacker and saw him drop off into the strong side, and the weak-side linebacker blitzed. Elijah Pitts picked him up with a great block and, as is supposed to happen, the split end, Max McGee, came open. He made a great fake on the cornerback, driving toward the post and then cut to the corner. Starr, behind great blocking, lofted a beauty into McGee's arms on the goal line for the touchdown. It was a fitting climax to an excellent drive, and everyone read their keys properly and perfection resulted.

X & Y wing zigout

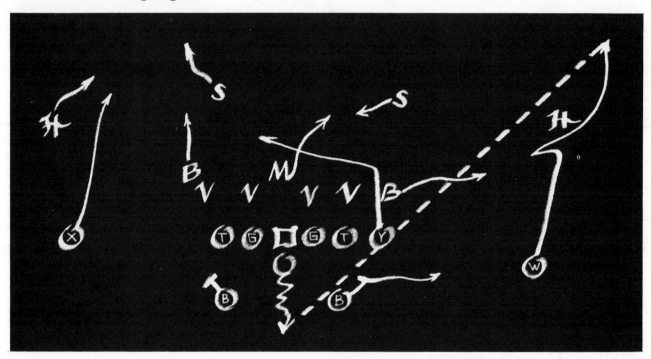

This is a pass used when the strong-side defensive back covering the wingback on the X and Y wing trail has been over-playing the wingback looking for the inside break.

The split end runs the same pattern that he did in the X and Y wing trail. He splits 7 yards and goes deep, again running a split to an area midway between the weak-side halfback and the safety man. His object again is to occupy both of them.

The Y end runs the same pattern as he did in the X and

Y wing trail. He goes 3 to 4 yards downfield with an inside release on the strong-side linebacker and runs an over pattern, forcing over to the opposite side of the field.

The wingback goes down about 10 to 12 yards. He makes a good, hard break to the inside. He fakes that trail route, then plants his left foot and breaks back deep to the outside.

The quarterback usually does no keying here and will throw to the wingback. If the wingback is well covered deep on the break to the outside the quarterback will lead him back toward the sideline, bringing the wingback back to the ball.

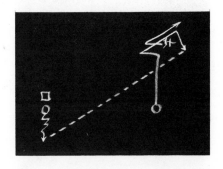

Fake sweep wing fly

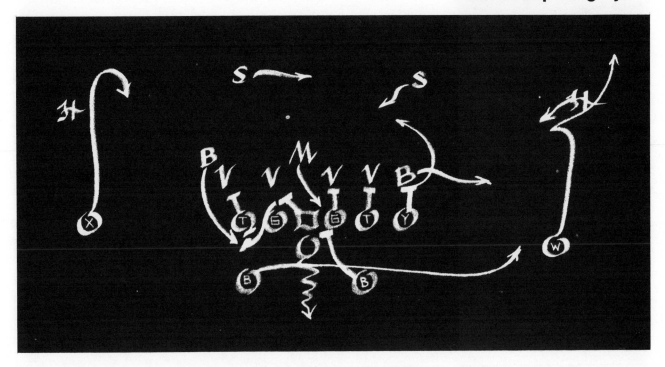

An excellent play against readers, the defensive secondary that is looking into the line and backfield for keys, is what we call our fake sweep wing fly, built off our fullback series, with the fullback hitting up the middle. It's a good call in short-yardage situations, it's a good first-down play, and I have even used it to open games.

The Y end blocks aggressively on the strong-side linebacker, influencing him to think it is a run, and also to get the strong-side halfback and strong-side safety to think run.

The right tackle drive-blocks on the defensive end, simulating run. The right guard drives into the defensive left tackle. The center on an even-man line blocks to his left, away from the play. The left guard leads with his right foot, steps into the defensive right tackle, then drops back to the outside looking for the weak-side linebacker to pick him up if he blitzes. If not, the left guard helps the center with the right tackle. The left tackle drives into the defensive right end and then recovers.

The fullback drives over the left leg of the center, taking a slight fake from the quarterback, to block the middle linebacker if he blitzes. If the middle linebacker is not blitzing, the fullback hangs or fills as an option blocker.

The left halfback comes across the backfield to the strong side between the quarterback and the offensive line. He picks up anybody who leaks through. If none, he becomes

The receiver, Carroll Dale, has beaten the cornerback on the fake sweep wing fly pass play.

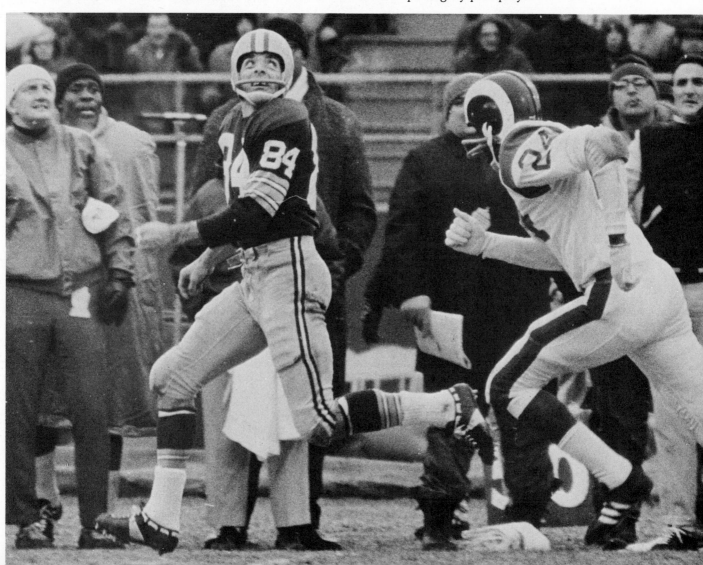

an optional receiver in the flat.

The split end, set out 5 to 6 yards, runs a deep turn-in at approximately 10 to 12 yards.

The wingback drives downfield, looking to the inside just as he does on the run, looking for the strong-side safety. He makes a slight fake to the inside, hoping to draw the strong-side halfback up or lull him as he does on the run. Then he breaks outside and up.

The quarterback pivots to his left, makes a slight fake to the fullback, and sprints deep to allow the halfback to cross underneath him. He sets up at 8 yards and throws to the wingback. The ball leaves the quarterback's hands by the time the receiver is 10 to 15 yards downfield. So this is a semiquick pass.

If the wingback is covered the quarterback has two outlets: the split end on a turn-in or the halfback in the flank.

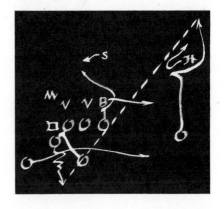

Dale has ignored the hands of the defensive back and makes the catch in the end zone for the touchdown.

Y and wing turn-in

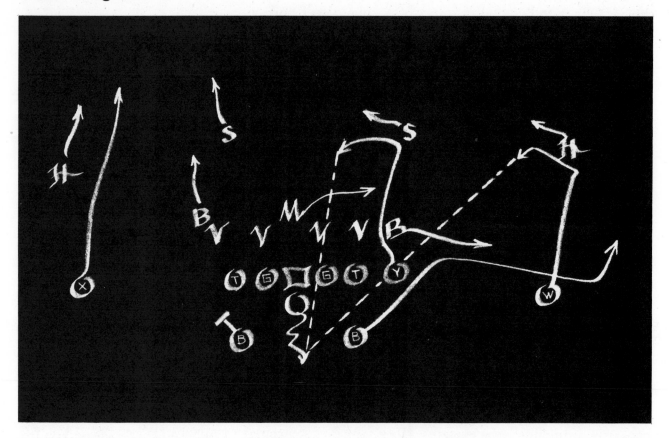

Another very successful pass play that we have employed so many times over the years is a rather simple play which we call a Y and wing turn-in. It's excellent, we think, because it's good against most defenses and it puts a great burden upon the middle linebacker.

On the Y and wing turn-in, as the name signifies, the wingback and the Y do simple turn-in maneuvers.

The fullback in this particular case runs a flat route. He runs right at the strong-side linebacker and then out into the flat. As he reaches the sideline, as he does in all flat routes, he turns upfield if he does not get the ball in the flat. With the action of the fullback running a wide route, usually the strong-side linebacker has to move out to attempt to cover him, which allows the Y end to release inside the linebacker. He releases inside and runs right at that safety man, driving the safety man back. As he drives him back he fakes to the outside and then starts his turn-in maneuver. As soon as he starts his turn-in he must key the middle linebacker.

The middle linebacker is coached to do a number of things. One is to shut off the turn-in, to play the Y end, to prevent the pass from being thrown to the Y end. If he does that, then the Y end continues to force, and he brings the middle linebacker back to him across the middle. The wingback, as he's coming off the line of scrimmage, drives the halfback back. He has a number of maneuvers he can make before he starts his turn-in. The wingback can fake a fly to drive back the halfback and then quickly break it off and do the turn-in; he can fake a sideline pattern and then bring it back to make a turn-in; or, a great maneuver and one that we've used successfully, is to come out hard and start a post maneuver which brings the halfback quickly to the inside, and then he breaks it off and does a turn-in.

We don't worry about the defensive halfback. That halfback has got too much to be concerned about—fly routes, post patterns and everything else. So he's really "deep" conscious. We are concerned with the strong-side linebacker. The fullback, if you remember, has caused the strong-side linebacker to move to the flat to cover him, and as the wingback makes his turn-in after any one of those maneuvers, he looks to the inside and must be conscious of where that linebacker is. If the linebacker is out with the fullback, he comes right inside that linebacker, underneath the halfback. And the middle linebacker is concerned with the Y end, and a tremendous hole opens up for the quarterback to throw to the wingback.

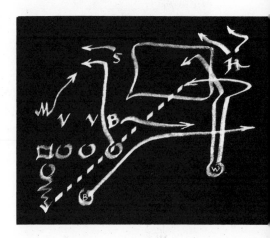

Now, what else can a middle linebacker do? The middle linebacker, of course, can ignore the Y end. The middle linebacker can go to a hook zone, which many teams are coached to do, and if he does that the Y end comes right in his inside. Now the ball is thrown to the Y end over the middle.

One other thing: on a zone defense, or on any kind of a defense where the middle linebacker goes weak regardless of what the fullback does, the Y end, conscious of this, will pull up in the middle, underneath the strong-side safety. When the middle linebacker goes weak the safety man usually goes into the hole.

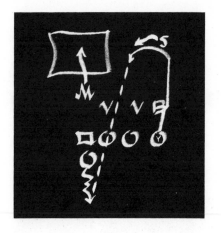

A simple maneuver by the X end—we ask the X end to run a split so as to take the defensive halfback and possibly the safety man deep.

Flood left X delay

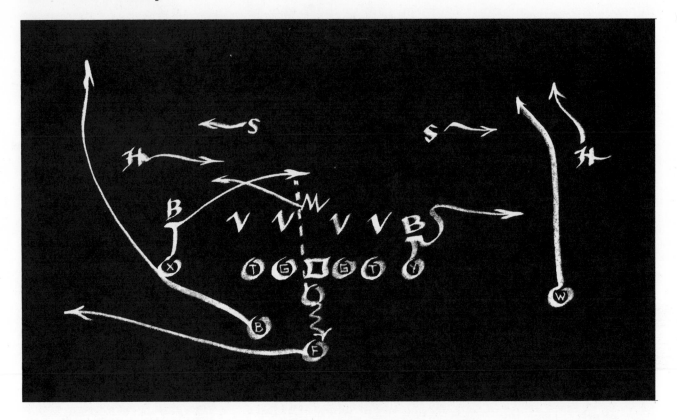

This is very effective against a middle linebacker who is quick to read and cover a fullback. The Y end delays on the strong-side linebacker and runs a quick drag outside. The X end opens up approximately 6 to 8 feet, blocks the weak-side linebacker aggressively for two counts and then delays over the middle in the area vacated by the middle linebacker, who will be going with the flood or with the fullback.

The left halfback runs a fly outside, outside the X end, being careful not to get pulled down by the linebacker. The halfback's job is to make both the outside linebacker and the defensive halfback aware of him. The fullback has no blocking responsibility but flows wide. The quarterback keys the middle linebacker, drops back 7 to 9 yards, and the middle linebacker vacates the area.

The quarterback hits the split end over the middle. If the middle linebacker does not go with the fullback, and the weak-side safety stays, the secondary receiver is the wing-back or the Y end in the flat.

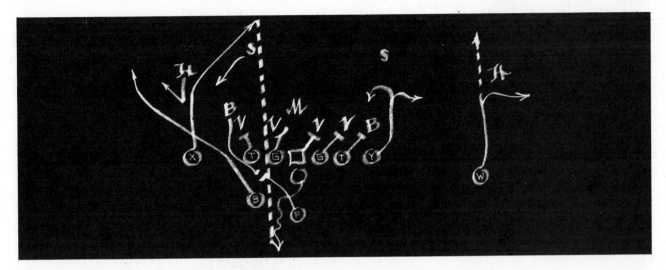

Now I want to give you a play that has proved itself to me time and time again. It's a great call in a short-yardage situation, third and 2, third and 1, or on the goal line. And since the fullback slant is a lead short-yardage running play, the defense must be geared to stop it. This play is a takeoff on that slant, and we have worked it successfully in championship games as well as in the Super Bowl games. That's why I deem the fullback slant X post a great pass play. Before we discuss the routes of the receivers or the play fake itself on the fullback slant X post, I'd like to cover the pass blocking, because it is a little bit different from the pass blocking we use in the regular situation. This is a short-yardage situation. What we do is to slide the line away from the play fake. I mean, since the play fake is to the left, we slide all of the linemen to the right. In other words, the right tackle will drive on the linebacker or the first man who is outside. He just drives right out on him. The right guard will drive on the first man to his outside, the defensive end. The center will drive to his right away from the play fake, the offensive left guard will cut off the man over him, the man who is inside, and the offensive tackle will drive the defensive end who's over him.

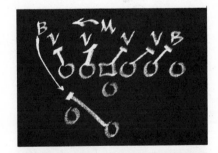

The route that the wingback runs on the fullback slant X post is either a square out or a fly. His job is to hold the cornerback, and possibly the strong-side safety. The Y end releases either inside or outside the strong-side linebacker, who is usually blitzing in this particular situation, and he must try to hold the strong-side safety either by hooking with the turn-out or turn-in.

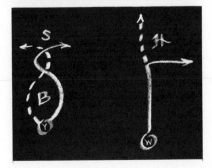

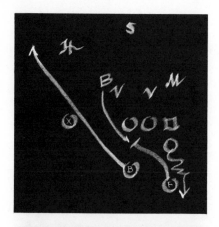

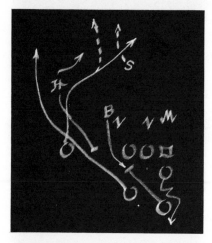

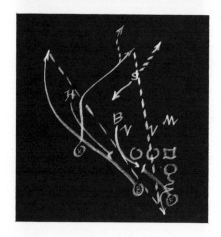

The quarterback reverse-pivots exactly as he does on the fullback slant. You've got to remember that we want to make this play look as much like the running play as we possibly can. He actually puts that ball into the fullback's stomach, who leads for the outside leg of his tackle. The ball is taken from his stomach and the fullback simulates run and drives on that weak-side linebacker. He blocks that linebacker who is blitzing or coming across hard in a short-yardage situation. The halfback drives for the outside leg of the linebacker just as he does on the run as if he's going to block him, and then flattens out and runs a sideline route.

The X end, the lead receiver, comes down the field. He is split, 3 yards at a maximum, and takes the same position as on the run. Ordinarily on the run he either blocks on the halfback or he blocks on the safety man, the first man to show on the run.

In this particular case he drives downfield and then runs a quick post right into the area usually covered by the weak-side safety. He actually keys that safety man. If the safety man comes up to play the run, or if he comes up to cover the halfback who is flying down the sideline, the split end runs that post almost directly behind the position that the safety man has vacated. If the safety man drops back, in other words, if he smells pass, the X end will now run a fly downfield.

Someone has to come up and play the fullback for the run. The halfback, as he comes out and goes for the flat, runs a sideline route, the split end runs a post.

The quarterback, after he makes his fake, drops back into the pocket and keys the weak-side safety man. If the safety man goes up to cover the run, or the safety man is out to cover the halfback on the sideline route, he hits the split end, usually for a very, very sizable gain.

One peculiar thing about this pass: usually if the split end is open, the halfback is open. Invariably you'll find that both men are open. In other words, if the split end is open the halfback is open, if the split end is covered usually the halfback is still open.

They are calling the fullback slant X post the "Bart Starr special" these days. He made it famous and it should be named after him. Calling the play at the right time and executing it properly are what make it Starr's play. I remember in the early years he was criticized in the papers for not being as daring as Unitas or Tittle or Layne. But Starr did have a gambler's streak, only he gambled when he had the odds in his favor. And, after all, isn't this what it's all about —make as few mistakes as possible, cut down your errors, and win!

For the Starr special to work, everyone on that offensive team must execute perfectly and, of course, they must read their keys properly.

In the '67 championship game against Dallas in Green Bay, the temperature was 13° below zero at kickoff. We scored early on a short pass from Starr to Dowler, and in the second quarter we started another drive. Three running plays had picked up a first down, and now it was third and 1 on the Cowboys' 43. We lined up in the Brown formation that we use in the fullback slant. Starr took the snap, reverse-pivoted as he does in the slant, and faked the ball to the full-back. The weak-side linebacker blitzed and was picked up by the fullback. The weak-side safety, Mel Renfro, came up hard to help on the tackle, and Dowler was by him in a flash. Starr, keying the safety, threw a beautiful lead pass, and Dowler ran under it and caught it on about the 20 and took it the rest of the way.

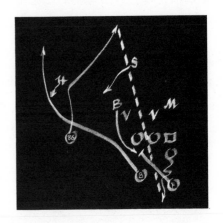

It was a fine call and, again, everyone did his job. Dowler and Starr got the headlines, but the blockers and the backs who picked up those linebackers deserved as much credit.

The passing game is practice and it is precision. That's obvious. What isn't obvious is the persistence: the persistence of the practice field, the persistence of the play book, the persistence of the quarterback and receivers who must read those defenses and read them correctly, the persistence of those unsung linemen up front who must put on those pass blocks and make them stick, the persistence of the end and flanker and back who must run a route precisely to move their defender to clear an area for the receiver, and the persistence of that receiver to get clear and catch that ball.

That's the passing game, and that is why, from original concept to final execution, every phase of the passing game must be perfected to the utmost.

10
Defense Against the Pass

One of the most beautiful plays in football is the completed pass, but not when it's completed against you.

The successful passing offense is built around timing and precision. That's where it begins and it follows that the successful defense against the pass must begin with the effort of those men up front—the defensive line—who must destroy the timing and the precision of the pass, and they destroy it by their pass rush.

And, of course, the rush comes from, first, the defensive ends, and second, the defensive tackles. In football today the defensive ends are first and foremost pass rushers, and secondly, concerned with the defense against the run. Those are the two people who have got to put the great pressure on the passer. They're the ones who have to get in there and get in there quickly. They have more freedom to maneuver than the defensive tackles and they are the people who have the very good moves—strong in the shoulders and with the quick feet. They've got to be strong in the shoulders so they can throw off those blockers. Their primary function is to get to that passer.

The defensive tackle forces the quarterback to pull the ball down by raising his arms as he charges.

The defensive tackles are also pass rushers and their primary job is to force the pocket deep, to push it back toward the quarterback and to allow the ends to get in there so the quarterback cannot set up. If they force the pocket deep then it means the quarterback cannot step up into the pocket and get away from the ends.

After the front four the responsibility for the pass defense belongs to the linebackers and those defensive backs. It's a frustrating job that those defensive halfbacks have and I have seen many of them cry. I've seen big, tough defensive linemen cry, too, but for defensive backs theirs is the real burden and I don't care how hard you try to make their job easier, it's still a greater burden than any of the defensive players face.

The trouble with that job is that it's all out in the open. The defensive back makes one mistake and they complete a pass over him for a touchdown and millions watch him on television running after the other guy looking like a fool.

It used to be that you would draft your halfbacks as offensive backs and convert them to defense when you got them up into the pros. Today, the coaching in colleges has improved greatly and more often now you find defensive backs being drafted as defensive backs. If they play defense in college it is probably some comparatively simple zone, but the problems up here in the pros are mental as well as physical.

You cannot play defensive halfback or safety without knowing where your help is at all times, so you must not

When that lineman gets to that quarterback, he wants that quarterback to remember him.

only know your own job but all the assignments of the other three defensive backs and the assignments of the three linebackers as well.

In this league, though, there is also a time factor that the defensive halfbacks have to learn to use. On a pass the quarterback has, on the average, 3.5 seconds to unload that ball, and good defensive backs know that. They must be like good jockeys and have a clock in their head. From ex-

The hard rush by the defensive end (No. 87) forces the quarterback to run out of his pocket and into the arms of the blitzing linebacker (No. 60) at right.

perience they should know when that 3 seconds are up, and if the quarterback hasn't unloaded the ball they should start to drift in the direction where the quarterback is now looking. That's why good defensive backs are so hard to come by and why, when you get a new one who looks if he may make it, you are so reluctant to let him alone. You want to work with him all the time, but there are thirty-nine others who need you.

We did not blitz much in Super Bowl I, but in the second half a blitz was responsible for an interception which helped break the game open.

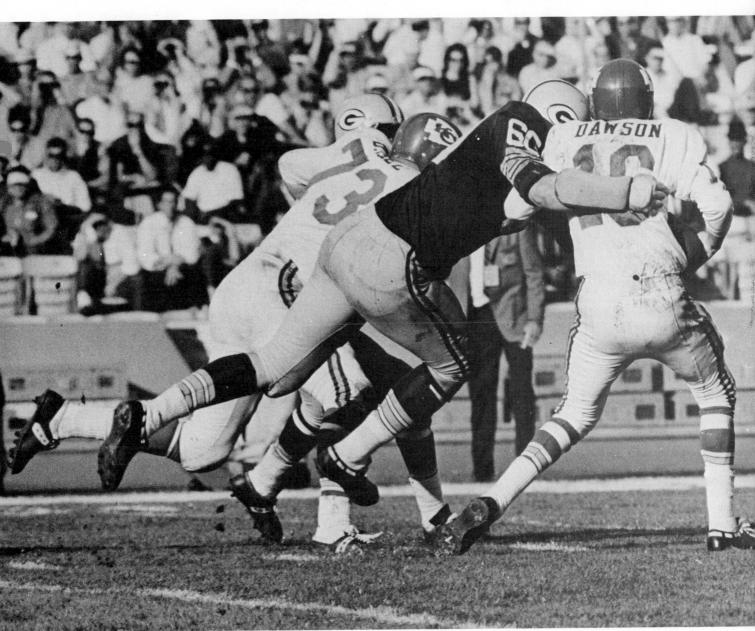

The interception has been made by the cornerback, Herb Adderley (No. 26). He breaks to the outside to return the interception.

One of the best that ever played the game at corner-back played for me in Green Bay, and his name is Herb Adderley. Genius that I am supposed to be, I almost ruined him by trying to make an offensive halfback out of him. He was our first draft choice in 1961, out of Michigan State where he'd been an All-American running back. With his size, his fine speed and open-field talent I wanted him for an offensive back or a flanker, but when we put him into a game nothing happened. So I finally went to him to find out what

Good blocking by his teammates has cleared the way for him and you can see No. 26 racing down the sidelines for a touchdown.

was wrong and he told me that he wanted to be a defensive back.

For half a season I had been so stubborn I had been trying the impossible—to make something of him that he did not want to be—so we turned him over to the defense and later on in his rookie year he made a key interception against the Lions in the Thanksgiving game that sealed the win for us. He made many key plays for us in his career at Green Bay.

PASS DEFENSE

In today's game there are a number of pass defenses, and each has its strengths and its weaknesses. But I have always been partial to the man-to-man pass defense. Not all teams have the personnel to play a man-to-man most of the time, and there are many reasons for that. First and foremost, you have to have a secondary made up of people who have exceptional speed, quickness and toughness, plus the intelligence to read their keys properly so they can react quickly.

To be able to play the man-to-man defense effectively, you have to get that good pass rush up front and have those big, fast linebackers who can cover the backs and the tight end. The man-to-man pass defense is a most demanding defense since each defender is responsible for his man alone and the completion of the pass cannot be excused by claiming someone was not covering his area properly. It puts a premium on mental as well as physical ability.

The Detroit Lions in the early '60s had one defensive back, Nighttrain Lane, who was then as good as our Herb Adderley. Lane had a habit of letting you complete those short ones inside of him, and as soon as that quarterback and receiver thought they could keep throwing against him, he'd pick one off for a touchdown. He was a special one.

And when these backs become that great, teams just avoid them. Adderley sometimes played two or three consecutive games without a pass being thrown in his area or to the man he covered. In fact, sometimes we did not even have to have his uniform cleaned after the game!

The safety, Willie Wood (No. 24), intercepts down near the goal line to stop this drive in our NFL title game in 1961.

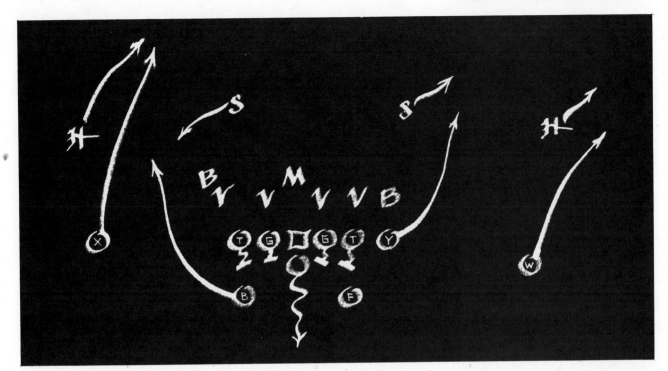

In the man-to-man defense, the four deep backs—the defensive secondary—cover the ends, the flanker and the weak-side halfback man-to-man. The strong-side defensive halfback covers the wingback man-to-man wherever he goes. The strong-side safety covers the Y or tight end man-to-man wherever he goes. The weak-side safety covers the weak-side halfback man-to-man wherever he goes. The weak-side defensive halfback covers the X end or the split end man-to-man wherever he goes.

The position that they line up in is for the defensive halfback to be 4 to 7 yards deep, approximately 1 yard outside the outside shoulder of the X end. The weak-side defensive halfback takes the same position: 4 to 7 yards deep, 1 yard outside the outside shoulder of the X end or flanker. COACHING POINT: The defensive halfbacks in the man-to-man defense should take advantage of the sidelines wherever possible. By this I mean that if the defensive back playing on the outside in the man-to-man defense has the sidelines to his close side he should be able to play his receiver stronger to the post, knowing that the receiver does not have much maneuverability outside of him.

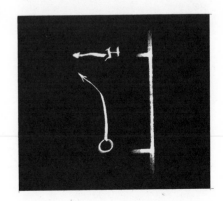

The three linebackers are back in the pass defense and No. 60 has picked off the ball as his teammates turn upfield to start looking for those offensive players to knock down.

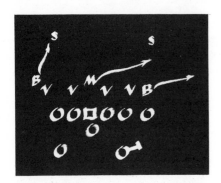

The strong-side safety is 8 to 10 yards deep and 1 yard outside the outside shoulder of the Y end or tight end. The weak-side safety splits the outside leg of the offensive halfback about 8 to 10 yards deep.

The linebackers—strong-side linebacker, middle linebacker and weak-side linebacker—key the fullback. In a man-to-man defense they will move in the direction of the fullback. If the fullback goes strong they will go to the strong side. If the fullback goes weak they will go to the weak side. They will cover that fullback man-to-man if he comes into their zone, leaving the other two linebackers free either for zone coverage or underneath coverage or some other assignment such as blitzing.

We spoke of the linebackers moving in the direction of the fullback, so what happens if the fullback blocks? The fullback does not go out on a pass pattern but stays in his position and blocks. Now, a predetermined choice is made by these three linebackers depending on what team we are facing that week. For example, if the strength of the passing game of the opponent is in the wingback area, or to the strong side, then, when the fullback blocks in the man-to-man defense against that particular team, we will move the linebackers to the strong side, with the middle linebacker and the strong-side linebacker going strong, or to the strength of the formation, and the weak-side linebacker going back into a hook-zone position.

If the strength of the passing game of that week's opponent is on the weak side—that is, their primary receiver is the split end—when the fullback blocks, we will move the linebackers toward the weak side. This gives underneath coverage to help the weak-side defensive halfback. Therefore, the weak-side linebacker would move out into the weak-side zone to help underneath for the defensive halfback. We would also move the middle linebacker to the weak-side zone to help in the hook zone underneath the weak-side safety, and we would move the strong-side linebacker straight back to help in a hook zone underneath the strong-side safety.

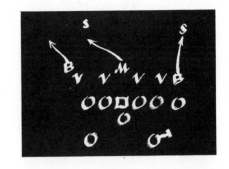

When the fullback flares strong, or goes to the strong side, the linebackers keying the fullback move to the same side or to the strength of the offensive formation. The strong-side linebacker will move out at a 45° angle to come underneath the defensive halfback. The strong-side linebacker does not come up real tight on the fullback, but that is his man in the flare area. If the ball is thrown out there to the fullback the strong-side linebacker has got to come up and tackle him.

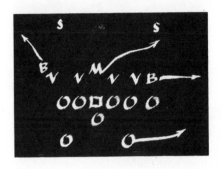

The middle linebacker, also keying the fullback, will now move into the strong-side hook-zone position to help underneath the strong-side safety man. The weak-side linebacker, also keying the fullback, will move into the hook position underneath the weak-side defensive halfback.

If the fullback were to go to the weak side it would move the linebackers to the weak side, with the weak-side linebacker coming underneath to help the weak-side defensive halfback. He also moves at a 45° angle just as the strong-side linebacker did, and covers that fullback man-to-man.

The middle linebacker would also move to the weak side into the weak-side hook zone, and the strong-side linebacker would move into a hook zone underneath the strong-side safety man.

If the fullback were to flare strong but in a circle route, since the middle linebacker is keying him, the fullback would move right into the middle linebacker's zone and he would be covered man-to-man by the middle linebacker.

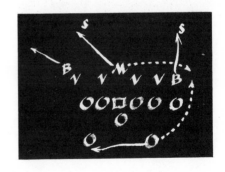

If the fullback were to move weak and come through the line, since the middle linebacker is still keying the fullback, he would again be picked up by the middle linebacker if he came into that weak-side hook zone.

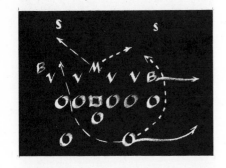

COACHING POINT: I'd like to reemphasize one point. That is, when the fullback moves in a direction into a zone that is covered by a linebacker, that linebacker picks him up man-to-man. For example, when the fullback moves wide to the strong side he is picked up by the strong-side linebacker when he comes into that linebacker's zone. If the fullback were to move in a circle route, he'd be picked up by the middle linebacker when he moves into the middle linebacker's zone. If the fullback were to go out to the weak side and then come through the line, say between his tackle and end, he would be picked up by the middle linebacker when he comes into that zone.

Throughout all of these maneuvers where the linebackers are covering the fullback, the deep secondary is man-to-man on the ends and on the weak-side offensive halfback. The strong-side defensive halfback is man-to-man on the wingback wherever he goes. The strong-side defensive halfback's primary key for run or pass is the Y end. A secondary key for run or pass is the offensive guard. Another key used is that, if the halfback, the weak-side offensive halfback, blocks, the strong-side defensive halfback knows that he will get help from the weak-side safety, who is now released when the offensive halfback blocks. So the strong-side defensive halfback knows he will have help on the post patterns of the wingback and, therefore, he can play that wingback much stronger on the outside.

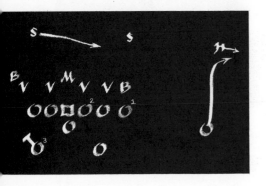

I mentioned his primary key being the Y end. If he sees the Y end block down on the defensive end he plays run. If he sees the Y end try to release and come to the outside he plays pass. The secondary key of the offensive guard means that if the offensive guard sets as to pass, the defensive halfback plays pass. If the guard pulls as to trap or sweep he plays run. Of course, he's making the decision on a split-second's notice as he's not only watching his man come off the line of scrimmage but looking into the offensive formation for his keys.

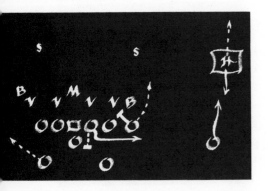

The strong-side safety is man-to-man on the Y end or tight end and is on him wherever he goes. In this defense, whether it's run or pass, the strong-side safety keys the Y end. His second key for run or pass is the offensive guards.

A third key for him, as for the strong-side defensive halfback, is the weak-side offensive halfback. The strong-side safety knows that if the weak-side offensive halfback blocks, the weak-side safety is now free, and he will get help to the inside; therefore, he can play the Y end much stronger to the outside.

The weak-side defensive safety keys the weak-side offensive halfback all the way. He has the same run or pass key with the weak-side offensive tackle. But if the offensive halfback blocks, the weak-side defensive safety immediately releases right to the middle to help anybody who comes into that post area or zone. Of course, if that halfback comes out either flaring or going deep, the weak-side defensive safety picks him up man-to-man.

The weak-side defensive halfback covers the split end man-to-man all the way. His key as to run or pass is the weak-side offensive tackle. That tackle must show run or pass immediately, and if he blocks down, the weak-side defensive halfback plays run. If he sets as for pass-blocking, that weak-side defensive half plays pass. The secondary key for the weak-side defensive halfback is the motion of the offensive halfback; if that back blocks, he plays pass; if that back starts out in a flare or circle route, that's a key to pass. He also knows that if that halfback stays in to block, he has help to the post from the weak-side safety so he can play the split end tougher to the outside.

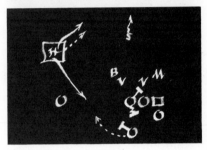

This is another interception by Wood, and his defensive mate Herb Adderley leads the interference for him upfield.

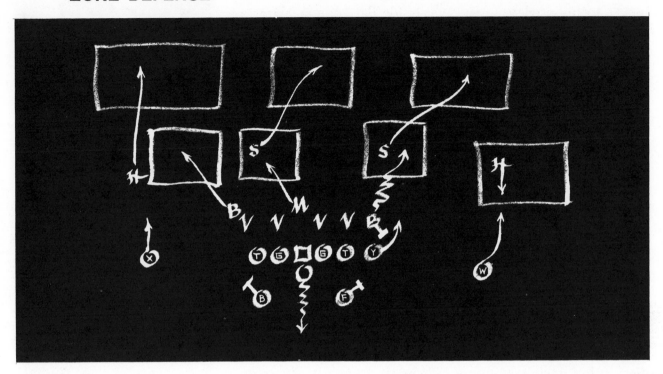

In the zone pass coverage, the linebackers have predetermined positions to go to as soon as they recognize pass, rather than have the fullback determine that position as it was in the man-to-man defense. As soon as the strong-side linebacker recognizes pass he moves to his predetermined zone, but before that he must chuck that Y end and chuck him hard, never allowing the Y end to release inside cleanly. On recognition of pass, after chucking the end, the strong-side defensive linebacker moves to his hook zone about 12 yards deep into the area directly behind his own defensive end. The strong-side linebacker gets no help in the circle area. He's responsible for that circle area from the fullback or halfback coming into that area, and he's responsible for all passes into that area to other receivers.

Middle linebacker: On the snap of the ball, as soon as pass is recognized, the middle linebacker moves to his predetermined weak-side zone and covers that area.

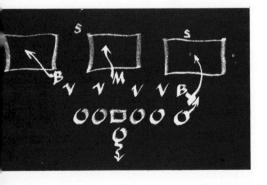

Weak-side linebacker: As soon as pass is recognized he moves to his predetermined weak-side flat zone at about a 45° angle, at least 12 yards deep, and he is responsible for that flat underneath the weak-side defensive halfback.

Deep secondary: The four-deep secondary coverage in the zone defense means, as the name signifies, that all of the four deep men have areas to which they go and which are predetermined. However, the original lineup shown to the offense is exactly the same as it is in the man-to-man. For example, the strong-side defensive halfback is 4 to 7 yards deep from the wide receiver and, on the snap of the ball, he is responsible for the short flat zone in that area. He will jostle the wide receiver as he comes down the field and try to knock him off stride to spoil the rhythm of the pass-route precision. If the flanker were to go to the inside, the strong-side defensive halfback will yell to the strong-side linebacker to warn him of the flanker coming to the inside.

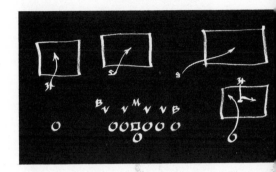

Strong-side safety: On the snap of the ball, and as soon as pass is recognized, the strong-side safety will move to cover deep behind the strong-side defensive halfback and cover that zone no matter what happens. He will drop into an area approximately 20 to 25 yards from the line of scrimmage.

Weak-side safety: As soon as pass is recognized, he will move from his area to the middle of the field to cover that zone. He'll cover the middle one-third of the field.

Weak-side defensive halfback: As soon as pass is recognized, he will cover the deep outside zone, covering his one-third.

So, in summary, it is one-third covered by the strong-side safety, one-third covered by the weak-side safety and one-third covered by the weak-side halfback, with the strong-side defensive halfback coming up to cover the flat near the line of scrimmage. The strong-side halfback is responsible for anyone who comes out into that flat zone. That is his zone. He is responsible for the fullback flaring out, for hitches, for roll-outs, for screen passes—anything that moves out into the flat.

The basic differences between the zone defense and the man-to-man defense is that in the man-to-man defense the defender glues himself to his receiver wherever he goes. He's on him and he never looks to the ball until the receiver makes his final break. In the zone coverage, the defensive back moves to his zone and immediately picks up the quarterback and the ball and reacts to the ball.

Combination defense

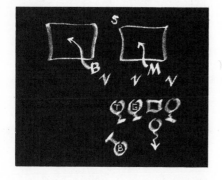

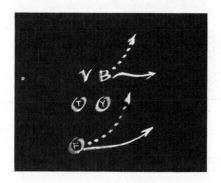

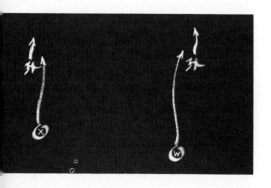

The combination defense is identified by two characteristics: 1) it's a combination of zone and man-to-man coverage, and 2) it's a defense where two defensive men are assigned to cover one offensive receiver.

In the combination defense the middle linebacker and the weak-side linebacker play zone immediately. They have no keys! They have the same rules as they have in the regular zone coverage so, on the snap of the ball, and as soon as pass is recognized, they move to their predetermined zones; the middle linebacker to the weak-side hook zone and the weak-side linebacker at a 45° angle moving out underneath to help out the defensive halfback on the weak-outside flat zone.

In the combination defense the strong-side linebacker is man-to-man on the near back, or the back closest to him. In a Red formation, it would probably be the fullback. In a Brown formation, it could be the halfback. He takes that receiver wherever that man goes. If it's the fullback and the fullback flares out, the strong-side linebacker moves out with him, retreating at a 45° angle, but he still covers that fullback man-to-man. If the ball is thrown to the fullback, the strong-side linebacker must come up and make the tackle. If the fullback circles, the strong-side linebacker is with him man-to-man. If the fullback comes down the field all the way in a long route, the strong-side linebacker is with him man-to-man.

The strong-side defensive halfback is man-to-man on the wingback wherever he goes, and that halfback also knows that, in a combination defense, he has help to the inside from either the strong-side safety or the weak-side safety. Therefore, he can be real strong to the outside in covering the wingback.

The weak-side halfback is man-to-man on the X receiver, the split end. He can also be very strong to the outside. He's got that man wherever he goes. He's man-to-man but he knows he's got help to the inside from either the weak-side safety or the strong-side safety.

The two safeties in the combination defense, if we're combining on the tight end, are inside-outside on the tight end or the Y end. And I mean if the Y end releases outside then the strong-side safety is on him man-to-man, releasing the weak-side safety to cover a deep zone area to help out the strong-side defensive halfback or the wingback, who may break to the post, or to help out the weak-side defensive half-back on the split end, who may also break to the post.

However, if the Y releases inside, he is the responsibility of the weak-side defensive safety, who now takes him man-to-man all the way, releasing the strong-side defensive safety to help in the middle zone against the post patterns of either the flanker or the split end.

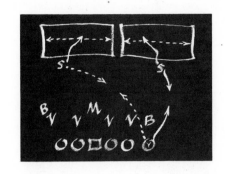

COACHING POINT: The responsibility of the strong-side line-backer is to chuck that tight end and keep him from releasing inside. He cannot always do that. For example, if the Y end splits out 5 to 9 yards from his offensive tackle it's very difficult for this strong-side linebacker to chuck him and to keep him from releasing inside, but he must make it as difficult as possible for the Y end to release inside, always trying to force him to the outside.

The two safety men also have a secondary key, and that is the near back or, in most formations, the fullback. If the fullback blocks, and there's an outside release by the Y end, the weak-side safety immediately retreats for the middle zone.

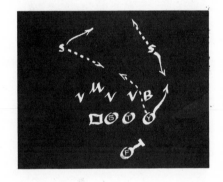

If the near back blocks and there's an inside release by the Y end, the strong-side safety can now release for the middle zone.

If the fullback were to come to the outside the strong-side safety's retreat into that zone would be more of a straight drop back rather than cutting diagonally over to the middle.

An additional point here is that in the combination defense we may determine that the most dangerous receiver is not the Y end, but either the flanker or the X end, and we may want to combine on him rather than the Y end. Let's assume that the best receiver, the one we want to combine on, is not the split end but the flanker. On an inside release by the Y end, the Y end is picked up immediately by the weak-side safety, which now releases the strong-side safety to combine with the strong-side halfback on the flanker or the wing-back.

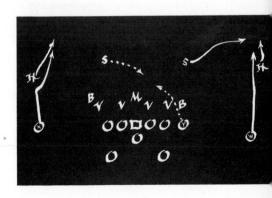

There is one big danger here, however, that everyone should be aware of. This means that now the weak-side half-back is all alone on the split end, and he must know that. He has to key the release of the Y end. As soon as that Y end releases inside, the weak-side defensive halfback knows that he has no help on the inside on the split end. That's the danger and, of course, any time you change the defense to become stronger against one man than it is against another a weakness shows up. In this particular case, the weakness is that the weak-side defensive halfback is man-to-man against the split end.

Free-safety defense

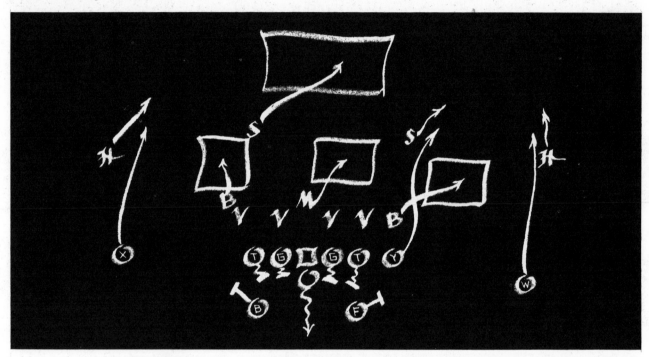

One of the most popular pass defenses in use today is the free-safety type of defense. We mean by this that on the snap of the ball the weak-side safety, without regard to what the offensive backfield does, must move immediately to the center zone, and he covers that center one-third of the field. He moves immediately upon the snap of the ball to that area—as soon as he has recognized pass, of course.

The linebackers—the strong-side linebacker and the middle linebacker—now key the fullback just as they do in the man-to-man coverage. If the fullback fans to the strong side the strong-side linebacker moves out into the outside flat zone, covering the fullback. The middle linebacker also keys the fullback and, with the move of the fullback to the outside, drops into the hook zone.

If the fullback blocks, the linebackers move to the strong side. In other words, as long as the fullback stays on the strong side of the field the action of the linebackers, whether the fullback flares or whether he stays in to block, is to move to the strong side.

If the fullback were to circle and come through the line, then, of course, the middle linebacker would come up just as he does on the man-to-man defense and cover him.

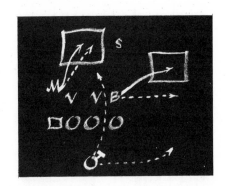

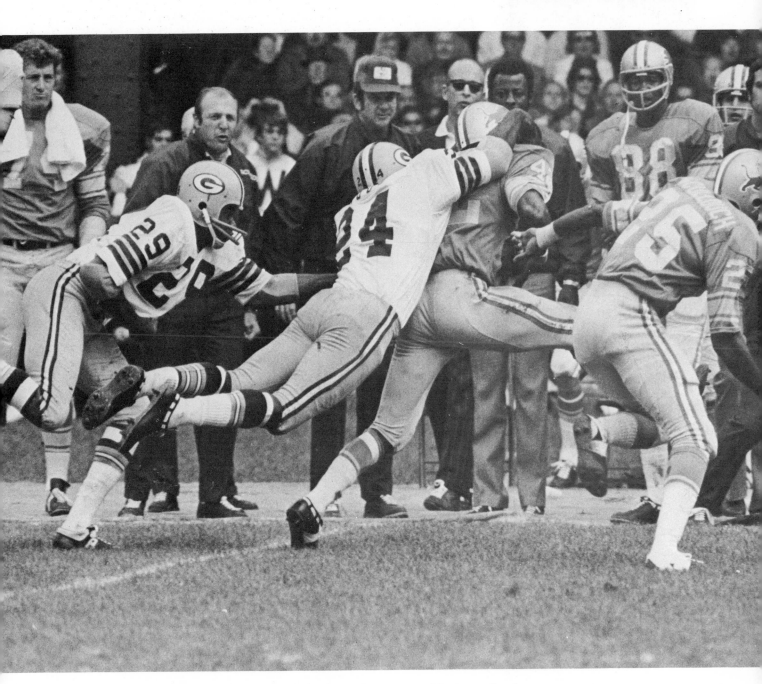

The receiver has caught the ball but the defender is there to stop him immediately.

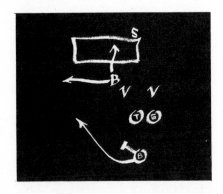

One of the differences between the free-safety defense and the man-to-man defense is the weak-side linebacker. The weak-side linebacker is now man-to-man on the halfback remaining in the backfield. He'll cover that halfback wherever he goes. If the halfback blocks, however, the weak-side linebacker moves to the hook zone; but he's got to be aware of that halfback and come up on him, should he fake a block and come out to the outside either in a delay or leaking through the line of scrimmage or flaring out. If that back comes out,

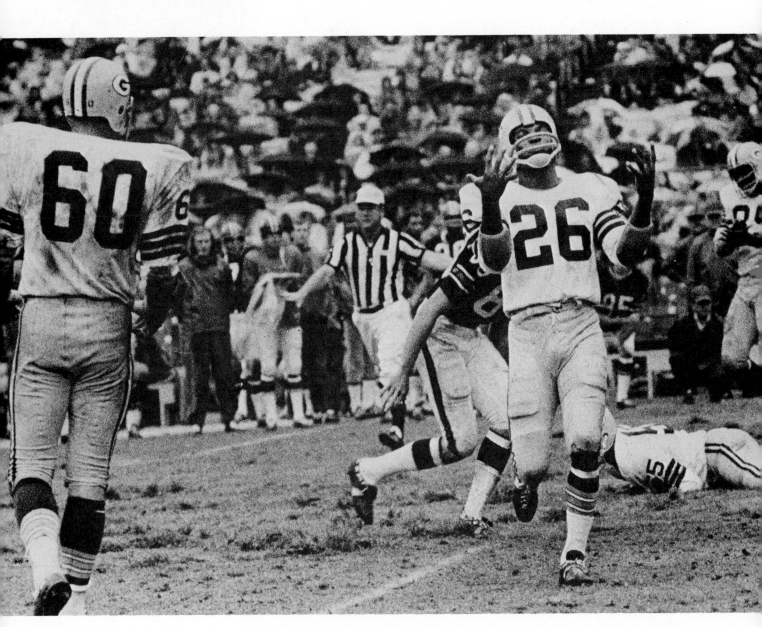

Sometimes even the best of defensive backs drops a sure interception.

the weak-side linebacker must take that halfback man-to-man. He's covering him man-to-man all the way. The strong-side halfback is man-to-man on the flanker. The strong-side safety is man-to-man on the Y end, and the weak-side halfback is man-to-man on the split end.

The big plus in this defense is that the defensive halfbacks, both of our cornermen, and the strong-side safety who are man-to-man on the flanker, the Y end and the split end know that, regardless of what happens, they've got help to the inside from the weak-side safety. They've got help against that post pattern. If any of the receivers, the flanker, the Y end or the split end, were to cut to the post, the man defending against that particular man would know that the weak-side safety is going to help him.

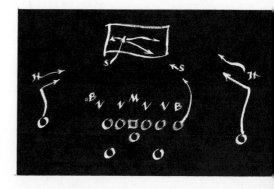

If the flanker were to come down hard and then break to the post, the defensive strong-side halfback knows that the weak-side safety is going to help him. Because of that the strong-side safety, as well as the weak-side halfback, also know that they've got help to the inside. For instance, if the Y end were to break hard to run a post pattern, the strong-side safety knows that the weak-side safety is going to be helping him, so now they can be a lot stronger in their coverage on the outside on the flanker, on the Y end and on the split end.

Should the offensive backs go to the weak side in this kind of defense, the play of the defensive backs or the defensive secondary would not be affected at all. However, with the offensive backs going weak, it does affect the play or the action of the linebacker. When the fullback goes weak, the strong-side linebacker now covers the hook zone directly behind the strong-side defensive end about 12 yards deep. With the fullback going weak the middle linebacker now drops off to the weak-side zone, and the weak-side linebacker still covers the flat zone to his side, taking the halfback as he comes out. That's the only difference in the free-safety coverage.

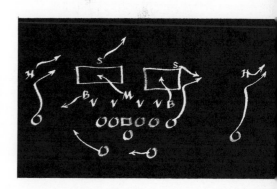

To reiterate, with the movement of the fullback to the weak side or the strong side, the coverage of the defensive secondary is not affected. The fullback does affect the movement of the linebackers.

The Nickel Defense

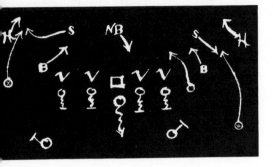

One of the most controversial new pass defenses is the so-called nickel defense. Some coaches feel that in an obvious passing situation the best defense is a prevent defense. They introduced a fifth defensive back to the pass defense, hence the term "nickel defense."

Personally, I don't agree with the theory of a prevent or a nickel defense. Your defense should always be trying to prevent the other team from scoring, and by adding a fifth defensive back and taking out a linebacker, usually the middle linebacker, I feel you weaken the integrity of your defense. Your defense is an integrated unit of eleven men that work and practice and perform together during the game. Each man knows his responsibility on each play and in the defense called. To take out the key man in your defense, the middle linebacker, just to add one defensive back for one play, breaks down the continuity of your overall defense and also tells your middle linebacker that he can't handle pass defense.

Another reason I'm against the nickel defense is that you open yourself to attack by the passer in that wide-open area vacated by the middle linebacker and underneath the "nickel," back who is usually assigned a deep-safety position. Additionally, quarterbacks at this level are so good that unless you can pressure the passer, he'll pick you apart no matter how many defensive backs you have.

The strength of the nickel defense, theoretically, is that you can double-team the wide receivers with your cornerbacks and safeties, leaving the nickel back to take care of the tight or Y end. Your outside linebackers are responsible for any backs coming out of the backfield. If no backs come out, the linebackers can drop off and help underneath. If the defense feels that the tight or Y end is the key receiver, then the nickel allows the defense to double up on that receiver, with the strong-side linebacker and the nickel back taking the tight or Y end inside-out. The cornerbacks and safties can still double-team the wide receivers. However, one of the defensive backs must be aware of any backs coming out on flare patterns and break off and pick up that back.

If the defense called for is a zone coverage, then the nickel back would assume the area that the middle linebacker would occupy in a regular zone defense.

Pass defense is predicated upon the coordination of all eleven men on that defensive team to get to that passer and, at the very least, destroy his rhythm. Then the linebackers and the defensive backs come into play.

The big play for the pass defense is the interception. However, the interception is just the apex upon which the structure of pass defense rests. That structure is four-sided, like a pyramid, and the base of that pyramid is the rush of the defensive front four. It is the men up front who must put on that aggressive pass rush to get to the quarterback and throw him for a loss, shaking his confidence in himself and in his pass protection. At the very least, that pass rush must force that passer to hurry his throw and to throw off balance.

One side of that pyramid is the practiced patience and the acquired knowledge of the linebackers and defensive backs, who must first read and read correctly before they react. They must analyze or read before they react. In their case it is better to be a little late than to be too quick to react.

Another side of that pyramid of defense is the correct reading of those keys of the offensive players by the defensive team. This requires experience, knowledge and intelligence.

And the fourth side of the structure, our pyramid of pass defense, is the proper playing of the receivers by the defensive backs and linebackers that leads to the apex of the structure: the interception. For it is here, the interception, where we may turn the game around—maybe even the season.

So, once again, the success of the defense against the passing attack, as in every phase of football, begins with and depends upon the absolute determination of the individuals. Each individual must perfect to the utmost his given talents and work in coordination with his teammates to get as close to perfection as is possible.

SUMMARY

11

The Kicking Game and the Special Teams

One of the most important parts of football is the kicking game. It is also one that gets the least attention in the press and in the reporting by the experts who cover the games on radio and television. But without a sound kicking game and also the excellent specialty teams that make the kicking game successful, the chances of winning a championship are slight.

Your kicking game is part of your offensive arsenal and part of your defensive strength. The field goal is a major scoring weapon for most teams and those that do not have a good field-goal team are indeed handicapped. Also, the ability of your special team—that defense against the field goal, to block an attempt or rush the kicker so that the attempt fails—is a major factor in the defense of your goal line.

On kickoffs and punt returns, your special teams, through their efforts, can get you that long run for the touchdown that can turn the game around. The kickoff and punt-coverage teams can stop the opponent deep in his territory and set up your defense in good field position.

I've seen my teams take command of a game when, after the opposition has scored to go ahead and we seem to be losing our momentum, because of the efforts of that kickoff specialty crew, we break that kickoff for a long one and we are back in the ball game.

During our drive for the third NFL title, in 1967, we played the Cardinals in a night game in St. Louis. The game was a bitterly fought contest with some great hitting on both sides. Late in the third quarter the Cardinals took the lead, and also the momentum. They kicked off and a rookie, Travis Williams, caught the ball on the 5-yard line and headed straight upfield for his blocking wedge. At about the 20 he broke through the first group of defenders, got a great block from Gale Gillingham at about the 35 and was gone. His run gave us back the lead, the defense shut off St. Louis and we scored later to put it away. That run and those blocks sparked us and we won a very tough ball game.

There have been two overtime games in the NFL before its merger with the AFL. I have been involved in both and field goals helped decide both. The first was in Yankee Stadium in 1958. I was the offensive coach for the Giants and we played the Baltimore Colts for the NFL title. With time running out, John Unitas took the Colts down the field to our 17-yard line and, with about 18 seconds to play, Steve Myra came in and kicked the tying field goal to send the game into overtime, and the Colts finally won, 23–17.

In 1965 we had a playoff with those Colts again in Green Bay for the the Western Conference championship. This time Unitas was injured and they had Tom Matte, a halfback, playing quarterback, and we were favored. We evened things up for them when, on the first play from scrimmage, Bart Starr threw a completed pass in the flat to our tight end, good for the first down. But the end was hit hard, fumbled, and one of the Colts picked up the ball and ran it in. Bart Starr tried to tackle him and got his ribs busted for his efforts. So we began a championship game by giving the opponents an easy seven points and also knocking out our quarterback. After that it was a real street fight. Their defense was just great and stopped us most of the day. They got into our territory close enough to get a field goal. We scored in the

Travis Williams is hurdling his blockers as he starts upfield on a kickoff return against the Bears.

third quarter, but it was not until late in the fourth quarter that we went for the field goal to tie. Don Chandler hit it from the 27-yard line and we went into overtime.

In the overtime the Colts missed their only attempt, a long shot from 47 yards away, but Zeke Bratkowski, who replaced Starr and did a fine job, took us downfield where Chandler ended the overtime with his field goal from the 25-yard line, giving us a 13–10 triumph. It was a fitting climax to a fine football game.

It is very important that when a team gets into the opposition's area from the 20-yard line on back to the 40 they come away with at least three points. There's nothing more disconcerting to an offense than to drive almost the length of the field, be stopped by the defense, and then have the field-goal kicker come in and blow one. In Super Bowl II, Don Chandler kicked field goals four times and each time it came after a long drive downfield.

Fundamentals of kicking —the center snap

The center, in addition to his responsibilities of snapping the ball on the proper snap signal to the quarterback and then blocking, must also learn to perfect the techniques of snapping the ball for punts and for field goals and extra points. As you remember, for the snap of the ball to the quarterback the feet of the center are staggered, with the right foot slightly back of the left foot. For the long snap on punts the center's feet now are no longer staggered but on a line parallel to each other and wide enough apart to allow both of his elbows to pass freely through his legs as he makes the snap. The ball should be positioned with the laces close to the ground on the right.

The center grips the ball on the laces with his right hand as a passer would. His left hand is at the back of the ball and is his guiding hand. As he becomes more experienced he'll be able to move that left hand forward to add more power and speed but until then he must sacrifice some of that speed for accuracy. As the ball is centered it is spun so that it reaches the kicker on a spiral, arriving at that belt-high level on line with the kicking leg.

The scoreboard tells the story and in the picture below Don Chandler kicks the winning field goal, to give us the victory, 13-10.

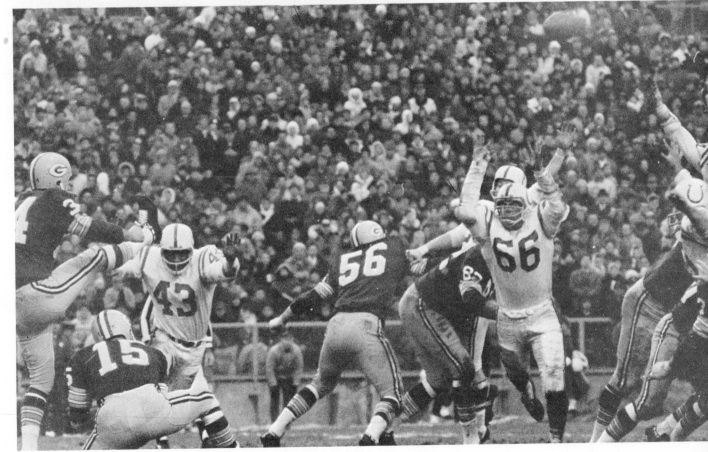

The punter
A primary rule for a punter is that at no time should he ever be concerned with a rush from the defense. He has enough to concentrate on without being worried about that rush. Of course there are times that the rush will get to the punter and when that happens a blocked kick results, but the odds against that are very high.

Once the ball is received from the center it should be brought into position quickly in front of and across the body at about the level of the right hip. The heel of the ball should be covered with the palm of the right hand and the thumb is at the midseam. The nose should be cradled

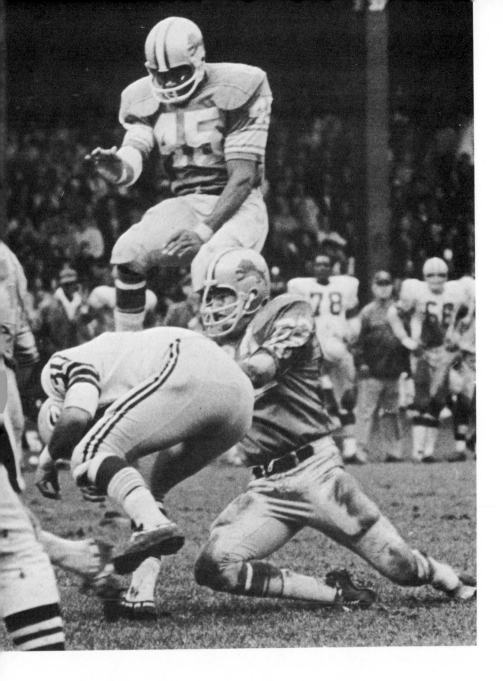

Here you see what the kicker faces as he concentrates on getting that punt away. There are four men rushing, trying to block that punt. Many times on an all-out rush like this by the defense, a roughing-the-kicker penalty will be called, and a drive that was stalled will be saved.

in the left hand. This must be done quickly, as no more than 2 seconds can be allowed to get the punt on its way.

Dropping the ball to the foot becomes one of the most important phases of punting. A proper drop will result in a good kick and a bad drop will result in the punt being spun off the side of the foot. The right hand always controls the ball and acts as a guide for the release. The left hand acts only as a support.

The number of steps a punter may take will vary but usually it is three steps. The first stride is somewhat of a half step moving in the direction of the intended flight of the ball, and the second step brings the kicking foot into action, the hands moving up simultaneously to get the ball in position for the drop. The third step involves the cocking of the kicking leg and ankle, with the toes pointed inward and downward.

On a normal kick the ball should be released just below waist level; the contact with the foot takes place just above knee height. If an especially high kick is desired to take advantage of a strong tail wind, the nose of the ball should be placed upward and the ball should be released above the waist, with the contact taking place at about thigh level. For a low kick into the wind the ball should be dropped at about the thigh, and the contact should take place just below the knee.

If the punt is properly executed, a good long spiraling kick can be heard as well as seen; it will sound more like a thud than a big boom.

Once the ball has been contacted it must receive proper follow-through to attain maximum distance. Often punters will just hit the ball and not follow through, and the ball takes off pretty well but doesn't get that maximum distance. The follow-through must be accomplished with stability and balance, which is not always easy because of that strong, whipping leg action. The right foot ends up near the kicker's head and the arms must be used as a balancing factor. But the strong follow-through is a must for all punters just as it is in all sports, whether it be baseball, golf or tennis.

It is important for punters to get the maximum distance out of their punts, particularly if they can achieve great height with their kicks. However, I feel it's more important to have height than distance. Too many times I have seen the punter boom one 50 or 60 yards downfield and the return back pick that ball off and bring it back for a long gain. Most of the time, when a punter kicks it high, his rush is able to get downfield to contain the runner and to hold it for no return. It is more important for a punt not to be returned than it is for it to be kicked far. In our '67 championship season the opposition averaged only about 1 to 2 yards on punt returns, which is an enormously satisfying figure.

Many times during the course of a season a punter can pull a team out of a hole by faking the punt and either passing or running. The fake pass is usually a play that is called from the sidelines, whereas the fake punt more often than not is an individual maneuver where the punter, noticing that the rush is not coming, pulls the ball down and just takes off. However, with the fake kick and pass there are definite responsibilities.

The kicker assumes the same distance as he does on the punt, 14 yards back from the center. With the snap of the ball the offensive linemen block aggressively just as they do on the punt. Usually the pass will go to one of the backs who are in the backfield to help on the protection of the kicker, and it will be called from the sidelines either left or right. What happens is that, at the snap of the ball, with the rush of the defense, the kicker takes the ball, takes two steps forward, brings the ball up to shoulder height to pass, and one of the blockers, either left or right, will peel out from the protection and go out into the flat area where the kicker will throw the ball. It's a very effective play, but it takes a great deal of practice and deception to make it operate effectively.

The punter as a runner is, as I said, an individual technique, and he has to have that good judgment and experience to know when he can pull the ball down and run with it. This play is very, very seldom called from the sideline.

The blocking team lines up in the spread formation. The punter is back 15 yards and he will have approximately 2.5 seconds from the time he gets the snap from center to get rid of the ball. So that snap has to be very accurate.

Your two guards split about a yard from the center. They are your principal blockers, while your tackles are combination blockers and coverage men. The two ends rarely have a responsibility to block and they're mainly coverage-containment men, responsible for the outside against the run-back. Two yards back of the ball and in the gaps between the guards and center are two fast halfbacks. You have a safety man, usually a fullback, who is stationed up in front of the

Punter as runner & passer

Blocking for punter

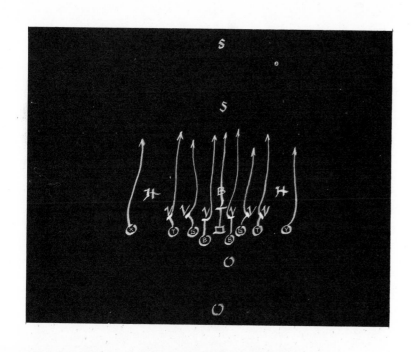

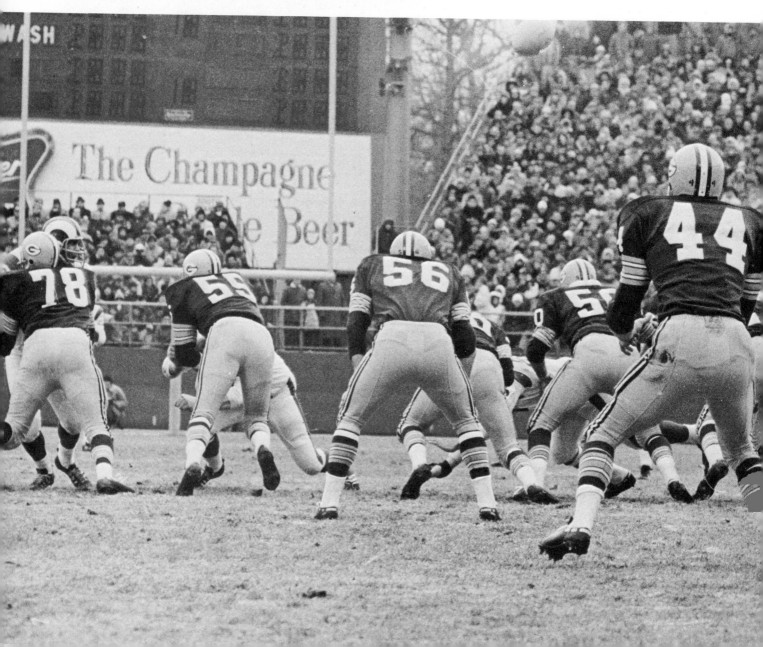

kicker. Usually you don't put a fullback in this spot, you put one of your linebackers, who is bigger and better able to handle any of those crashing linemen who might break through. With the snap of the ball the interior linemen, the guards, block, and keep their blocks. The offensive tackles block and then release and start downfield. The ends break to the outside and come downfield to force the return up the center. Your backs and your fullback stay in until the ball is released, then they release downfield and your punter now becomes the safety against any breakaway.

This is how it looks to the punter. As he keeps his eyes on the ball his blockers are making contact and the center (No. 50) is already releasing to go downfield. The fullback (No. 56) is waiting to pick up anybody who might penetrate.

Field goals & extra points

No snap can be too fast for the center on centering for a punt. For points after touchdown and field goals, however, the center cuts back somewhat on the speed of the snap. On the snap for extra points and field goals the center's stance and hand position are the same as they are for the punt. The distance of this snap is now 7 yards and his target is the numbers of the holder who is down on one knee, arms and hands extended and ready. If the center aims at the kicking alley and misses, there will be no chance for recovery, but by aiming at the numbers the holder gets a chance if the snap is off the mark.

The holder for the kicker should have good hands, and is usually either the quarterback or one of the defensive backs. The kicker has approximately 1.3 seconds from the time of the snap to get the ball off, so the holder has to have those good hands to be able to catch that ball and not fumble it.

The holder lines up with his left knee on the ground opposite the spot from which the kicker is going to boot

Paul Hornung, in this sequence, shows the proper form for kicking a field goal. The placement of the ball by the holder is excellent.

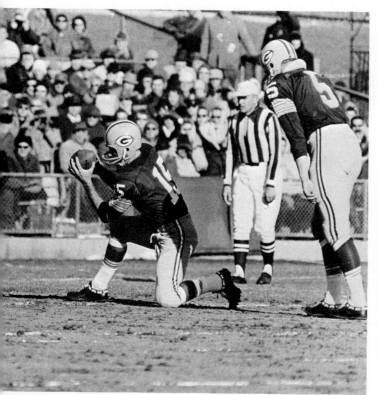

the ball, and he puts the fingertips of his left hand on the spot where the ball will be placed. He then extends his right hand about 2 feet off the ground toward the center, to give him that target at which to shoot, just as a baseball catcher gives the pitcher a target with his mitt. The center then snaps the ball to this hand or to the numbers. The holder should never take the marking hand off the ground until the ball is snapped so he can give that kicker a mark to aim at. The snap should come back as low to the ground as possible, and when the holder gets it, it should be just about knee-high. If the ball comes back much higher than that it could throw the whole timing off. The holder then grabs the ball and puts it down, placing it practically straight up and down. Most kickers prefer to have the ball line up so that the laces are away from the kicker and he has a smooth surface to kick at. With the ball on the ground, only the index finger holds the ball on the top and applies just enough pressure to keep it upright. The ball should not be pressed into the ground but held firmly enough so it's upright.

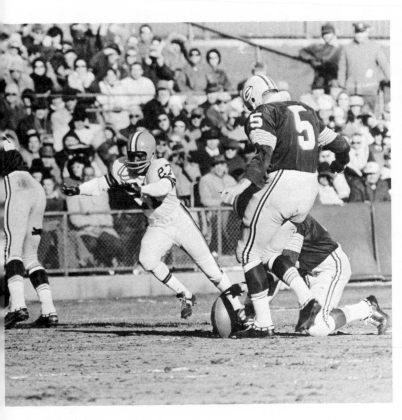

With excellent blocking, the field-goal kicker, Don Chandler, gets the ball away for 3 points.

In blocking for the field-goal kicker or extra points the team has no reason to rush downfield, so you bring everybody in very tight. The center lines up with his head back of the ball so he is not offside, the guards line up close to the center, the tackles close to the guards, and the offensive ends are now replaced by a couple of defensive linemen. Instead of having your backs in there to block on either one of the ends you replace them with linemen, and they take a position directly behind the blocking ends, about a foot off the rear of their teammate facing the outside rushers. These are the key men who must prevent any penetration by those swift halfbacks crashing in from the outside.

Many teams try to come right over the top of the center, since he is the lowest point, and the center has a very difficult play here. He must concentrate on that snap, that is all that counts. He must not let that big lineman over him intimidate him. In fact we tell our centers to ignore the man over him, just concentrate on getting that ball into the holder's hands as fast as he can. After he's done that then he can worry about the man over him. It takes only a split second for him to get that ball off and then to block, so he has plenty of time to make the good snap before that man can charge him. The guards lock one foot almost directly behind the center. By that I mean they will be a little bit deeper off the line of scrimmage. The tackles line up shoulder to shoulder with the guards, and the ends line up shoulder to shoulder with the tackles. This forms that cup to give that kicker time enough to get that ball away.

Note the excellent follow-through by the kicker as his foot comes up to his chin.

Kicking off

The kickoff is one of the most exciting parts of football, whether it be the opening kickoff or after a team has scored a touchdown. And here is where those great breakaway backs, those great running backs, can mean so much to a team. They can break open a ball game. They can give a team the inspiration to come back. They can give you that quick score that can turn a game around.

The long runback on a kickoff is such a beautiful play and, even though I've hated those that have been run back against my team, I would never want to see anything done to the game that would eliminate this excitement. To my way of thinking, the kickers have improved to such an extent that too many kickoffs are going so deep into the end zone that the runback is going the way of the quick kick. Of course, if your team is doing that you're happy, but I can remember days in Green Bay that, when we would kick off, after the tackle had been made on the ball carrier, I would be tempted to send in our goal-line defense. But as a fan, if the kick-off team were moved back to the 35-yard line to insure more runbacks, I'd applaud.

In my years with Green Bay we had a number of great running backs who ran kickoffs back for us, and one of them was our superb defensive back Herb Adderley, who a couple of times took it the length of the field. But we really didn't have that kind of breakaway speed until 1967 when Travis Williams joined us. That year he set an NFL record for kickoff returns for touchdowns, and I remember one game against Cleveland when he returned two in a row in the first quarter as we jumped off to a 35 to 7 lead. Williams had that great breakaway speed that is so necessary to be able to run kickoffs the length of the field. He had the strength in the legs and in the shoulders to be able to get past the tacklers, and was able to spot the daylight and run to it.

In receiving the kickoff we try to keep our blockers spaced so that they can pick off the opposing men and then form the wedge in which the runner can run behind. The return team distributes itself on the 40-yard line facing the kicking team. The center in the middle of the field has the job of knocking down the other team's kicker. The two guards are on either side of him, spaced about 10 yards, and they drop back and then crisscross with the kickoff. They are responsible for the first men lined up on either side of the kicker, and by having them crisscross you are giving them an angle they need to drive those two men to the outside. The two ends are on the 30-yard line and their job is to loop back and in, and they drive the two men who are third out from the kicker to the outside. On the 20-yard line you have three big tackles who form the center of the wedge. Behind the middle tackle is a fullback, he's on about the 10-yard line, and if the kick is short he usually will get it. And then down on the goal line will be your two receivers.

If the kickoff is to the right safety man, the fullback will move to the right and outside the tackle on that side. The left safety man will then come up to complete the left side of the wedge. If the kick is to the left safety man, the fullback moves to the left and the right safety man moves up to the flank on the right side.

The receiver is to follow the wedge until he sees an opening, and the safety men know that any kick that goes deeper than 5 yards in the end zone is to be left there, but only after it has been caught or picked up. The exception is that they may run it out if it is a low kick and there's lots of daylight still showing between those tacklers charging downfield and the blockers.

Punt returns

Each time we send in a punt-return team we send in the word with them that we want the return to be to the right or to the left. By that we mean that we want the blockers to try to set up a wall either to the right side or to the left side of the field for that runner to run behind. Up the middle is the shortest way to the other goal line, but on a punt return, unlike the kickoff return, the defensive line is right on top of your running back and you can seldom get to the center of the field. Also, on the kickoff return, you've got time to form a wedge and take advantage of the better blocking.

Because the punt has a high arc and the defense has time to get downfield, it is almost impossible to return punts straight upfield. So what you try to do is set up a wall of blockers to either side, have the return man drop back after receiving the punt, giving ground so he can move to the outside and get behind that screen or wall of blockers. By dropping back, the runner also gives his blockers time to form that screen. In setting up that screen you can use a minimum of three men or a maximum of five, and your instructions to

Returning the kickoff is a very exciting but tough part of the game of football. Here you see the running back catch the ball near his goal line and break upfield. The wedge forms in front of him. Those big offensive linemen must root out those defenders and open a lane for the ball carrier. In the picture at bottom right, you see the blockers have made contact, the defenders are closing in, and the ball carrier is breaking to the daylight for a long runback.

those men are to get outside the colors of the other teams or to get outside the other team's jerseys. You have to have two men rush the punter and these men are usually lined up as your defensive ends on either side of the line. They must make sure that the punter does punt and does not pull the ball down and run with it. The rest of that line holds up the coverage of the punt by hitting the blockers and then releasing to form the screen for the runner. Some teams, particularly the Bears, like to send all nine men on the line in to rush the punter. This forces the kicking team to keep all of its blockers in to protect the punter. But even though you eliminate any big rush downfield, you also eliminate the blockers, and that receiver is all alone.

So what you have to do most of the time is strike a happy balance. Rush the punter with those two defensive ends, hold up the rush downfield with those interior linemen, hitting and then releasing to form the screen, and drop back one man to help the receiver determine whether to fair-catch the ball or catch it and run with it. That man also becomes the first blocker, trying to hook in the first coverage man.

Defense against field goals

One of the plays that can really turn it around for a team is when the defense blocks a field-goal attempt by your opposition. You try to get your men to be able to penetrate on that field-goal attempt but there is no way that any play can be set up to be used. More often than not the defeat of the field goal is through sheer individual effort, individual brilliance by one of your players. One of the great efforts for the Packers took place in 1963 in the key game against the Minnesota Vikings. We were leading 28-27 with 2 minutes to go when the Vikings had taken the ball to about our 15-yard line, and they set up for a field goal. With the snap of the ball, Herb Adderley came hurtling in from the left side, blocked the ball, and it was picked up by Hank Gremminger and run the length of the field for a touchdown, insuring the win.

Another instance where blocking a field goal helped turn a game around was in our Western Conference playoff game against the Rams in '67. I knew we were going to win that game, but the Rams had grabbed an early 7 to 0 lead and in the beginning of the second quarter had taken the ball down to our 20 and lined up for a field goal, and a score here would have made it more difficult for us, but Dave Robinson and Hank Jordan made a great charge and blocked the field goal. We recovered and, after a couple of changes of the ball, we took over the game and were magnificent, beating the Rams 28 to 7.

Blocking field goals and punts, running back kickoffs and punt returns for touchdowns, are all part of the individual commitment to excellence that a player must make. The running back who breaks one for a long run gets the glory but those ten other men must do their job if he's going to break it. The same thing with that man who may block the field goal. Every other man on that team must be doing the job to allow him to get in there. So it is with the kicking game as it is with every phase of football, that a commitment by every player at every minute of the game to do his best is necessary for any team to be victorious.

This picture captures the total determination by Adderley to get to that ball to block the field goal against the Vikings that saved the victory for us.

Epilogue

Vince Lombardi died on Sept. 3, 1970. The football records have been chronicled in these two volumes and elsewhere, but the legacy of Vince Lombardi is more than first downs and championships, and a lot more important. For what he was as a man, there can be no end.

The qualities of his life are reflected in the principles he lived by and the words he used to motivate his men and those others who came in contact with him. He taught hard work, personal sacrifice, a dedication to principles, love and respect of his fellow man, country and God; in essence, a personal commitment to excellence. And even though he is gone, what he stood for is still with us, and these qualities of life are what made America great.

There was another Vince Lombardi; one that was seldom seen by the public and almost never portrayed by the media. He was a man of great charm, modest to the point of shyness, fun-loving and full of laughter, a great companion and warm friend. Those who knew him closely miss him more for those characteristics than for all the football glory.

But it will be as "the coach" that Vince Lombardi will be remembered, and the message of dedication and faith that he taught is not only for football but for all of us no matter what we do. He belongs with the giants that this great nation has produced. His friend and collaborator, W. C. Heinz, expressed it best: "I have my Armageddon platoon—those men that you have met in life that you want with you at your side in that 'last' battle. Vince Lombardi is not only on that platoon, he is the leader."

George L. Flynn

Acknowledgements

Vince Lombardi on Football is the result of the cooperation and work of many people. From its initial conception to its final publication, there are many people the publisher depended on to make the idea a reality. We wish to thank them now.

Dan Sibley put together the best editorial and production staff it has ever been our pleasure to work with. This two-volume set was published in less than seven months, and without Dan Sibley it could have been seventeen months.

Earle Kersh designed both volumes and supervised the overall layout and makeup of the books and, as they show, did a superb job.

Hilda Edson and Rachel Tuckerman made sure every 't' was crossed and every comma placed correctly, and then kept the printer in line and on schedule.

Lee Nevitt helped on layouts and saved those editorial mistakes with her marvelous patch work on the mechanicals.

The publisher had a great deal of help in the selection of the color illustrations from Dr. Elisabeth L. Flynn of the art department of Longwood College, Farmville, Va.

Frank Mullins did the line drawings for this set, and worked long and closely with the publisher in making sure that every 'x' and 'o' corresponded with the text.

Don Ackland of the New York Graphic Society and Dick Berleth of Sports Illustrated Book Club had the foresight and courage to back this venture with the commitment of their companies.

Richard Hirsh of American Book-Stratford Press made sure that our extremely tight schedule was met and completed before deadline.

Rodney Finn of Marquette Paper Co. delivered the paper necessary for the books in these days of the paper shortage.

The publisher also wants to thank Joe Lombardi, Vince's brother, who gave such strong encouragement to us, and Peter Campbell Brown, the coach's close friend and attorney, whose early enthusiasm and help greatly benefited us.

Thanks to Red Smith and Bart Starr for their forewords to *Vince Lombardi on Football*. There are no two finer people in the world.

W.C. Heinz could not join us in this project, even though he wanted to, but his encouragement and cooperation greatly assisted the publisher.

And to Vernon Biever, whose photographs so complement the text, a special thanks for his talent and his help throughout the production.

The publisher is indeed fortunate to have so many talented and wonderful people work with him on this project.

WALLYNN, INC.
George L. Flynn, Editor
James J. Walsh, Publisher

Credits

From the book "RUN TO DAYLIGHT" by VINCE LOMBARDI with W.C. HEINZ. © 1963 by VINCENT LOMBARDI, W.C. HEINZ and ROBERT RIGER. Published by PRENTICE-HALL, INC., Englewood Cliff, N.J.

162, 163 — LIFE/TIME INC. ARTHUR RICKERBY
221 — SPORTS ILLUSTRATED photo by NEIL LEIFER © TIME INC.

Index